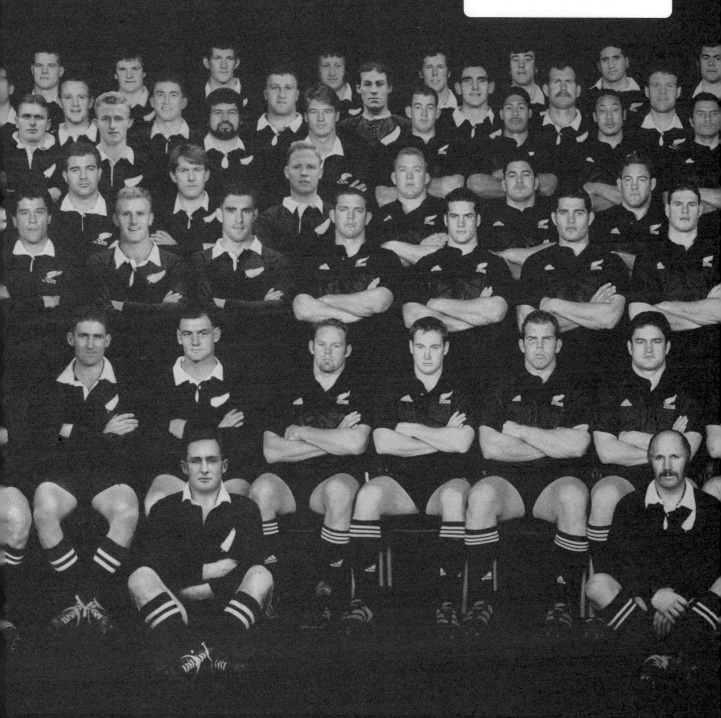

THE JERSEY

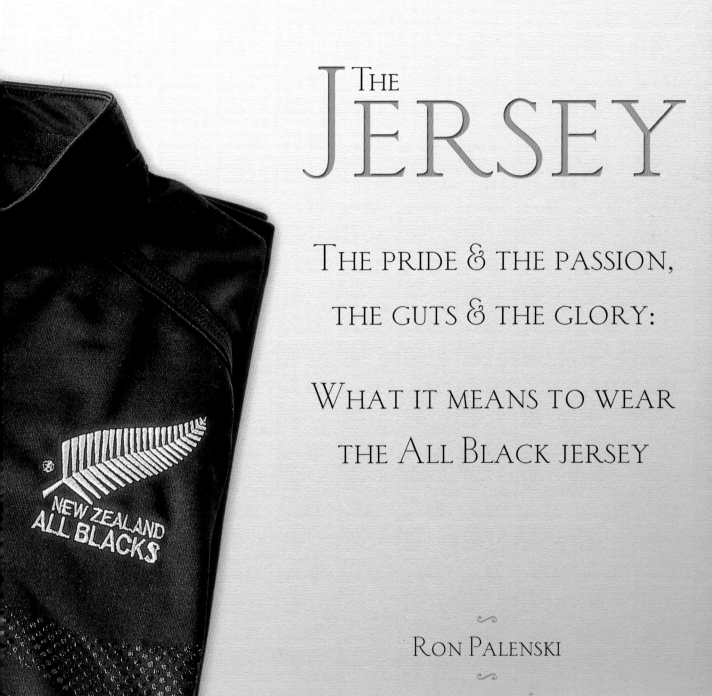

THE JERSEY

THE PRIDE & THE PASSION, THE GUTS & THE GLORY:

WHAT IT MEANS TO WEAR THE ALL BLACK JERSEY

RON PALENSKI

Hodder Moa Beckett

ACKNOWLEDGEMENTS

The photographs in this book came from many sources. Special thanks to Peter Bush, Bob Luxford, curator of the New Zealand Rugby Museum in Palmerston North, Andrew Cornaga (Photosport, Auckland) and Ron Palenski. Thanks also to News Media, Auckland, Ross Wiggins, Craig Baxter, Fotopress and Getty Images.

The author and publishers would also like to acknowledge the assistance of adidas (NZ) and the New Zealand Rugby Football Union.

ENDPAPERS
The past and present mingle in this computer-generated All Black poster produced by adidas.

P4-5
The Australians are challenged at the Exhibition Ground in Brisbane in 1932. The haka worked — the All Blacks won 21–3.
PALENSKI COLLECTION

P6-7
A man for generations — Colin Meads against France in 1968.
PALENSKI COLLECTION

P10-11
The Original All Blacks line up at Crystal Palace in London for their test against England. Captain Dave Gallaher has the ball (plus shinpads outside his socks).
NEW ZEALAND RUGBY MUSEUM

ISBN 1-86958-877-0

© 2001 Text — Ron Palenski
The moral rights of the author have been asserted

© 2001 Design and format — Hodder Moa Beckett Publishers Ltd
First Published in 2001
Reprinted 2001

Published in 2001 by Hodder Moa Beckett Publishers Ltd
[a member of the Hodder Headline Group],
4 Whetu Place, Mairangi Bay, Auckland, New Zealand

Designed and produced by Hodder Moa Beckett Publishers Ltd
Film and colour separations by Microdot, Auckland
Printed by Toppan Printing Co. (Hong Kong)

To all who have worn The Jersey
and for those who will

CONTENTS

PREFACE

It was two or three years ago that I decided to count the number of All Blacks. What motivated this burst of enthusiasm escapes me, although it would have seemed like a good idea at the time. Anyway, I was surprised to learn that there were then 900 and something. Without the counting, if I'd had to guess how many All Blacks there had been since 1884, I would have figured well over 1000. But no.

The knowledge the 1000th All Black would be chosen within the next few years was filed away, one thing led to another, as things do, and this book was born of a late-night discussion with Kevin Chapman and Warren Adler of the publishers, Hodder Moa Beckett. Since the All Blacks meant so much to New Zealand, the 1000th couldn't go by without recognition of some kind.

The 1000th All Black is a bit like, if you'll forgive the analogy, the one millionth customer into a shop who gets a week's free groceries: the one millionth on its own wouldn't exist if it wasn't for the preceding 999,999. So it was with the All Blacks. We decided what needed to be marked was 1000 All Blacks, not the 1000th.

Logistics, timeframes and gestation periods, not to mention blank screens, all have to be factored into the author's side of book production. The 1000th All Black, we figured, would be named sometime in 2001. That was the easy part. Jason O'Halloran became the 998th against Italy at the end of the All Black tour last year and, according to the dictates of history, form and logic, there surely would be two more in 2001.

Publishers, however, quite rightly want books on sale when they're likely to sell the most and this means between September and Christmas. For a book to be in shops in September, say, it needed to be written within the first four months of the year, allowing enough time for all the things that book publishers do, as well as printing the thing. And herein lay a problem. How could I write a book about 1000 All Blacks by the end of April if the men responsible for that milestone, the All Black selectors, weren't picking their first team of the year until after the Super 12? Could I whisper sweetly in the ears of Wayne Smith, Tony Gilbert and Peter Thorburn? I did, as a matter of fact, but it did me no good. Could I reasonably assume that they would pick two new All Blacks at some stage before the book became available? Yes, I thought I could. And if they didn't? Well, you've got before you a book that celebrates 998 All Blacks.

The point of the book remains unchanged, to celebrate anecdotally one of the most recognisable sporting teams in the world and one that is dear to the heart of all New Zealanders (and if it isn't, it should be because of what the All Blacks mean to the well-being of New Zealand).

The 500th All Black passed into history unnoticed. That was on the 1949 tour of South Africa when 16 new All Blacks were named, taking the total to 500. The last two of them to take the field were the Auckland halfback, Bill Conrad, and the South Canterbury fullback, Jack Goddard. The debut of each was delayed until the third game and since C comes before G in the alphabet, Conrad was deemed to be the 500th. It's probably of no significance whatsoever, but the first 500 All Blacks took 65 years to come along, and the second 500 just 52 years.

Much has changed in rugby since the first New Zealand team, not known as the All Blacks, was formed in 1884 and went off to Australia to show them how the game should be played. All Blacks of today wouldn't recognise the game as it was played 117 years ago and, if the truth be known, wouldn't recognise it as it was played even 20 years ago. Not too long ago, I watched a video of the 1987 World Cup final with a recent All Black and he marvelled at the space the players had. The name is the same, it's still rugby (and not "union" as some would have it), there are still 15 blokes in each team, but the dynamics of the game change year by year.

What doesn't change is what the All Blacks mean to New Zealand, and mean to the rest of the rugby world, and what it means to be an All Black. There's sadly no way of knowing of course, but I wouldn't mind betting that Billy Wallace had the same overwhelming feeling of pride when he pulled on the black jersey for the first time as any modern All Black does. The same feelings of pride, responsibility and apprehension would have been felt by Todd Blackadder when he first led the All Blacks onto the field in a test match and by Dave Gallaher when he walked his team of Originals on against Scotland in the first test of their tour in 1905.

The crowds that waited outside Parliament and outside newspaper offices for news of early All Black matches would have waited with the same anticipation and hope that people now feel as they head off to the ground or, the majority, sit down in front of their television sets.

The despair, depression, even anger, that the nation feels when the All Blacks lose knows no constraints of time: 21st century or 19th century, the feelings would have been the same.

The All Blacks in one sense are no different from any other group of highly trained athletes representing their country in their chosen sport. A woman who plays hockey for New Zealand, a man who plays soccer for New Zealand, attains the same pinnacle as the man who plays rugby for New Zealand. But, in another sense, the All Blacks go beyond mere representation on the playing field. The All Blacks, because of the status rugby has in New Zealand and because of their record of enduring excellence, represent also what we are as a nation. That's not putting too great an importance on mere sport. It is a fact, palatable or not, that the All Blacks are capable of defining the mood of the nation. They are our signpost for the rest of the world, they are our vehicle for telling the rest of the world that this is what we're good at, this is the exemplar of New Zealand achievement.

We have always been demanding of All Blacks. The Originals led the way. They lost just one of their matches in Britain — and a loss with a consoling sniff of controversy — and all succeeding teams have had to match that yardstick, whether in Britain or anywhere else. The fact that most teams have been able to match or even exceed that has just raised our expectations. Of course there have been losses along the way, and of course there have been bleak periods, but such is the nature of sport. When the All Blacks play, there is an expectation, almost a public demand, that they must win. Our self-esteem as a country requires it.

It seems now, in the seventh year of professional rugby, that New Zealanders have become even more demanding of the All Blacks, simply because they're paid. They get heaps of money and get cossetted in any number of ways, the argument goes, so they should jolly well win. Oh that it were that simple. The money in the game, while it has boosted our expectations, has also allowed other countries to develop their games so that the natural gap that formerly existed between them and New Zealand has narrowed. Their greater resources allow them to do this as well as buy the expertise and experience that New Zealand players and coaches possess. While the demands on the All Blacks increase, the All Blacks' chances of maintaining their unmatched record of excellence have become less.

It is an unforgiving world, and one that is not getting any less forgiving. But enough of the crystal ball. This book is intended to be a celebration of what's been, not of what may be to come. It pays homage to the All Blacks who have brought us joy and national pride, who have thrust us into the depths of despair, who have frustrated us at times and who have also overwhelmed us with their brilliance. It is a book about a New Zealand institution, about a club of which there are 1000 members, a club to which many aspire and a club that in a very real sense shapes what we are.

As I said, Kevin Chapman and Warren Adler came up with the idea of the book and guided and cajoled me through it with their usual professionalism and enthusiasm. I'm grateful to Adrian Hill of Napier for first drawing my attention to the fact early rugby teams were known by the colours of their jerseys (leading inexorably to All Blacks) and to Geoff Miller of Hamilton for so willingly and efficiently supplying statistics which I sought. I would advise readers never to get into a rugby quiz with Geoff on the opposing side. Clive Akers, who also readily offered his help, would be another to avoid.

I thank all those players to whom I spoke for cheerfully sharing their experiences and their feelings. Some were interviewed specifically for this book. Others have been interviewed over time in various places. A series of video interviews conducted on behalf of the New Zealand Rugby Football Union on the occasion of its centenary also provided much resource material and I also thank the union for making available at various times scrapbooks and documents which have helped round out the story of the All Blacks.

The works of earlier authors such as Sir Terence McLean and Alex Veysey have also been of valued assistance.

Again, I thank my family for knowing when to stay silent and knowing why I was sometimes silent as I continued this masochistic urge to be at a keyboard.

Most of all, though, I thank all the All Blacks — just for being All Blacks. As I said in the preface to *Men In Black*, it is they who have created and sustained the heritage. Only they know the full worth of The Jersey.

Ron Palenski
Dunedin, April 2001

INTRODUCTION

Wilson Whineray, one of the finest of All Black captains, once wrote of a man he knew who had been a player of rugby, a coach and a distinguished administrator of many years standing who had been made a life member of the New Zealand union. In accepting such a high honour, the administrator said he would have exchanged it all just to have worn the black jersey once.

Every New Zealander, or certainly every New Zealand male, would have known how that man felt.

There are other New Zealanders who acknowledge the passing of their years in direct relationship to the All Blacks. They consider themselves young when they're younger than, or at least the same age as, most of the All Blacks. They know they're getting on in life when the All Blacks are younger than them and they acknowledge to themselves that they will never be one. In their deeper, private moments, they may also acknowledge they should never have been one.

The All Blacks are a touchstone of our being. Their success is our success, their lack of success when it occurs has an impact on all New Zealanders.

When the New Zealand Rugby Football Union celebrated its 75th anniversary at a dinner in 1967, the guest speaker was the New Zealand Chief Justice at the time, Sir Richard Wild. He happened to have been a very good rugby player and his younger brother, Peter, was a member of the New Zealand union council and a driving force 25 years later when the New Zealand union celebrated its centenary.

Sir Richard told the assembled guests, which included as many All Blacks as could attend, including three survivors of the Originals of 1905, why New Zealand became so good at rugby.

"Rugby exactly suited our climate and our soil," he said, "and it matches the temperament of the New Zealander and in large measure it has moulded the national character. It is the team element which provides a spur for the weaker spirit, a curb for the selfish and a discipline for all. It treats every man as an equal from whatever background he comes; there's no yielding to status in a tackle, there's no privilege in a scrum."

Sir Richard told of a schoolboy sick in bed who whiled away his time by writing a poem about sport and he quoted the boy's prose when he got to rugby:

But we always turn back to rugby, when our worst is never too bad;
And the arguments go on unceasing as to the best side we ever had.
Was it Gallaher's, Aitken's or Porter's, Manchester's, Brownlie's or Reid's,
Whineray's, Kilby's or Mitchell's, Allen's, Stuart's or Duff's?
Oh I could tell you some tales of matches in Wales,

Or at Twickenham, Newlands and Sydney,
Of Williams and Wooller and Morkel and Muller,
All players of similar kidney.
Of opponents like Osler, Obolensky, O'Reilly,
Were Svensson and Steel any better?
Of Ulyatt and Uttley and Wild Bill Cerutti,
And of Skinner's affection for Becker.
Oh I could sing you a song till the night is far gone,
Of the glorious running of Jarden,
Of the surge of the scrum when the game's nearly done,
And the forwards are begging no pardon,
Of the spiralling arc of a goal by Clarke,
Or of Nepia launched for the kill,
Of the courage of Elvidge, the strength of Dalzell,
And the lightning of Jimmy Mill.
Of the cunning of Nicholls, the magic of Cooke,
And the thrill you feel in your bones,
At the might of the Whites and the deeds of the Meads,
And the language of Peter Jones.

Sir Richard didn't say who the schoolboy was but there was a suspicion that Sir Richard himself was the anonymous poet; an august jurist showing the little bit of the schoolboy that remains in all of us, especially as far as the All Blacks are concerned.

Different generations have seen and followed the All Blacks in different ways. From the first, when the name "All Blacks" had not caught on, people pored over newspaper accounts, pages and pages of the big matches. The more significant stories bore layer upon layer of headlines and each newspaper proudly proclaimed, "By latest telegraph" or some other device to tell its readers that it had the latest news it was possible to have. Premier Richard Seddon apparently liked to proclaim the results of the Originals' matches from the steps of Parliament. Nothing, it seemed, that the All Blacks did was left unsaid or unread. Hotel menus were reprinted, innocuous conversations repeated at length, every word and every deed of match day was lovingly recorded. And there were often the poems, paeans of praise for the players, or more generally for the team, such as the first verse of this one after the Originals had played a game in England:

From these faraway lands in the distant Pacific,
Where nature's fair bounties are lavishly spread,
And the sweet goddess Flora in measure prolific,
Lays her carpet below — hangs her curtain o'erhead;
From Aotearoa, the long cloud so white,
Came the All Blacks, Tana, their kinsmen to fight.

There were the black and white years when rugby, as John Mulgan wrote, was the best of all our pleasures. When George Nepia guarded the gate, when Bert Cooke and Mark Nicholls glided through gaps we couldn't see, when we'd pack Eden Park or Athletic Park or Lancaster Park or Carisbrook in our homburgs and long overcoats, cigarette smoke curling up into grey skies, swearing that this All

Black team was the best of all or, if there was a loss, just swearing . . . swearing revenge and demanding changes.

Teams came and went and the All Blacks went away and came home again and always we thrilled to their deeds, revelled in their presence, marvelled at their skills, indulged vicariously in their successes. And if the All Blacks lost, as lose they did, we felt for them and with them and we made jokes about the 1937 Springboks being the best team to ever leave New Zealand.

Then after the war, a deadlier game in which we took great pride in our team spirit and nationalism as if such things transferred naturally and smoothly from rugby field to battlefield, there were new generations of players and new generations of followers, some lamenting the past, others looking toward a brighter future. Always at the centre of our being were the All Blacks with their black-as-ebony jerseys with the contrasting white of the "silver" fern, the big numbers on their backs — one for fullback, two for a wing in those days — and their shorts that came down almost to their knees, showing a bit of muddied skin before the two white hoops on the tops of the black socks.

There were dark days, and there was none darker than in 1949 when the All Blacks lost six tests and, horror of historical horrors, two of them on the same day! But there were brighter days around the corner and the sun shone for all New Zealanders in 1956 when the defeats by Springboks past were finally and

A crowd outside the St George Hotel in Wellington in 1956 waiting for a glimpse of the Springboks.

INTRODUCTION

irrevocably exorcised. Dwell a little on the New Zealand that was in 1956. An age of trams and Morrises and Austins, of Aunt Daisy and a young Queen, of the hockey-playing prime minister, Sid Holland, of queuing at picture theatres to see newsreels of the latest matches, of waiting at dairies on Saturday nights for the arrival of the sports papers bringing us the news of the afternoon's matches, of crouching over mantel radios and waiting for the magical cry of McCarthy, "Listen . . . wait for it . . . it's a goal!"

That year was a year of learning the name of every Springbok, of having photos cut from the *Weekly News* and the *Free Lance* pinned up on the wall, of collecting team photos laid out in the shape of a rugby ball, of knowing as much, or thinking we knew as much, about the All Blacks and potential All Blacks as the selectors. It was waiting patiently for the test matches with an excited tension that no Christmas morning ever knew, of queuing for tickets overnight outside the ground, Royal Stewart tartan rug providing the outer warmth and a Thermos providing the inner. Of buying black and white ribbons or rosettes from sellers outside the ground and waiting, fidgeting, for the gates to open, then rushing onto the open terraces and there claiming your territory, there to remain for the next six or seven hours. Of curtainraiser after curtainraiser, their passage marked not by the quality of their play but by writing the scores in the programme and knowing each brought the test match closer. Of the hubbub as the teams arrived separately, the players in their street clothes, hands in pockets, inspecting the ground and watching a curtainraiser in a perfunctory manner, then taking their seats in the stand until it was time to go below.

Winston McCarthy, the voice of rugby in the 50s, in working pose at Athletic Park.

Then, at last, the curtainraisers are over, the band plays its last tune and the St John men and the ball boys come out from under the stand to take up their match stations. Then an assortment of other match people. Then the two teams, side by side, grim-faced captain alongside grim-faced captain, the pristine green and white of the Springboks contrasting greatly with the fresh, new blackness of the All Black jersey and shorts. The referee all in white, with just as grim a visage as the players. Then the anthems, the players standing where they happened to be at the time, scattered about the field randomly, the odd one flexing or stretching a muscle. The referee calls them to the middle, the kicker prepares, the teams line out, the shrill of the whistle . . . the days and weeks and months of anticipation all come down to the next 80 minutes.

The matches seemed to go by in a blur, for the spectators and for the players. As history unfolds before your eyes, it's sometimes hard to comprehend it. With each All Black score, a huge roar goes up from the crowd, programmes and whatever may have been in hands gets tossed in the air, neighbour hugs neighbour and throats get a little hoarser.

There's that uplifting feeling of elation that we've done it again, we've won. Such a contrast to the deep depression that follows a loss. We've won, the sun is

CHARL VISSER COLLECTION

shining — if waning — there's a late afternoon nip in the air, all is well with the world. Out of the park and on to a pub or to home and there or wherever to relive the match with friends and neighbours, say what you saw and listen to what they saw, tell how the ball bounced near you and how Ron Jarden slithered into touch right alongside you, so close you could have reached out and touched him but you dared not. Down to their dairies to buy the sports papers and there to have confirmed in black and white what you saw with your own eyes that afternoon.

Then after the black and white days came the days of colour, the days of the scarlet of the jerseys of the Lions, the bottle green of the Australians until it changed to gold, then the white of England, the scarlet of Wales, the blue of France, and all the while the one constancy in our rugby lives, the black of New Zealand.

The success of the 60s, the turning back of all pretenders at home and the vanquishing of all foes abroad, the feeling of invincibility, the rock-solidity of the forwards and the speed and creativeness of the backs. A feeling that All Black dominance was something we had and something that we could have forever, that whatever else we did in the world, whatever else we aspired to, we always had the

Springbok centre Wilf Rosenberg on the attack in the third test of the epic 1956 series. Halfback Ponty Reid and captain Bob Duff show they're well aware of the danger.

INTRODUCTION

All Blacks. We had the men like Meads and Lochore and others who would come down from their farms, tough as teak, to do their best for their country and you always knew their best would be good enough, far better than any opponent's.

But then the days of doubt returned. A tour of South Africa that was successful in all but what mattered, the test matches, followed by the unprecedented events of 1971 when a Lions side — a Lions side(!) usually all forward brawn and back brain and never the twain would meet — out-thought us and outplayed us, when a Scottish doctor, Doug Smith, baffled us with his talk of circadian disrhythmia while all the while he and his Welsh cohort, Carwyn James, conned New Zealand. It was when we saw for the first time how successful a round-the-corner kicker could be and by the end of the tour, even we on the losing end were singing the praises of King John and his acolytes, men such as Gareth Edwards and Mike Gibson, of Ian McLauchlan and Mervyn Davies.

Whenever an All Black side has been down, it picks itself up again but in the 70s the picking up took a little longer. When we were able to see a test match on the other side of the world live in our own homes for the first time, the All Blacks beat Wales as we always knew they would, and we marvelled at the strength and commitment of Keith Murdoch as he scored his try. But then we wondered and worried as he was sent

Men who came down from their farms, tough as teak. Brian Lochore and Colin Meads in Lochore's comeback test in 1971.

home and the rest of the team seemed to lose a little faith in themselves, though they still went within a hair's breadth of achieving the grand slam in Britain for the first time. It was AM (after Meads) rugby and it was a worrying time.

The 70s were not moments to remember all that fondly, though wins still came. So did losses, one to England at Eden Park, then the slow climb back up during 1974 when the All Blacks were in Australia and Ireland, then 1975 in the wet test at Eden Park, then once again in South Africa, another lost series, more complaints about South African refereeing, and this time some disquiet about whether the All Blacks should have been there at all.

The Lions again in 1977, not a patch on the 1971 side though probably better in the forwards than the All Blacks, we were alarmed to note, especially when the All Blacks put down a three-man scrum in the test in Auckland. What's this? The mighty All Blacks, whose success had been founded on forward power, conceding they weren't up to it against the Lions? A regathering of forces in France later in the year, especially in the second test in Paris when we were astounded by a penalty goal from Gary Seear, gratified by a dropped goal from Brian McKechnie and thrilled by a try from Stu Wilson, all combined to put the world to rights again: the All Blacks were back on top.

There was a successful series against Australia, even if the last test was dropped by an embarrassing 30–16 when one of the Aussies, Greg Cornelsen, was somehow allowed to score four tries. But we forgot about that aberration

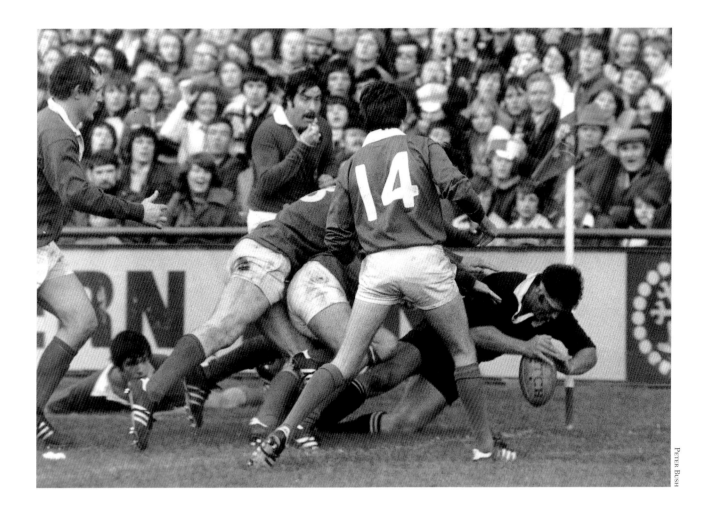

when, by the end of the year, the All Blacks achieved the grand slam for the first time. We knew they weren't the greatest of All Black teams and the players themselves would concede that, but what they lacked in individual talent they made up for with team spirit and discipline. They were a smoothly efficient side. We wondered when they were beaten by Munster on that mad day in Limerick and we wondered even more the following Saturday when they were very nearly beaten by Ireland, being saved just in the last minutes by Mark Donaldson darting around the front of a lineout and Andy Dalton getting across to score. From then, the Grand Slam was a possibility. But nothing comes easy in an All Black's life, including wins against Wales. This was when we were amused and appalled all at once by the shenanigans in the lineout that cost Wales the match, how Andy Haden dived and wasn't caught but how Geoff Wheel climbed all over Frank Oliver and was caught. And how Brian McKechnie, not wanted for the tour in the first place, then not wanted for the match in the second place, calmly kicked the goal to win the match and set Welsh teeth gnashing. After the heart-stoppers of Ireland and Wales, England and Scotland were relatively plain sailing although at Murrayfield our hearts were in our mouths when Ian McGeechan attempted a dropped goal, but all was well when the All Blacks charged it down and roamed through the gloaming for Bruce Robertson to score.

These were what could be called the Mourie years, when the All Blacks were

The first leg of the grand slam is assured by this last-minute try by Andy Dalton against Ireland.

INTRODUCTION

Captain Graham Mourie
and coach Jack Gleeson
before the grand slam test
against Wales.

PETER BUSH

led by Graham Mourie and coached first by Jack Gleeson and then by Eric Watson. They were not wholly successful years because tests were lost, but they were satisfying years. They were the years when the Australians won in Sydney and rediscovered the Bledisloe Cup and paraded it around the Sydney Cricket Ground as if it was the prize bull that had just won the grand parade at the Easter Show. The Wallabies kept the cup the following year, in 1980, but the equilibrium was restored later in that year when the All Blacks beat Wales in a match that was staged to mark the Welsh union's centenary. It was a stunning display of All Black gifts and one of the players, Andy Haden, went so far as to suggest that it was one of the great All Black teams of all time. But by then we knew Haden well and knew that he shouldn't always be taken that seriously. Nevertheless, it was an emphatic victory and one in which were displayed the extraordinary gifts of an All Black with a tragically short career, Nicky Allen.

And in the early 80s, we worried about rugby. We worried because New Zealand seemed split in two about whether the South Africans should tour in 1981. It may have grown beyond a merely rugby issue to one of law and order, to one of some people challenging authority, but rugby was still at the core of it and it was a sad time for rugby. The All Blacks won the barbed wire series and they revelled in it and so too did those who followed the All Blacks come what may, but for many others, perhaps for the first time, there were things that were more important than rugby, more important than the All Blacks winning a series. It became a time of questioning the government, of questioning the rugby union and of questioning ourselves and wondering whether the game was worth it if it was dividing the country. Many decided it wasn't.

But happy times always follow the sad times because such is life and the Bledisloe Cup was regained the following year. In between times, the All Blacks had toured France and won the series there and broken new ground with a test match in Bucharest, of all places. A year later the Lions again visited and this time, as in 1966, were beaten four tests to nil. We weren't kidding ourselves that New Zealand rugby was at its peak because we knew it wasn't and a depleted All Black team later in 1983 was held to a draw by Scotland and beaten by England. There were still concerns in 1984 with a harrowing win against France and then a narrow series victory against Australia, and all the while on the horizon was the issue that seemed as if it would never go away, South Africa.

The All Blacks were due to go to South Africa in 1985 and we watched and wondered when two men challenged the New Zealand union in the High Court. When they won the first stage of their action and an injunction against the tour was issued, the old sores reappeared. One half of New Zealand wanted the tour, one half didn't. The All Blacks instead went off to Argentina for a not very satisfying tour and early in 1986 laid their plans for going to South Africa anyway, as the Cavaliers.

It was a time when loyalty to the jersey, loyalty to all that the All Blacks meant, was sorely tested. Go most of them did, and the All Black team that played France became known as the Baby Blacks.

They were reunited for the series against Australia and the end of year tour of France, but there was a rift between those who went to South Africa and those who stayed at home. The rift, we could see from afar, healed during the French tour and especially after the second test in Nantes, which was lost.

The dawn of a new era for rugby was at hand. The first World Cup, staged in New Zealand and Australia in May and June of 1987, changed the face of international rugby forever. It was the catalyst for all the change that was to follow, including the momentous events of eight years later when the old amateur regulations were declared redundant. It was a catalyst for change to the All Blacks too and how we thrilled to their new style of play, their commitment and their free-flowing movements as they thrust aside all opponents in their pursuit of the cup. They took rugby to a higher plane; they showed they were ready for and had prepared for the cup and they showed that the rest of the world had got left behind.

The cup win and the succeeding years were exciting times for All Black rugby, a team to rival the successes of the 60s and of the 20s, a team that was hailed as one

The 1987 All Blacks with David Kirk as their on-field leader took rugby to a new plane . . . and took the World Cup as well.

of the greatest in All Black history, a team that no one, it seemed, could stop. Australia beaten, Wales slaughtered, France and Argentina put in their places, Ireland swept aside. They were days of constant sorrow for other international sides, days in which we marvelled at the skills of players such as John Gallagher and John Kirwan, Joe Stanley and Warwick Taylor, Grant Fox, Wayne Shelford, Gary Whetton and Murray Pierce, Alan Whetton and the front row of Richard Loe, Sean Fitzpatrick and Steve McDowell and, with them most of the time, a player who surely has gone as close to being peerless as any player, Michael Jones. There were others during this unbeaten period of the late 80s when the result of an All Black test was never in question, only how much they would win by.

Nothing lasts forever and certainly not in the fickle world of sport and by 1990, the rest of the world — or at least the Australians — had caught up and we'd just recovered from the bombshell of Shelford being dumped as captain in favour of Gary Whetton when we had to suffer the shock of the third test loss to Australia in Wellington. It was the end of the golden weather and there was more murk to come.

What followed was not a happy time for the All Blacks and the All Blacks, evidently, were not a happy team. After a French tour at the end of 1990, there was a tour of Argentina in 1991 which counted for not much in the wider scheme of things, a loss to Australia and then an uninspiring win, and then the disappointment of the second World Cup.

That was when we were supposed to retain the cup but New Zealanders knew

INTRODUCTION

Jonah Lomu at the World Cup in 1995, a once-in-two-lifetimes player.

that some players had gone a test or a tour too far, that there was no longer the gap between New Zealand and the rest and, perhaps the most telling blow, the appointment of Alex Wyllie and John Hart as co-coaches was never going to work. And it didn't. It wasn't too much of a surprise when the All Blacks were eliminated by Australia in the semi-final in Dublin, when David Campese — who had first crossed swords with the All Blacks in 1982 — showed that special magic he had and conjured up tries that sank New Zealand.

Did we despair, did we wallow in self-pity and wonder where we had gone wrong and where we were going? Well, yes we did. But the good thing about sport is that there's always a tomorrow and there's always a chance to redeem. Rugby by now had fallen into the four-year cycle of the World Cup and everything was geared towards the next cup: the selection of coaches, the grooming and selection of players, all was done with the distant goal of the cup in mind. Well, that's what we were told, but there were still the intermediary goals of beating every opponent thrust in our way. The thing about those was if the occasional test was lost, it could always be rationalised away as part of the grand plan to win the cup. And were we sucked in by this? On the whole, no. We're too proud of the All Blacks and too jealous of their record to allow any test to get away, no matter how it's painted.

So there were losses along the way to the next World Cup, a series to Australia here, a series to France there, a test against the Lions, even another test against England, and how that grated with All Blacks, but there were compensations when we got to the next World Cup. Once again, it was revealed, the All Blacks were at a different level to other teams. They played the game with more speed, their support play was better and more organised and, what's more, there was a once-in-two-lifetimes player on the wing for the All Blacks, Jonah Lomu. Complementing him, as if he needed complementing, were players of special talent — perhaps they were players of just one lifetime — such as Jeff Wilson, Josh Kronfeld and Andrew Mehrtens.

How we smiled with quiet satisfaction when Wales and Ireland were put away, and how the smiles became broader when we racked up 145 points against the Japanese and then beat the Scots. And how the smiles turned to guffaws of laughter when the All Blacks and Lomu in particular steamrolled all over England and there we were in the final, hardly having raised a sweat. And then how the smiles turned to tears, how the joy transformed into despair as the All Blacks were beaten by the Springboks in the extra-time tryless final. The food poisoning business was the thimble of consolation to grasp at but that became a bit of a joke in the end as shaky fingers were pointed at such diverse objects as British bookmakers and a Johannesburg waitress. We were done, that's all there was to it. The best team there, but we were done. It happens.

So into the next cycle. New coach. New players. It was becoming a familiar routine. It was also a new era. The amateur days had gone, the professional ones were upon us. But the All Blacks had always been professional in the sense of their attitude and preparation so all that changed was they were being paid for their time. Money for jam for some of them.

And how upbeat the new cycle began. In the first year wins against Samoa and Scotland, then an exhaustive series of matches against Australia and South Africa, combining the new tri-nations with a three-test tour of South Africa. The holy grail. The sought-after prize of every All Black. Many had tried, all had failed. But not this time. The tri-nations was dealt with first. Four tests, four wins. Then the series. Match one in Durban. Yes! Match two in Pretoria. Yes! The series was ours. Who cared about the third test in Johannesburg, the All Blacks had won a series in South Africa for the first time. Well, we should have cared more and the Springboks did care more and they won it. We won the series, but it would have been better to wipe them three-blot.

Next year, more of the same. Fiji and Argentina brushed aside, then the tri-nations wrapped up without a loss. Easy-peasy. Then on to Britain and Ireland for a reality check because things never quite go according to plan there, as any number of All Black teams have discovered. Ireland and Wales disposed of comfortably enough but the All Blacks didn't look their dominant selves against England, not in the 25–8 win at Old Trafford and certainly not in the 26–26 draw at Twickenham. England regard a draw against the All Blacks as a triumph. All Blacks regard a draw against anyone as disaster.

So were there signs in 1997 of what was to come in 1998? Some say yes, some

PETER BUSH

say no. There was no Sean Fitzpatrick any more, no Frank Bunce, no Zinzan Brooke. All three were missed to a greater or lesser degree. Everyone in New Zealand, as always, had an opinion. Whatever the reasons, the all-conquering team of 1996 and 1997 was now nothing like conquering. Five losses in a row harked back to the bad old days of 1949. It was not a happy year.

The next was even less happy, though it started well enough. We breathed a sigh of relief when the run of outs was stopped against Samoa and then France, Australia and South Africa were beaten in short order. But whoops. Australia won in the new Olympic Stadium in Sydney. Was that a sign of things to come or an uncharacteristic loss? The former, we were to discover, rather than the latter. Once again we thrilled to the All Blacks beating England in a World Cup match but once again elation turned to despair. Because the England match was so crucial in terms of the later draw, did the All Blacks subconsciously regard that match as their final and drop their guard later? Did they take France too lightly? Who knows? Every All Black would have his own reasons for the semi-final loss to France, just as everyone it seemed in New Zealand was able to adroitly put their finger on the cause. Some blamed the All Blacks, some blamed the money-driven Rugby Union, some blamed the team culture, but it was all to no avail. Whatever the reasons, the All Blacks were beaten by France and, once again, have to sit out four years until the next cup.

So another cycle. New coaches, new players. Losses to Australia and South Africa, a loss to France. Some apprehension about what lies ahead, some concerns about the depth of New Zealand rugby talent, some concerns that the money in the game has allowed other countries to close the gap on New Zealand.

Concerns, always concerns.

Much has changed in the 117 years since a New Zealand rugby team first took the field. Much more will undoubtedly change. What hasn't changed is the hold the black jersey with the silver fern has on us all.

BLACK TO THE START

He can be old and he can be young. He's past tense or present tense. If the latter, he'll ward off the former as long as he has breath in his body. He's told that he's revered or has been revered, but that is a relative term. Revered in a general sense perhaps, but in the specific sense he may sometimes be revered, sometimes reviled; his every move is open to inspection, examination, dissection and comment. No politician, no person in public life, no celebrity with a claim to fame at anything other than being a celebrity, is studied so minutely and so repetitively through the lens of the public microscope.

He is one. He is many. He is one of a thousand. He is an All Black.

He is a man in black. He's clad in black because that's the colour of his being: the colour of his past, his present and his future. Black can be a forbidding colour, it is the colour of night; it is the colour of dark forces, it is the colour of the louring sky, it is the colour that is the antithesis of the purity and innocence that is white. An All Black is Darth Vader in rugby boots. He is proud to be in black because it is his country's colour and when he wears the black jersey he is wearing his country on his sleeve and on his heart.

Those who line up against him, those who would attempt to defeat him, are first confronted with the black: the black of the jersey, the black of the shorts, the black of the socks. They are confronted not by 15 players clad in black but by a panoply of the present with the past ranged out mystically behind them, generation layered upon generation of men in black who have gone before, ghostily riding with the current custodians just as those current custodians will one day (some sooner than they wish) also ride in the rear, urging their successors on in the name of all those who have come before.

But they are more. Not just the players of the past or of the present, but with them always (or mostly always) is a vast armada of support carried along on the tide of success and of hope that has been the hallmark of All Blacks since and even before the name first entered the rugby lexicon. They have fashioned their own burdens, the All Blacks, and they carry them willingly and proudly. The burdens are their successes and the constant expectations and demands by their followers for more and more success. Alone among New Zealand sports teams, they are expected to win. It is required of them. A team from any other sport may lose, and lose often, and be praised for being valiant in the attempt; but not so the All Blacks. They lose, as the caprices of sport demand they must, but the losses just add to their burdens. They are not supposed to lose. Losing is for others and especially for their opponents. They are All Blacks and history demands that they win. And history shows that they've met those demands more than any others (not that there are many others which have such demands placed upon them).

All Blacks began life in circumstances that were not propitious and for a team with such a storied history as the All Blacks, it was a most unlikely beginning. The first New Zealand team played in 1884 against Wellington as a shakedown match before heading for Australia. The game was delayed a day because of terrible weather and when they played the next day on Newtown Park, the conditions were still so bad that the match was reduced to 25 minutes each way. It was only when they got to Australia that they played their first proper match, at Parramatta in the west of Sydney.

An historic tour or a misnomer? They regarded themselves as a New Zealand team even though there was no such thing then as the New Zealand Rugby Football Union and the tour was organised by the secretary of the Canterbury union, William Millton, and a Dunedin businessman and rugby entrepreneur, Samuel Sleigh. The players were from only Auckland, Wellington, Canterbury and Otago. The spread was slightly wider when it is considered that Wellington then included Wairarapa and Southland was part of Otago.

Though the tour of Australia (plus that one truncated game in Wellington) marked the first successful foray by a national rugby team, there are some who say they should not have been regarded as All Blacks — that the 19 players who played nine matches for nine wins were just rugby opportunists and should have no place in the ranks of the One Thousand. The argument, a retrospective one, is that they should not be regarded as All Blacks because there was no national union and because the team was not chosen from all the provinces then in existence. But, by Jove, as they probably would have said at the time, they *felt* as if they were representing their country — or their colony as it was then — and it could hardly be laid at the players' door if there was no national union. They were regarded as All Blacks, or at least as New Zealand representatives, by recorders of rugby at the time and subsequently by the chroniclers of New Zealand rugby history, men such as Arthur Swan, Arthur Carman, Rod Chester and Neville McMillan. The last two even wrote a book, *Centenary*, based on the premise that the first New Zealand team was in 1884. And since the names of the 19 players have forevermore appeared in All Black lists, and maybe somewhere descendants still treasure a fading jersey or a tasselled cap, how is All Blackdom, once conferred, removed? How is an All Black unAll Blacked? They're not. Once someone has taken the field for New Zealand, they're an All Black. It could be for just 20 seconds. Never mind. An All Black he is. The revisionist argument, it should be emphasised, is not about the calibre of these 19 pioneers but against the status of the team as a collective, that it did not truly represent all of New Zealand and was not chosen by a central body representing all of New Zealand. It's an argument with no answer. History has decided.

So All Blacks they were (though it was to be some years before that name became attached) and All Blacks they remained, the oldest of the serried ranks upon ranks that have marched through history to form the One Thousand.

PALENSKI COLLECTION

But All Blacks they weren't, if you want to be picky about it. The first team didn't wear black at all. The jerseys they chose, perhaps reflecting the Otago origins of their energetic organiser, Sleigh, were dark blue with a gold fernleaf on the left breast. (Sleigh himself recorded the details of the jersey so it's curious therefore that a studio photo of the 1884 team decked out in their playing gear shows dark jerseys with nothing on them at all.)

Neither were they the best of the few provinces from which they were picked. It all happened like this. New South Wales had sent a team to New Zealand in 1882 and though they played what were then the main provinces, they didn't play a national team. In 1883, Wellington, Canterbury and Otago played a three-way tournament in Wellington — nothing new about the tri-series concept — and yarning into the night, men such as Sleigh and Millton, who was Canterbury secretary as well as being in Sleigh's words "a steady dribbling forward, always near the leather", hit upon the idea of repaying the New South Wales visit.

Sleigh was entrusted with the organisation and Millton, who got about the country because he also played cricket for Canterbury, was delegated the task of sounding out likely players. He found and persuaded 19 of them to join the first New Zealand team but over the summer and into the autumn seven of them had to pull out for various reasons, mostly because they weren't given time off by their employers. This number included the prospective captain, George Campbell of Wellington, so when the team assembled for departure from Wellington, the captaincy was put to the vote and Millton found himself with the job. One of the replacement players he had found was none other than his younger brother Edward who, though also from Canterbury, played for

Wellington in the pre-sailing match against the new national team. That was far from being the only sibling selection in those days. The Native team that went on an odyssey to Britain and Australia in 1888 included captain Joe Warbrick and his four brothers, plus three Wynyard brothers.

Millton nearly had to find another replacement. The Otago wing forward, James O'Donnell, was merrily whiling away his time on the train taking him from Invercargill to Dunedin on his way to joining the tour when it made an unscheduled stop at Clinton in south Otago. A policeman climbed on board, arrested him for unpaid debts, and escorted him back to Southland where he was confronted by a range of creditors with their hands out. They had taken out the arrest warrant fearing he intended to skip the country without paying his bills. How they could possibly have formed that suspicion has not been recorded. That minor matter taken care of, O'Donnell resumed his journey and made it to Wellington in time to join his team-mates. Lo and behold, O'Donnell stayed in Sydney at the end of the tour, never to return to New Zealand. He later played for Australia, becoming the first All Black to play for another country. (There must be something about Southland All Blacks heading for Australia. Jock Richardson, one of the giants of the Invincibles' tour in 1924–25, became the secretary-accountant of the Southland union after the tour and he too headed for Aussie in the late 20s, not to return until the NZRFU brought him back when he was 93 for its round of centenary dinners in 1992.)

New Zealand rugby proclaimed its arrival in Australia by an unusual means — as the good ship *Hauroto* steamed up Sydney Harbour, a football was hoisted up the main mast. As Sleigh recorded, "The football was rampant and the crowd at the . . . wharf, who recognised their loved ball aloft, gave three hearty ringing cheers for the visitors."

Three weeks later, the New Zealanders having played nine and won nine, there was another bout of ringing cheers as they left Sydney. There was also some Australian soul-searching. "Football will never become with us a leading game in the same sense as cricket," the *Sportsman* bemoaned. "The New Zealanders seem to furnish a type of the excellence required. They are a fine body of men, well-built, and with their muscular powers fully developed, although their dark uniforms made them appear thinner than they really were."

The *Sydney Telegraph* said the New South Wales "muffs" (a curious word that seemed to have derived from the NSW players muffing their chances) were taught how to play by the strangers from across the sea. "There is a natural affinity," it said, "between the climate of New Zealand and the robust character of this outdoor sport."

So were formed the first impressions of the strength of New Zealand rugby and first impressions, so it is said, are the ones that last. This inferiority complex, at least in terms of New Zealand rugby, was to stay with the Australians for the next 80-odd years. Alas, it is no longer.

New Zealand rugby must have had a self-satisfied, smug air about it after the tour because it had tested itself against its brother colony and had come away victorious. There seemed to have been a natural desire to have a go at someone else which was the raison d'être for the Natives' tour, so called because it was supposed to comprise only Maori, though five Pakeha were included and two of them had not been born in New Zealand. New Zealand rugby had another chance too, between April and October 1888, when a British team toured. It didn't play a national team, however, and for all its missionary purpose, the New Zealanders didn't learn a lot from it as one of the Natives, Tom Ellison, of whom more anon, rather sniffily commented.

Rugby was moving apace despite the difficult and sometimes hazardous methods of getting around New Zealand. A young journalist who was keen on sport, first in the Bay of Plenty and later in Hawke's Bay, Ernest Hoben, was enthusiastically fired with the idea of uniting the various and scattered provincial unions into a national body and he fired off letters here, there and everywhere in pursuit of his goal. His reasoning made a lot of sense to most of the unions, but not to Southland (by then a separate union), Otago and Canterbury, who didn't want a bar of a central organisation based in Wellington and much preferred to remain answerable to the English union, which then ruled the rugby roost and legislated not just for English clubs but for anyone happy to tug a forelock in their direction.

Hoben's big day came on 16 April, 1892, when delegates from around the country settled in the Club Hotel in Wellington — much of the business of early New Zealand sport was conducted in pubs — and decided to form the New Zealand Rugby Football Union. Hoben had most of the say and became the first secretary of the union and he successfully proposed George Campbell, the prospective captain of the 1884 team who couldn't get leave from his work at the Audit Department, as the first chairman.

Now that New Zealand had a national union, it was time to set about getting a national team, and deciding on colours for it. At the first annual meeting a year later, the union decided on both. Among the felicitous greetings from kindred organisations were one each from New South Wales and Queensland, not just saying how jolly good it was that there was such a thing as a New Zealand union but also suggesting they send a team across the Tasman (obviously having forgotten how it was New Zealand 1, Australia 0 nine years before).

In the arcane language of minute writers, "your committee" decided to accept the invitations. Then there was the matter of what the team would wear. Up popped Ellison, lawyer, innovative rugby player of note and one of the Wellington delegates.

The NZRFU's minutes gravely record, replete with liberal capitalisation: "It was resolved that the New Zealand Representative colours should be Black Jersey with Silver Fernleaf, Black Cap with Silver Monogram, White Knickerbockers and Black Stockings, on the motion of Mr Ellison, seconded by Mr King."

For the jersey, Ellison chose the style that the Native team, of which he had been such a prominent member, had adopted, which itself was an extension (blue to black and gold to silver fern) of the jersey worn by the 1884 New Zealand team.

Thus were the All Blacks born. Well, not quite. There was still the matter of the white knickerbockers, which the team that went to Australia three months after the NZRFU annual meeting wore. That team, which was fittingly captained by Ellison, played 10 games and lost one, to New South Wales.

The 1893 team, like its predecessor in 1884, wasn't fully representative of New Zealand rugby either, because players from Canterbury and Otago weren't

PALENSKI COLLECTION

The first New Zealanders to go to Britain were the 1888–89 Native team, tasselled caps and all.

BLACK TO THE START

considered since those unions were still against the idea of a New Zealand union. Ellison, originally an Otago man, called the attitude of the unions peculiar and said their efforts to undermine the validity of the New Zealand union had been notorious.

Were the knickerbockers really knickerbockers, that quintessentially American piece of apparel so beloved of baseballers? Of New York origin, they were "shorts" that were gathered in just below the knee or at the calf. Did All Blacks really wear such items or did New Zealanders use the word knickerbockers for shorts, as we would know them?

Pictorial evidence suggests that All Blacks did indeed look like New Yorkers. The only photos in existence of the 1893 team show them in street wear — what players now would call their number ones — but *The Queenslander* magazine carried a series of sketches which clearly depicted the All Blacks in long tight "shorts" that met their socks: knickerbockers.

By the following year, however, when New South Wales paid a return visit, the New Zealanders wore what were demonstrably white shorts, even if they did look like the baggy Bombay bloomers of the 1940s. In 1896 against Queensland at home, New Zealand also wore white shorts.

And when did the white become black? Sadly, it's not recorded. The only photos of the 1897 team that went to Australia show the players in their natty number ones, complete with bow ties, boaters and each player with a cane. They looked more prepared for a music hall routine than a rugby match.

The next time the All Blacks took the field was at home against New South

The 1897 team in natty number ones.

Wales in 1901 and by then they were definitely in black shorts, flapping around below the knees it is true, but shorts they were and black they were.

The All Blacks played a test for the first time on 15 August, 1903, and there were indications then of the attitude that would permeate all succeeding All Black teams: a competitiveness and an obsession to protect their own line. The manager of the first test team wrote in his report, "Each member of the team seemed to be imbued with one main object, viz, to use every legitimate means to uphold the traditions of New Zealand rugby football. . ."

A newspaper report after the test at the Sydney Cricket Ground, won 22–3, reflected on the competitiveness of the All Blacks: "The great difference, perhaps the greatest, between the two teams is that the New Zealanders go right on with the game, irrespective of forward passes, knockons, or other breaches of the rules: Australians if they observe a forward pass pause and momentarily relax their efforts."

Oh that that were still the case.

It's a hoary old quiz question: how many All Blacks made their test debut in 1903? Anyone who can't answer should be sent back to rugby quiz school.

A better question would be: how many New Zealanders made their test debuts when the All Blacks played their first test in 1903? The answer is 18. One of the Australians, Bill Hardcastle, was a Wellingtonian who had been an All Black in 1897, and the two wings, Sid Riley and Charlie Redwood, were both New Zealanders.

While the All Blacks had by then sorted out their colours if not their unofficial

The team that played New Zealand's first test in 1903 in Sydney. Captain Jimmy Duncan is in the middle wearing a beanie that covers his bald head.

BLACK TO THE START

The Originals line up on their goal-line at Crystal Palace before their test against England.

Once more into the breach . . . the Originals take the field before another capacity crowd.

THE JERSEY

name, the Australians were still bereft of national colours. The Australian team in that first test (it was Australia's fifth test after they'd played Britain four times in 1899) wore the light blue jerseys of New South Wales.

Those years had been what could be described as the formative years of the national New Zealand rugby team. The great adventure was now upon New Zealand rugby.

The British tour of 1905–06 was what established the All Blacks in the eyes of the rugby world as the team that set the standards in terms of playing organisation, player fitness, tour procedures, and it also added the words "All Blacks" to the rugby vocabulary.

A British tour, a desire to show the "mother country" how well the farflung offspring had developed, had been mooted for several years and even at the first annual general meeting of the New Zealand union in 1893 it had been noted there had been considerable correspondence with the English union.

After a few false starts and some concerns by the English about whether the New Zealanders were true-blue amateurs, unsullied by sordid money, agreement was finally reached for the 1905 tour. It was, by any yardstick, a stunning success.

An indication of the importance New Zealanders left at home invested in the tour was given by Premier Richard John Seddon, who likened the tour to the recently completed Boer War.

"As indicating public interest here," Seddon wrote to the *Daily Mail,* "information of the contests taking place in Great Britain is awaited almost as eagerly as news of the late war in South Africa. The results have been received with great enthusiasm."

And in an attempt, one of many over the years, to explain why New Zealanders should be good at rugby, Seddon added: "The natural and healthy conditions of colonial life produce the stalwart and athletic sons of whom New Zealand and the Empire may be justly proud."

Seddon's envoy in London, William Pember Reeves, a man of many parts including a stint as a Canterbury footballer, elaborated on his boss's words.

"As Mr Seddon points out," he said, "the conditions of life in New Zealand are especially favourable to the production of a fine body of footballers . . . the climate is a great factor. It is brisk, breezy and bracing, with a combination of sea and mountain air. Our country is peopled with a race inheriting the sporting instincts of a British stock with vaster opportunities and inducements to practice open air games."

He could have added, but didn't, that the Maori flair and passion brought an added dimension to rugby in New Zealand and had he lived long enough, he surely would have added that the dimension was widened even more by the advent of other Polynesians later in the century.

The Originals astounded the people of Britain with how they had brought order, organisation and fitness to the game. "The visitors played together as a perfect piece of machinery," one paper commented after the opening win against Devon. "Every member of the team had his appointed place and could be relied on always to be in it, ready to carry on the attack without hesitation."

The New Zealanders, this enthusiast went on, "exhibited wonderful vigour, activity and stamina and this alone would have given them the victory even had other things been equal, but they were not."

So the All Blacks, as they gradually came to be known, entered history in the northern hemisphere. Praise was heaped upon more praise as the tour developed but there were some reservations and, of course, an infamous reverse. The reservations centred mostly on the play of that distinctive New Zealand invention, the wing forward, a sort of unattached flanker whose prime role at scrum time was to prevent the opposition halfback from getting round and interfering with an All Black ball. This contentious role, which New Zealand clung to until it was legislated out of the game in 1931, was noticed right from the outset. "The wing forward completely spoiled [Devon halfback] Jago on the few occasions that Devon managed to get the ball in the scrum," the Devon *Express and Echo* complained. "[He] ought to have been frequently penalised for offside and wilful obstruction."

Those complaints echoed throughout the tour and in the following years until finally the British lawmakers decided they'd had enough. The Originals' captain, Dave Gallaher, was the wing forward who earned the most invective but he was able to laugh about it when he was watching one of the games from the stand. A spectator behind him shouted at regular intervals as the All Black wing forward did his business, "Gallaher you cheat, you're offside again" and other imprecations about the man sitting in front of him.

The reverse was the match against Wales lost 3–0 in which Bob Deans did or did not score. He said he did but was pulled back across the line before the referee huffed and puffed into position; the Welsh said he forced the ball short. The try would have brought the scores level and Billy Wallace would likely have kicked the conversion to turn the Originals into Invincibles. It was an unsolvable argument that resounded for years whenever Welsh and New Zealand rugby was discussed and players in the game were said to have croaked on their deathbeds that Deans did (or didn't) score, depending on which nationality was doing the dying.

The piece of Cardiff Arms Park ground on which Deans was said to have lain prone, ball firmly under his chest, was pointed out to visitors for years afterward. The ground was realigned and a new stand was built over the original goal-line but still the Welsh would mischievously point to a piece of the new ground and tell visiting New Zealanders that was where Deans didn't score, and the New Zealanders would dig up a bit of the turf and smuggle it back home.

In New Zealand eyes, the referee got the blame, as referees do. This one was a Scot, John Dallas, and history tells us that he was dressed pretty much in street clothes and ordinary shoes and, lacking the fitness of the players, he struggled to keep up with the play. By the time he arrived on the scene, so the story goes, Deans had been pulled back across the line and no try was awarded.

Dallas left Cardiff soon after the game on a train for London, thence to return to Edinburgh, and he wasn't aware of the fuss until a few days later. When he heard, he put pen to paper. "I was astonished," he wrote, "at the suggestion that Deans had scored a try which I had disallowed."

When the ball went to Deans, he said, Deans veered toward the touchline. "I kept going hard ahead and when Deans was tackled by Teddy Morgan, he grounded the ball 6–12 inches short of the line. At that moment he could neither pass nor play it. As I passed between the Welsh goalposts, my whistle went shrill and loud."

That whistle, with Dallas' written explanation, now lies in the Cardiff Rugby Museum.

If such an event happened today, Dallas would have described a square with his hands and looked for guidance from a television match official sitting glued

NEW ZEALAND RUGBY MUSEUM

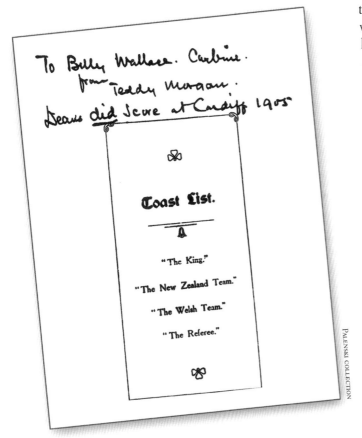

To Billy Wallace. Carbine.
from Teddy Morgan.
Deans did Score at Cardiff 1905

The celebrated 1924 menu on which Welsh wing Teddy Morgan wrote his confessional message about Bob Deans scoring in 1905.

(menu text)

Toast List.

"The King."

"The New Zealand Team."

"The Welsh Team."

"The Referee."

to a monitor somewhere. The players would have watched it on the replay screen, the word would have come down from on high and the referee, supposedly still the sole judge of fact, would have signalled a try or a scrum. The crowd would have accepted the video evidence before them and gone away satisfied or dissatisfied, depending on allegiance. It may still have been talked about for years, but the lore of the game would have been different.

For all the impact the All Blacks had on their all-but-unbeaten tour, and for all the new heights to which they took the game, they were still not universally admired. They were being paid three shillings a day expenses money and became known as "three bob a day men" and this didn't sit well with the well-heeled custodians of the amateur ethos, which decreed that chaps should play their sport for the sheer love of the game. The Scots in particular were affronted by what they saw as veiled professionalism and they were even more put out when they realised they had underestimated the popularity of the All Blacks. The New Zealand union financed the tour itself and sought guarantees from the various opponents to cover their expenses. The Scots wouldn't guarantee anything for the test against Scotland but agreed that New Zealand could have the whole of the gate, less expenses.

By the time of the Scottish test, the All Blacks were drawing huge crowds everywhere and the Scots lost both the match and the money. That and their criticism of the All Blacks being "paid" rankled for years and was said to have been a contributing factor to their not agreeing to play New Zealand on the 1924–25 tour. By then, the Scots also had another argument, this one against their more ancient enemy, England. The English had taken it upon themselves to organise itineraries for touring teams and the Scots didn't want any part of being told by the English when they could play or against whom. So they didn't play the Invincibles, ironically at a time when Scottish rugby was strong and may have offered Scotland their best chance of beating the All Blacks. They're still waiting for that first victory.

It's curious how selective memories and morality can be. The Scots bemoaned the All Blacks being paid three bob a day, and forced through a resolution at an International Rugby Board meeting in 1909 that such payments were against the spirit of amateur rugby. They must have forgotten that, five years before, a British team in New Zealand, captained by a Scot, was paid two shillings a day "wine money".

A New Zealander living in Scotland also fell foul of the Scots. Nolan Fell was a wing who had played for Nelson and Otago and decided to continue his medical studies at Edinburgh University. The Scottish selectors snapped him up and he played seven times for Scotland before the All Blacks arrived. He was also chosen to play against New Zealand but withdrew, saying it wouldn't be right to play against his fellow countrymen. The Scottish selectors never knocked on his door again.

The occasional controversies aside, the Originals were a seminal team in the history of rugby and such was the respect for the way they played the game that their captain, Gallaher, and his vice-captain, Billy Stead, were persuaded to write a book to share their knowledge and understanding of the game. They combined on the work, *The Complete Rugby Footballer*, in the last few weeks of the tour, Stead doing the bulk of the writing while Gallaher found photos and read proofs. The book is still regarded as one of the best on the game, a textbook for excellence.

It is for that very commodity, excellence, for which All Blacks continue to strive. The Originals set the benchmark for all New Zealand teams. When the 1924–25 team went to Britain, they went with the avowed aim of avenging the one loss suffered by their predecessors. And they did. Every following team, from Jack Manchester's side of 1935 to the most recent team to tour Britain, is judged by that benchmark. The success of All Black teams anywhere is judged not by the number of games they win, but by the number they lose. The more losses, no matter the circumstances, the less kindly the team is judged, either by contemporary critics or by history. Losing is the dirty word of All Black history.

In the years since the pioneers of 1884, as the One Thousand have ranged far and wide in pursuit of their excellence and in pursuit of the elusive perfect game, the All Blacks have an overall success rate in tests against all countries of nearly 72 per cent. That is astonishingly high over such a period. By comparison, the next best is by South Africa at 64 per cent and only three other countries, France, Wales and England, are above 50 per cent. Another comparison could be made with a perennially successful national sports team, Australian cricket. Although there are more variables because of the higher percentage of draws in cricket, the Australians' overall success rate in tests is 43.4 per cent.

In all matches by the All Blacks, 1063 of them to the end of 2000, the success rate is 84 per cent.

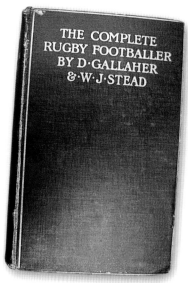

Still regarded as a classic of rugby writing, Dave Gallaher and Billy Stead's *The Complete Rugby Footballer*.

INTERNATIONAL TEST WINNING PERCENTAGES

	Played	Won	Winning %
New Zealand	346	248	71.7
South Africa	268	172	64.2
France	541	289	53.4
Wales	495	264	53.3
England	517	265	51.3
Australia	358	177	49.4
Samoa	108	47	43.4
Scotland	491	211	43.0
Ireland	485	178	38.0

STATISTICS ACCURATE TILL 31 DECEMBER, 2000

BLACK TO THE START

ALL BLACKS —
THE CHRISTENING

The enduring myth about how the New Zealand rugby team came to be known as the All Blacks was that it was a result of a printer's interference, that a reporter wrote "all backs" because of the way they played but that the printer inserted an "l".

There is no evidence to support this often-told story but plenty to suggest that it's just a myth.

Myths were two a penny in the 19th century. In rugby, the other big one was that William Webb Ellis in a rush of his Irish blood snatched up the ball and ran with it and so invented rugby. English officials, so keen to claim the game as English, seized on that tale, plastered it on a wall at Rugby School and turned it into fact. Or tried to.

As a celebrated Prussian military strategist Helmuth Von Moltke once wrote, it was a duty of piety and patriotism not to destroy certain traditional accounts if they could be used for an inspirational end.

But myths are not facts and while a contemporary and less educated population may have walked with a lighter step with pride pumping in their chest because of the manufacture of myths, it's the duty of later recorders to cast a far more objective eye on the romantic fiction of the past.

In other words, it's well past time to spoil a good story with a few facts.

The story with which we grew up on our grandfathers' knees was recorded by one of the Originals, Billy Wallace, and perhaps because he lived longer than any of them and continued to repeat his story it became accepted as fact.

Where Wallace heard the story is not known — though there was one theory that the insertion of the "l" in "all backs" came not in a newspaper, but in a newspaper billboard before or after the game against Somerset, which was the 11th match of the tour.

This came two games after the All Blacks' 63–0 win against the Hartlepool Clubs, a match which was also said to have prompted the printer's

Billy Wallace, who repeated the myth about how the All Blacks got their name.

historic initiative.

But the facts tell a different story. First, some background. It was evidently a trend in rugby in the 1890s and early in the 20th century to refer to a team by the colour of its jerseys. Otago were the Dark Blues, for example. The first official New Zealand team in 1893 played its first match against a team chosen from southern North Island unions — an early version of the Hurricanes. The combined team wore a variety of jerseys but mostly red and a newspaper report wrote of a try by centre "Tabby" Wynyard: "Wynyard . . . with a determined effort got through the Red backs."

What's more, the Wellington Rugby Football Union *Annual* of 1894, referring to that first historic match, said, "The Blacks (ie, the New Zealand representatives) won . . ."

The parentheses were the *Annual* editor's.

Later in the same report, the writer said, "The Blacks now played up with great determination . . ." When referring to the multi-hued opponents, he talked about "the Colours".

The manager of the Originals, George Dixon, kept a diary throughout the tour and at times he referred to the players as "the Blacks", even while they were still on board ship and far from a keen printer's eye.

They played their first game against Devon at Exeter and walloped the locals 55–4. The next day, a local paper, *The Express and Echo*, recorded: "The All Blacks, as they are styled by reason of their sable and unrelieved costume, were under the guidance of their captain (Mr Gallaher) and their fine physiques favourably impressed the spectators."

So much for the free hand of a typographer or even the wit of a reporter coming up with a catchy phrase. By his reference, it was clear the team was known as the All Blacks before he happened along.

Now back to Hartlepool. The name "the All Blacks" seems not to have appeared in print again until the night of the win against Hartlepool when the *Northern Daily Mail,* Football Edition, got in on the act. This was one of those newspapers, like the old sports editions in New Zealand, which were rushed onto the streets for sale as soon after a match as possible. Its report of the match traversed 14 paragraphs before this introduction to a listing of the players' vital statistics: "A glance at the undermentioned weights of the invincible 'all blacks' will convey some idea of the calibre of the team . . ."

The name didn't recur in the paper's coverage, which filled two pages.

The next morning, the *Northern Daily Mail*'s parent paper, the London-based *Daily Mail*, took up the name. Its report recorded the score in the second paragraph and continued: "This is a record in the tour, which is yet barely a month old, exceeding as it does by eight points the 55 points

the 'All Blacks', as the Colonials are dubbed, piled up against Devon."

The *Daily Mail* was represented throughout the tour by JA Buttery and it is a reasonable assumption that he wrote the previous day's story in the *Northern Mail*.

The next paper to use the name was the Gloucester *Citizen* a week later and All Blacks first appeared in a heading in the *Daily Mail* on 19 October.

The next national newspaper to use the name was the *Daily Mirror*, on 6 November 1905. After that, everyone was using it.

The industrious Buttery included the name in his book of the tour, *Why the All Blacks Triumphed*, thus using it in a book title for the first time.

The New Zealand union took a long time to adopt the name in a formal sense. It was always regarded as a nickname for the team and was in wide common usage but officially it didn't exist.

One of the dominant men of New Zealand rugby for 40 years, Norman McKenzie, didn't like the name All Blacks at all. In fact, he didn't even like New Zealand teams being called New Zealand.

McKenzie was coach of the great Hawke's Bay →

The clipping from the *Express and Echo* in Devon which includes the first published reference to the team as the All Blacks.

BLACK TO THE START

team of the 1920s and an All Black selector for two terms, the first from 1924 until 1930 and the second from 1947 until 1949. He was also a prolific writer on the game.

On the eve of the first test against the 1959 Lions, McKenzie wrote that the New Zealand union "should take pains to announce subsequent selections as 'the New Zealand XV'."

"No one imagines that it is the best," he said, "but it is the New Zealand XV to play the visiting international XV whichever country it comes from."

His views on the term All Blacks were similarly novel: "I have always regarded the title 'All Blacks' as something that should be reserved solely to that band of pioneers who blazed the trail in the homeland in 1905–06 and were described as such, by reason of their sombre uniform, by the English press."

(That was a view similar to the Australian Rugby League's, which decided its national team would be called the Kangaroos only when touring Britain. It formally changed its corporate mind in 1994, decreeing that they could be the Kangaroos when touring New Zealand as well.)

A onetime chairman of the New Zealand union, Ces Blazey, once remarked that the team chosen was the New Zealand rugby football team and that the phrase, "All Blacks", was a journalists' phrase and had no official standing. This was in response to being asked if the team that went to Argentina in 1976 was an official All Black team.

When money got involved, that soon changed.

As the New Zealand union gradually realised it could make money out of the All Blacks through sponsorships and licensing arrangements, it also gradually realised that so could anyone else.

In 1986, at the urging of its marketing advisor, then none other than Andy Haden, a man who in that role was the classic poacher turned gamekeeper, the union had designed a stylised silver fern emblem and had it formally registered.

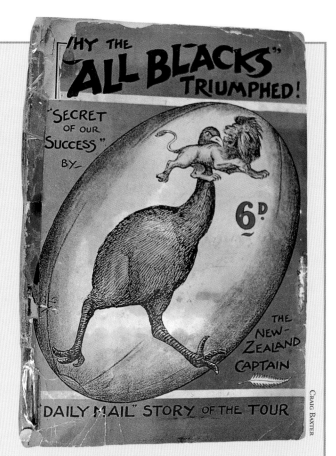

Reporter JA Buttery's book which made full use of the team's new name but it was not a name, as the myth has it, that he had a hand in coining.

A year later, the phrase "New Zealand All Blacks" was also registered, giving the union legal power to protect its use from predatory ambush marketers.

This gave rise to a few accusations of tautology among those who knew what tautology was. Why say the New Zealand All Blacks? What other All Blacks are there? The Israeli All Blacks? The Congo All Blacks?

No, but actually there are the Welsh All Blacks (that's the Neath club) and there's a team in South Africa that calls itself the All Blacks. And search the internet by providing just the keywords "All Blacks" and you'll get some surprising results. Up popped the All Black Lesbians. And the All Blacks, a gay Caribbean network.

Ah, but there is only one New Zealand All Blacks.

RECEIVING THE CALL

Try this for a contrast: flat, warm beer with chilled champagne; reheated and hardened battered fish with seafood crêpes; cheerios with beef Wellington (with a few honey-glazed carrots, broccoli and duchess potatoes piled alongside).

Such was the way with All Black team announcements. The beer, fish and cheerios came in the days of the old function room at Athletic Park when All Black aspirants jostled with All Black veterans for a bit of space in the crowded, smoke-filled room. The champagne (Moët, if you please), seafood crêpes and beef Wellington came in the first of the new days, when the All Black squad for the first World Cup was announced.

There were more contrasts. In the old days, a white-coated official (and if he didn't wear a white coat, his attitude was such that he should have) stood stolid sentry duty at the door, carefully inspecting each pass that would admit entry, even if its owner was more of a public figure than the prime minister, and even if he looked as if he'd just emerged from a shower (which he had) and was wearing a provincial blazer and clutching a gear bag.

Even if the owner of the pass was a figure who had passed through rugby's ages of man as player, coach and administrator over a period of 40 or 50 years and had probably helped paint the function room in some distant past, entry was not automatic.

Sometimes, a woman would be so audacious as to attempt entry. "Sorry madam, the room for the ladies is down the corridor." (The separate function room for the women had all the charm and space of a disused ticket collector's booth.)

Somehow, perhaps when the white coat's back was turned or when he was remonstrating with some other would-be gatecrasher, others, passless, would get in. Turn left inside the door to grab a jug or a bottle and a glass if there were any left, then push and shove and elbow into some space that may have been left in the outer reaches of the room.

There to await the announcement. There was no other cause or reason to be there. Certainly not for the delicacies of food and drink on offer.

But in Whangarei the night the first World Cup squad was announced, there was none of the old Athletic Park tradition. Not even passes to get in. Diners were invited, no less. "We would appreciate your attendance . . ." Appreciate! All the

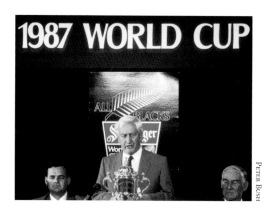

NZRFU chairman Russ Thomas at the champagne naming of the 1987 World Cup squad in the Grand Hotel in Whangarei.

PETER BUSH

The place best known for All Black team announcements was the much-maligned function room at Athletic Park where players sweated while waiting for selectors to finalise their teams. NZRFU chairman Jack Sullivan, up on the small platform that served as a stage, names the team to tour Britain in 1972-73 and below, players react. On the left are new All Blacks Kent Lambert (back to camera) and Graham Whiting. Ian Eliason, also named as an All Black for the first time, seems to be wiping away a tear while Frank Oliver, who wasn't chosen, looks pensive.

PETER BUSH

old white coats appreciated was the perks of their job of a few free beers, getting to hear an All Black team announcement, and telling journalists with as much unconcealed glee as they could muster that they had no right to be there.

The venue in Whangarei was the grand dame of hotels, the Grand, where for more than a century it had hosted the great and the good in sumptuous dining, where the Queen once sipped at toheroa soup.

The function room at Athletic Park had sparse decor but on one wall was a springbok head that may have been a souvenir of the New Zealand Universities' win against South Africa in 1956 or perhaps Wellington's win against the 1965 team; no one could remember which and, when a team announcement was pending, no one cared.

The dining room at the Grand had the crossed tusks of an elephant, a souvenir of some altogether more risky undertaking, and from the tusks hung a battered brass dinner gong, a far more effective method for rugby's muezzins than the back of a teaspoon banging on a seven-ounce beer glass.

For all the contrasts, there were still similarities. It was hot. Hot in the function room at Athletic Park because of the press of bodies of expectant humanity, hot in the dining room in Whangarei because of the presence of lights for television. Sweat rolled down the faces of players who had played in the final trial that afternoon, sweat because of the heat and sweat perhaps because of the apprehensive tension.

Another similarity was the chairman of the New Zealand union standing and reading the names of the chosen ones. At Athletic Park, on a stage that had room for only one man. In Whangarei, standing at a lectern alongside one of the dining tables, looking into a television camera that beamed the announcement live to homes throughout New Zealand. In Whangarei it was Russ Thomas. In earlier years, it had been Jack Sullivan, Tom Morrison, Cuth Hogg . . .

For the players, for all the change, it was much as before.

Friend sat alongside friend, one was in and one was not. Team-mates sat opposite team-mate, one was in and one was not.

At one table in the Whangarei dining room sat Bernie McCahill, Bruce Deans, Andy Earl and Brent Anderson. Three were in, one was not. McCahill was ecstatic, one of the genuine surprises in the team. Deans was stunned, barely able to comprehend what he'd just heard. Earl was relieved and moved that he'd again been entrusted with a place in the most respected of New Zealand sports teams. Anderson was bewildered, a little hurt, a little angry.

While other diners moved in on the table, slapping backs and shaking hands and laughing and all talking at once, Anderson sat there expressionless, perspiring and staring out at some distant point. He was leaned on, nudged, reached over, ignored as photographers joined the crowds of wellwishers.

There were similar scenes at other tables. Warwick Taylor, in, sat and talked quietly to Dean Kenny, not in. John Schuster, not in, leaned over a bottle of Moët and roughed the hair of Michael Jones, in.

As always, the trite but expected words came out. "I'm absolutely delighted", "I didn't think I had a show", "I'm over the moon", "This is a dream come true" and so on, words that have echoed down the years.

Nothing so trite for Bruce Deans, brother of All Black Rob, great-nephew of All Black Bob, who did or didn't score against Wales in 1905. With a television camera thrust in his face, reporters and photographers jostling each other around

It was the most public of All Black team announcements. Michael Jones (top) and John Gallagher react to being named in the World Cup squad in 1987.

him, he politely asked for time to compose himself.

Clearly moved, he later said how pleased he was not for himself but for his mother and father who had done so much for him, pleased also for older brother Rob and proud that he had been chosen to continue a noble family tradition.

The old way of doing things, the cattle market atmosphere of Athletic Park and the pedantry of the official announcements . . . "DB Clarke, Waikato . . ." had been criticised and bemoaned often enough. But the new way didn't win universal praise either.

The convenor of the selectors for the World Cup squad, Brian Lochore, sat at the top table and was a little saddened by what he saw and heard. The naming of an All Black team, while of great public interest, is also a private time for the players, those who make it and those who don't. Perhaps they don't mind their joy at selection being in the public gaze, but it's hard on players who somehow have to mask their disappointment, who sometimes may feel as if someone has just slipped a knife in their guts and twisted the handle.

It is a time for elation, joy and relief and the whole gamut that comes with being named in the All Blacks, but it is a time too for deep personal disappointment, for stoicism, for the brave face. It is a time when some of those who miss out can't hide their true feelings. More than one All Black has had a face like thunder after a team announcement, more than one has been known to slam a fist into a wall, to go to a private place for a brief outpouring of rage.

Some have had to put their emotions on hold. The team to go to Australia in 1938 was due to have been announced at Athletic Park after the North-South match but the New Zealand union, at a meeting the night before, decided to delay it. The reason was the Australians wanted the tour matches to be played under the laws then being used in Australia, which were different to international laws (one significant difference was the dispensation allowing Australia and New Zealand to restrict kicking into touch on the full to within a defending side's 25-yard line — a dispensation that became a universal law 30 years later).

The NZRFU said there would be no tour until Australia agreed. Hence, the inter-island players had their after-match function with none of the tension of a pending team announcement.

Five days later, the Australians agreed and the team was named. Even then, things didn't go smoothly. Aucklander John Dick, who had been an All Black the year before, had to withdraw because he had measles and sole selector Ted McKenzie chose Alan Wright of Wellington to go in his place. But no sooner had the All Blacks left for Australia than Dick pronounced himself well again and the Auckland union insisted he be reinstated.

No can do, replied the NZRFU. He's been replaced and the All Black complement is at the maximum the Australians will pay for. Undeterred, the Auckland union organised a whip-round and soon found enough money to dispatch Dick to Sydney. The New Zealand union said he could join, providing he had a medical clearance and that he left by a specific date. Eventually, the privately funded Dick did join the team in Australia and played in three of the last four matches, including the final test.

New South Wales captain Victor Richards (left) greets some of the All Blacks at a welcoming reception in the Hotel Metropole in Sydney in 1938. The All Blacks, from left, are Harold Milliken, Charlie Quaid, Ron King and Albert Bowman.

All Black wing Alan Wright is caught short of the line in the Queensland match in 1938 by Queensland and Australian centre Winston Ide.

At least McKenzie selected a team that played, even if one extra player did get added. The following year, he chose a team that didn't play. The All Blacks were due to tour South Africa in 1940 and when war broke out in September 1939, a series of trials was in full swing. The New Zealand union had a hurried consultation with the South African Rugby Board and they agreed that if the war was over by 1 January, the tour would still go ahead. If the war was still on, the tour wouldn't be. The war won.

McKenzie, so rugby folklore has it, still selected his team, though it was never made public and not even shown to anyone else. McKenzie died in 1946 and the names of the 1940 would-be All Blacks died with him; what didn't die was speculation about whether anyone else ever saw the list and who was on it. Even 40 and 50 years on, there was still speculation about who may or may not have been All Blacks in 1940, even though most of the speculators wouldn't have seen in action any or many of the players they championed. There was a widespread school of thought, for example, that halfback Charlie Saxton, who had been in Australia in 1938, would have captained the team. Maybe. McKenzie's brother Norman, another man of many rugby parts, chose for a newspaper his All Black test team based on the trial form he had seen in 1939 and his halfback was Eric Tindill, whose one test had been at first five-eighth against England in 1935. Norman McKenzie placed Saxton at first five-eighth and didn't name a captain.

Another said to be a certainty for the 1940 team was No 8 Ernie Todd, who was later a distinguished Wellington and New Zealand administrator who managed the 1972–73 All Blacks in Britain.

Selection in the All Blacks was once described as being like being chosen for a job: the matches that come before were likened to job interviews. "For many are called, but few are chosen." Only the All Blacks who have studied the scriptures would know that phrase comes from the Gospel According to Matthew. And those who have missed out should know that the preceding sentence in Matthew reads, "there shall be the weeping and gnashing of teeth".

While there are superficial similarities, selection for the All Blacks is not like being a successful job applicant at all. People apply for jobs to advance their careers and/or to earn more money or sometimes just for a change in scenery, direction or lifestyle. For rugby players, being named as an All Black is something they've set their hearts on, something to which they have aspired for many years. It is the reason for their being. Their rugby lives have been geared to the one ambition and the closer they get, the more significant it becomes. People can apply for a job, shrug when they miss out and look around for the next one. Missing out on the All Blacks is no time for shrugging and no player who ever uttered the phrase, "Oh well, there's always the next time", truly believed it or uttered it with conviction. Because for them, the next time is one step closer to retirement, one step closer to a younger player stepping up, one step closer to losing the edge that earned the trial or got him so close in the first place.

And no job applicant ever goes into an interview with the whole country following his every move and action, some willing him on, some saying he has no show. It is the most public of examinations.

Some announcements of All Black teams are more — or less — public than others. Take the naming of the team to go to South Africa in 1976, for example, a team in which there was the usual enormous public interest but also a wider interest because of the questioned wisdom of sending a team to a country in which a white minority ruled and disenfranchised the great majority.

That team was named on a Sunday morning in a hotel near Wellington airport that's undergone various name changes over the years and has been a base for All Blacks from time to time. The chairman of the union then was Jack Sullivan and he made it known he'd announce the team at 9.30 in the hotel bar. Most of the players who had played in a test against Ireland the previous day were still there.

Jack Sullivan, chairman of the NZRFU from 1969 until 1977, who was most associated with the deliberate naming of All Black teams.

A few of Sullivan's colleagues from the union council were there, plus a few journalists. It was not a big gathering and, given the time of day, it was a sober one.

There was no ceremony. Sullivan walked into the room with a sheaf of papers in one hand, went to a table and sat down. "This is the team," he said, "the selectors have chosen for the tour of South Africa." He then read it at a fairly brisk pace.

No cries of delight punctuated the naming, no cheers, no back-slapping. It was all very matter-of-fact except that when he got to the name of halfback Lin Davis, there was a shriek from outside the room. Since some of the players' wives were waiting outside, it was assumed the jubilation came from Davis' wife Alison who not only had supported Davis in his ambitions but had also been the willing recipient for hours and hours as he practised his passing.

Sullivan's voice was the one most associated in modern memories of the deliberate intonation of All Black teams. He it was who was associated with the punctilious pronunciation of players' initials, names and provinces. So it was that in the hotel that morning he read, "KL Fawcett, Auckland, LW Mains, Otago . . ." and so on through the favoured 30.

But Sullivan, wrongly known publicly in later years as a man of a few terse words, was merely continuing a tradition in which he too had grown up and 40 years before had heard his own name called, JL Sullivan, Taranaki.

With the naming of All Black teams, for all the traditions and for all that the players accepted as the way it was done, there were calls from time to time for more understanding of the players' personal feelings, for the announcements to be made in a less public way. This was occasioned more by the need to let some players down gently rather than protect those who were included in the team.

The naming of Andy Leslie to captain the All Blacks in Australia in 1974 was a case that led to calls for more courteous, sensitive announcements. Standing near Leslie in the Athletic Park function room when the team was named was Ian Kirkpatrick, who was, as everyone understood, the incumbent All Black captain. He'd led New Zealand in 1972–73 and the first he heard that he wouldn't be the

All Black captain and haka leader extraordinaire Wayne Shelford, dumped amid controversy in 1990.

leader any more was when the team was announced.

Dignified man that he is, Kirkpatrick immediately went to Leslie and offered his congratulations and support.

Even worse, three years later, Kirkpatrick, who was not wanted for the tour of France, apparently heard the composition of the team when boarding the Poverty Bay team's bus.

When another All Black captain, Wayne Shelford, was dropped, a mix-up between selectors Alex Wyllie and John Hart meant that all New Zealand heard the team at the same time as Shelford.

For all the misgivings about the systems used, there doesn't seem to have ever been a serious suggestion that New Zealand should follow the British example and send letters to the chosen ones. Theirs go along the lines of: "Dear Roger, You have been chosen to represent England against Scotland on . . . You are required to be at training on . . ."

A day after the letters were posted, the teams were publicly announced.

Some selections were much less formal than that. When the British were scouting around for players for the Anglo-Welsh team that toured New Zealand in 1908 (a team which the Scots and the Irish wanted nothing to do with), manager George Harnett wrote to Arthur O'Brien, a New Zealander who had been studying at Guy's Hospital in London. O'Brien, though a New Zealander, had played for (and managed) the British team in New Zealand in 1904 but, as the 1908 tour approached, he was planning on returning to work in New Zealand. Harnett's letter to him read:

My Dear AB,
I suppose you wouldn't play for us in New Zealand if we should need a ?. I am just sending you this line in case you would like to.
I hear from our good friend Mac that you are just off to the old home so am sending you these few lines to wish you every prosperity and good health and also to Mrs O'Brien. I trust the good Providence will allow us to meet some day. At any rate, it will always be a great pleasure to look back on the many happy days we have spent together. With all good wishes,
I remain, my dear old fellow, yours as always,
George Harnett.

Friend "Mac" was Pat McEvedy, another New Zealander studying at Guy's, who was vice-captain on the tour. He too later returned to New Zealand and became involved in rugby administration and was president of the New Zealand union in 1934. It's not known how O'Brien responded to Harnett's letter but, in any event, he never played.

There couldn't have been a greater contrast than 90 years later when All Black coach John Hart chose his first squad for 1999. It included a number of new players and Hart felt he had to let them know before the team was publicly announced. It happened that, at the time, several of them were in the Highlanders and they were in Cape Town for a Super 12 semi-final against the Stormers. Hart phoned the coach of the Highlanders, Tony Gilbert, and he brought each of the players to the phone to be given the news by Hart. The squad was then announced publicly while the Highlanders were on the way home.

But even that method of considering the players' feelings first had a drawback. The Highlanders had won their semi-final and were returning to a home final against the Crusaders. Being named as All Blacks just added to the pressure on the players who also had to cope with the normal demands of a final plus the shortened and disrupted buildup caused by the exhausting flight back home.

Receiving the call a second time can almost match the stunned thrill of the first . . . almost. Take the extraordinary case of Neil Wolfe, that 5 foot 6 inch (1.67m) bundle of lightning energy who played for the All Blacks in 1961 two years after leaving New Plymouth Boys High School. He played the three tests against France that year, another two against Australia in 1962, all at first five-eighth, then he popped up at second five-eighth in the one test against England in 1963.

After that, nothing. He and most others would have thought it was nothing until a strange set of circumstances in 1968.

Two trials were held at Athletic Park in May 1968 for the team to tour Australia and Wolfe was among the 10 reserves named for both teams. He sat through the first trial and wasn't required. A few minutes' break to stretch the legs, then it was back to the seat in the stand for the second trial (reserves always sat in the stand in those days, rugged up against the cold alongside their manager and coach).

The centre in the black-clad Possibles team, Grahame Thorne, was injured

All Black trialist Neil Wolfe
shows his class.

and had to leave the field and Wolfe thought his chance had come. But no, selectors Fred Allen, Ivan Vodanovich and Les George said they wanted a centre from the first trial, Tony Johnson of Waikato, to have another go. This was news to Johnson because, thinking his services would no longer be required, he'd showered and changed. He dashed down to the Colditz-like dressing room, rummaged around what gear was left, and appeared on the field eight minutes later in a black jersey — noticeably more faded than those of his new teammates — and white shorts (the others wore black).

Sticking out like the much-maligned sore thumb, Johnson went down in a thumping tackle by the Probables fullback, Mick Williment, and as halftime approached, an ailing Johnson told his captain, Colin Meads, that he didn't think he could continue.

Now, at last, Allen motioned towards Wolfe to get out there. He needed no second bidding and joined the Possibles at halftime. As what might be called a reserve-reserve, Wolfe decided that even the slightest opportunities should be taken and, in the final five minutes of the match, he scored two tries.

It was enough for the selectors to write his name down for the trip to Australia — five years after he'd last played for the All Blacks.

Wolfe said amid the contrasting congratulations and consolations in the function room at Athletic Park that he thought he'd gone from New Plymouth to Wellington just for the trip.

"I didn't think I had a show of getting in," he said. "I'm speechless, I just don't believe it. The tries were pure luck. It was just the bounce of the ball and there I was over the line."

Wolfe played three matches at first five-eighth in Australia and one at centre. He didn't play in the tests.

A couple of Taranaki men had a more-than-passing interest in Wolfe's surprise recall. When Wolfe was still at New Plymouth Boys High, the school's first XV coach, JJ Stewart, remarked to a few friends that the tiny Wolfe would one day be an All Black.

After a bit of scoffing, one of the friends, Gerry Monaghan by name, challenged Stewart: "A 4½ keg that he's not." The bet, being offered, was duly accepted.

Wolfe fulfilled Stewart's prophecy within two years but it was another couple of years before Stewart and Monaghan mentioned it again and the latter said to the former: "I owe you a 4½."

Stewart, in that slow deliberate way he has, thought a bit then said: "Make it double or quits."

Monaghan was quick to seize upon what seemed such a magnanimous offer, given that everyone in New Zealand *knew* Wolfe's All Black career was over.

Stewart just smiled . . . and was smiling even more a few years later when Monaghan fronted up and paid his dues. The nine-gallon keg was delivered and consumed during a social day for the Taranaki team on John Major's Inglewood farm. And Wolfe was among those who drank to Stewart's foresight.

Tremain's 'happy hour'

Picture the scene. It's late on a Saturday afternoon in 1959 and all over New Zealand pubs are serving beer through hoses at a terrific rate as the witching hour of six o'clock approaches.

The pub at Springston, out of Christchurch and near Lincoln College (as it then was), was typical of them all. A crowded bar, noisy drinkers retelling tales of the afternoon's rugby match, glasses being emptied and refilled at a desperate rate, drinkers with one eye on the clock and the other on whose round it was.

Among the drinkers in the public bar at the Springston pub was the Lincoln College B team, even more anxiously watching the clock because not only was six o'clock closing time, it was also the time that the evening meal was stopped back at the college.

Among the B team drinkers was a farm cadet, 21-year-old Kel Tremain, who usually played for the A team. But he'd had a game for the Bs because the As had a bye that weekend and he needed to get through a game to show the national selectors he'd recovered from a knee injury.

Bob Duff, a Canterbury stalwart and All Black captain just three years before, went out to Lincoln to check Tremain managed 80 minutes and he then phoned the convenor of the All Black selectors, Jack Sullivan, who that day had watched his old province, Taranaki, against the British Isles.

The All Blacks had won the first test in Dunedin 18–17, six goals by Don Clarke, and changes for the second test were expected.

The noisy revellers in the Springston pub were told at about five to six to shut up. A hush settled over the bar and someone reached up and

Kel Tremain.

increased the volume on the mantel radio.

Over the airwaves came the staid voice of the New Zealand Broadcasting Service announcer reading the All Black team for the second test that he'd just been handed. He read it in the traditional way with the fullback first and as the drinkers realised the selectors had made dramatic changes (eight of them) the quiet gave way to a growing murmur. The murmur became roars of approval when the twelfth name was read out . . . "KR Tremain . . . Canterbury . . ."

The rest of the team was barely heard as Tremain's back was slapped and both hands were shaken at the same time as celebratory beers were being thrust into them.

Six o'clock closing in the pub and dinner back at Lincoln were temporarily forgotten and the barman's time-honoured shout of "Time, gentlemen please" was either not shouted at all or not heard for the uproar.

Tremain recalled the night years later with clarity and said it was a delightful way to learn of selection in the All Blacks. The drinking didn't go on too long, though.

Tremain said they left the pub at about quarter past six for the two-minute drive back to the college, hoping that dinner was still on.

"But the matron had kept the meal on, knowing where we were and why we were late," he recalled. "So there was a tremendous reception back at Lincoln as well."

The test the following Saturday in Wellington was the start of one of New Zealand rugby's most illustrious careers. Tremain played 38 tests until 1968, and another 48 matches for New Zealand. He died in 1992, aged 54.

INVITE OF A LIFETIME

❧ Jamie Hendrie thought he was having his leg pulled when the president of the West Australian Rugby Union, Joe Lord, sidled up alongside him after a colts game and said, "How'd you like to play for the All Blacks tomorrow?"

It was the day after Hendrie's 19th birthday.

Hendrie, fresh from the field of play and almost as fresh arriving in Australia from Scotland, couldn't believe what he was hearing.

The All Blacks were in Perth on their way to South Africa in 1970 and were due to play twice the next day, once against a President's XV and once against the state team.

Since one of the All Black halfbacks was Sid Going, who didn't play on Sundays, All Black manager Ron Burk had asked Lord if there was a likely local lad who could fill in.

"I suppose I'd played reasonably well in this game on the Saturday and in any event must have caught Lord's eye," Hendrie recalled. "I must say I was an invitational All Black, not a meritorious one.

"Obviously it was a big thrill but I didn't know as much about the All Blacks then. It was only later that I came to understand more about what they meant and what it meant to be an All Black."

Hendrie recalled being welcomed into the dressing room before the game as if he was just any other player chosen to wear the black jersey. "They all came up to me and shook my hand. They were very friendly. My hand was not very big and here it was being shaken by these big paws."

He recalls, 30 years after the event, little of the game against the President's XV, which was won 52–3 by the All Blacks.

"I know I've never been better protected in my life," he said. "The All Black forwards, especially Colin Meads [who was captain for the match] did a great job of looking after their halfback, which was just fine by me. The only time I got hurt in the match was when Jazz Muller fell on me. He'd be a big man by today's standards. He was certainly big then."

The All Blacks tried to organise for Hendrie to

A 1992 photo of All Black for a day, Jamie Hendrie.

score a try but it didn't quite come off. "We were close to the line and someone shouted at me and they got the ball to me but I couldn't quite get through," he said.

Hendrie stayed with the team for the after-match function, at which the All Blacks were required to sing. They chose *Pokarekare Ana* but Hendrie confesses to just standing there with his mouth open, pretending to know the words. "I didn't have a clue," he said.

Hendrie recalled having aspirations, like any young man playing rugby in Australia, of one day playing for the Wallabies even though he knew it was just about mission impossible to get into the national team from Perth. "But as a kid, you have these dreams. In any event, a month or so after the All Black game I basically had a shoulder destroyed and I was never the same player again after that. I couldn't tackle properly whereas before tackling had been one of my strong points. After the injury, I just couldn't play rugby to any sort of standard that would get me further."

Hendrie was a medical student when he received his surprise callup to play his single game for the All Blacks. He now works as an emergency specialist in Melbourne.

Ship mates/team-mates

Jim Burrows and Geoff Alley, Canterbury friends and team-mates, would have left Athletic Park in the early evening of 8 October 1927, with the utmost reluctance. They'd just played in the winning team in the last of a seemingly interminable series of trials for the New Zealand tour of South Africa in 1928, the first visit there by an All Black team.

Thirteen players had been named in the touring squad four days previously after the inter-island match, won by the South Island, for whom Burrows and Alley also played, and the remaining 16 were due to be named after the last trial.

But Burrows and Alley, and other South Islanders who had played, couldn't wait to hear if they'd achieved the rugby player's ultimate goal. They had a boat to catch.

They were driven down to the inter-island wharf in Wellington while the six selectors pondered the balance of their team back at the park. With six selectors, no one was predicting an early announcement. It would be a long wait for people still at the park; an anxious voyage awaited Burrows, Alley and the others on the overnight ferry to Lyttelton.

In the time-honoured tradition of such voyages, players and other passengers would have sat around for a while in the lounges, perhaps playing cards, and others would have leaned on the rails until the lights of Wellington disappeared in the distance. Then they would have retired to bed, waiting for the wake-up call in the morning by a steward bearing sturdy cups with USS stamped on them and filled with tea so strong there would have been no chance of going back to sleep.

Burrows and Alley shared a cabin but they didn't have to wait for the dawn wake-up. Theirs came not long after retiring when a steward banged on their cabin door.

"The chap burst into the room and said, 'You are both in the team!'" Burrows later recalled.

There was no need to say which team.

"Whether we went to sleep after that I'm not sure," Burrows said.

Alley had been in the All Blacks before, in Australia in 1926, but it was a first for Burrows.

Given that the final trial was in October and the tour didn't start until the following April, it was a six-month summer of careful activity for all the All Blacks. No one would have been taking any chances with injury. "We were able to swank and live in our glory until we left," was how Burrows put it.

The team left for South Africa on Friday, 13 April — and much was made of an All Black team heading off on tour on Black Friday.

It wasn't the only acknowledgement of superstition for that team. It was the style of the day for playing jerseys to be numbered according to the number of players in the squad, their numbers being determined by the alphabetical order of their surnames. Alley thus wore No 1 though he was a lock; Burrows had No 3. There was not a No 13 though. The jerseys were numbered one to 12, and 14 to 30.

Jim Burrows suffered a rib injury early in the tour and played just nine matches on the tour, his only appearances in an All Black jersey. He also played cricket for Canterbury. He had a distinguished military career, being the only person to command all three of the 2nd New Zealand Division's infantry brigades in the Second World War, and was also in command of K-Force in Korea in 1950. Burrows died in 1991, aged 86.

Geoff Alley played 19 matches for New Zealand, including three tests in South Africa, and wrote a book about the 1930 tour of New Zealand by the British Isles. Alley died in 1986, aged 83.

Jim Burrows.

Invincible selections

⌐ All Black teams have been announced in ways that have seemed to be more for the convenience of rugby officialdom rather than any consideration for player sensitivities or anxieties.

Such was the case in 1924 when, after a series of trials, the All Black team to tour Britain and France — to become known as the Invincibles — was named in Wellington in two stages.

The first section was chosen after the annual inter-island match, in which the North had a 39–8 cakewalk, and the chairman of the New Zealand union, Stan Dean, named 16 at a team dinner in Barrett's Hotel. The hotel was for many years, with the Grand, a regular Wellington watering hole for visiting rugby teams.

The 16 were George Nepia, Gus Hart, Fred Lucas, Bert Cooke, Jack Steel, Mark Nicholls, Cliff Porter, Bull Irvine, Brian McCleary, the

Brownlie brothers Maurice and Cyril, Jim Parker, "Son" White, Jock Richardson, Ron Stewart and Ian Harvey.

It was a relief for the 16 chosen ones among the diners, but meant a few more days of worrying and wondering for the others.

A final trial was scheduled for the following Monday, King's Birthday, and a few of the certainties were included in the match, apparently in a bid to strengthen their teams. Cooke was not among them and he was sitting in the stand, rugged up in overcoat and hat.

"It was a dreadful day," he recalled, "rain coming down in bucketfuls and I was happy to be sitting up in the stand watching the others mudlarking. Then Louis Paewai broke a collarbone early in the second spell and instead of sending on Lucas, they called for me. I had to get changed and go on, not liking it a bit. However, I carefully kept clear of any danger. It wouldn't have done to get hurt before sailing."

The second half of the touring party was announced the night of the final trial at a dance in the Wellington Town Hall.

"I don't think any of the footballers enjoyed themselves much for the first hour or two," Cooke recalled, "the agonies of suspense being too painful. Finally, the names were put up on a board on the stage around 11 p.m. while everyone crowded around. The last name posted was that of Read Masters. He must have had some anxious moments."

Cooke said the "ins" as well as the "outs" celebrated long into the night.

A similar selection procedure was followed for the next big tour, that of South Africa in 1928. Cooke again was among the 16 certainties, despite having told Dean that he didn't want to tour because of business commitments (he'd recently opened a menswear store in Masterton).

"I let myself be talked into it," Cooke said. "Mr Dean's persuasiveness was chiefly

PALENSKI COLLECTION

Bert Cooke, the man regarded as the prince of centres.

responsible. He was very anxious for me to go and I appreciated the compliment."

Cooke played in the final trial though he still harboured misgivings and, finally, in February of 1928, he told Dean that he'd have to stick to his original decision and not go.

As in 1924, the names of the remaining touring players were put up on a blackboard at a team dance.

Cooke also told of how the certainties named for a tour would take extra good care of themselves if they were required to play, as he was, before the tour began. The certainties got together before the match, he said, and made a pact to look after each other and curb their competitive instincts.

Bert Cooke was regarded as the prince of centres but his team-mates called him "King". He played 44 matches for New Zealand, including eight tests, between 1924 and 1930. In a first-class career of 131 matches, he scored 121 tries. He also played rugby league for New Zealand. Cooke died in 1977, aged 75.

FAKE TEAM, BY GEORGE

੭ Great was the fuss in 1968 when it was suggested that several top rugby officials knew the All Black team to tour Australia before the final trials and, therefore, before the team was publicly announced.

What's the point, the Wellington *Evening Post* reasonably asked, of holding the trials if the selectors have not only already decided on their team but even told some members of the New Zealand union of its composition?

What indeed?

The sinister, however, was explained away as the banal.

The secretary of the New Zealand union, George Geddes, explained that he'd picked his own touring party of 28 so he could get the ball rolling on booking flights and accommodation.

When the official team was named after the trials, Geddes had to confess that he'd been eight out.

Bob Kidd, the Wellington tailor who for years outfitted All Black teams, had also had a crack at picking the team so he could run up the required number of blazers in time. Alas, he too was astray with his selections and a few blazers had to be hurriedly altered.

The chairman of the New Zealand union, Tom Morrison, was so horrified at the thought some people considered union officials were in the know before they should have been that he offered a public explanation:

"It has been suggested that there has been some skulduggery going on," he said. "To take advantage of the group travel discount we had to name what we thought would be the touring party some weeks before it was announced. We have done this for a number of years and have been astray every time."

George Geddes, professional secretary and amateur selector.

IN TIME OF CRISIS . . .

↬ Brian Lochore was retired. Fit, but retired. His career of 23 tests from 1964 until 1970, captain from 1966 until 1970, was at an end. It was one of the most distinguished of All Black careers. But it was over. So he thought.

It was 1971 and Lochore was still fit because he'd played early in the year in a series of matches to mark the centenary of the English union and, back home, he'd continued to play club rugby.

But he'd retired from international play. Not even a tour by the Lions could entice him into another year. "To be a good test player you've got to be hungry and I guess I wasn't hungry anymore," Lochore said.

So Lochore was content to play just club rugby for Masterton. But then a crisis in Wairarapa-Bush. They were short of a lock for their match against the Lions.

"They pleaded with me to play and I said, 'Ah well, okay, just this once', and I reckon I had reasonable reasons why I could play."

So Lochore played his one game for Wairarapa-Bush that year and that, he reckoned, was it.

But then another crisis. This time in the All Blacks on the eve of the third test in Wellington. The Lions had won the first test in Dunedin, the All Blacks the second in Christchurch.

The third test was critical. But captain Colin Meads was doubtful because of a rib injury and the other lock, Peter Whiting, had already withdrawn because of injury.

"I was working on the farm on the Friday, my wife had gone somewhere for the day with the children and I came home at lunchtime and the phone rang," Lochore recalled.

It was Bob Duff, one of the selectors.

Can you play tomorrow? Lochore was asked.

Well no, not really, was Lochore's reply.

Then he learned that Ian Kirkpatrick would captain the side if Meads couldn't play and that he too was doubtful because of injury.

"So they were not only looking for another lock, they were looking for a possible captain as

Brian Lochore pictured before his comeback test against the Lions in 1971.

NEWS MEDIA AUCKLAND

well if Meads and Kirkpatrick couldn't play. So really, as far as I was concerned, I had no option," Lochore said.

So Lochore went to Wellington and played. As it happened, Meads and Kirkpatrick also played. And the Lions won 13–3.

"I had no regrets about being asked or playing. A lot of people have been upset that I came back and that perhaps didn't do myself justice but that doesn't worry me at all. I did a job for New Zealand.

"How would I have felt with my conscience forever if I'd said no and they'd still lost by the same score and everyone in New Zealand would have known because you can't keep secrets like that? I would have felt a lot worse."

The Lochore recall provided one of those nice rugby tales that get handed down through generations. Since his wife Pam was out and Lochore couldn't get hold of her, he left a note on the kitchen table: "Gone to Wellington to play in test tomorrow. Ring you later. BJ."

FOR LEADER, READ LESLIE

One of the most talked-about team announcements under the stand at Athletic Park was in 1974 when the chairman of the New Zealand union, Jack Sullivan, named the team chosen to tour Australia.

It was a party of 25 for the three-test tour with an unofficial test against Fiji tacked on, and 15 of the chosen ones were newcomers.

The announcement drew more than the usual gasps and shouts of delight.

None was louder than when Andy Leslie was named. So often a trialist and so often picked by the pundits, he had so often been overlooked that most of his supporters had long since given up hope of his being an All Black.

Not only was he an All Black, he was also the captain, displacing Ian Kirkpatrick who had been captain since the 1972 internal tour.

Leslie remembered the day well. "I'd sat under the grandstand for quite a few teams being picked and the announcement was made and it got down to IN Stevens, then the next initials were out and they were AR . . . I was just expecting it to be AR Sutherland but it was AR Leslie and I fell over backwards. I didn't hear another word mentioned."

Amid the uproar, Ian Stevens picked up on the crucial word that Leslie had missed.

"The next thing I remember," Leslie said, "was Nectar [Stevens] hit me on the shoulder and said, 'You bastard, you're captain too!'"

Leslie recalled that after Stevens, Kirkpatrick was the next to congratulate him. "And then the first letter of congratulations I got was from Kirky's mother which I thought was real neat."

What Leslie didn't know — and what no one else in the crowded function room knew either — was how JJ Stewart and his fellow selectors, Jack Gleeson and Eric Watson, arrived at Leslie being captain.

Stewart in a television interview recalled what happened. "We picked the team and Sullivan kept popping in and saying, 'Are you finished yet?' and I kept saying no. 'Well, hurry up'. 'We will hurry up

Coach JJ Stewart and captain Andy Leslie in Australia in 1974.

if that's what you want or do you want the team?' 'You take as long as you like'. So off he'd go."

Stewart said Gleeson and Watson thought Kirkpatrick should be the captain because he was the incumbent, but Stewart had the impression that Kirkpatrick wasn't all that comfortable with the leadership.

"He's one of the greatest persons I've ever met," Stewart said, "certainly one of the greatest footballers you'd ever meet or have anything to do with. But I didn't feel that being captain was pleasing him and I said that and they said, 'Well, who else have we got?' Then we started to look at the list."

A general belief then and later was that Leslie had been chosen for his captaincy skills. But Stewart's story disproves that.

Leslie was in the team first before the selectors discussed the captaincy.

Stewart said he hardly knew Leslie and told a story against himself to prove it. He was at an aftermatch function following a Wanganui–Wellington game and talked for about five minutes to a player he thought was Leslie. "And then the person I was talking to said, 'I'm not Andy Leslie, I'm Dave Waller'."

Stewart conceded that naming Leslie captain was a gamble, "but I know now in retrospect the decision we made was very, very successful."

Leslie played 34 matches for the All Blacks, including 10 test matches, and captained them from his debut until his retirement after the 1976 tour of South Africa.

Queen's Birthday surprise

∽ It was the Saturday of the Queen's Birthday long weekend in June 1968 and Tony Kreft reckoned he'd go and watch the annual seven-a-side tournament at Ranfurly in the Maniototo district of inland Otago.

He was due to play for Ranfurly that afternoon against Alexandra but reckoned he had time to watch some of the sevens before the drive to Alexandra.

"I was just standing there watching when someone came up to me and said they'd had a phone call in the clubrooms wanting to know if Tony Kreft was there," he recalled. "The message I got was that I had to ring Charlie Saxton."

Saxton, All Black in 1938 and captain of the post-war Kiwis, had been the All Black manager in Britain the previous year and was a member of the New Zealand union council.

So Kreft walked over to the clubrooms and put the call through to Saxton, not knowing what it was all about.

"I didn't have an inkling," Kreft said. "Then Charlie came on the line and said I was wanted in the All Blacks and that I had to get to Australia. He wouldn't let me play in Alexandra that afternoon."

It was a rushed introduction to All Blackdom. In Dunedin on Sunday morning, Christchurch Sunday afternoon, Sydney and then Canberra on Sunday night. Training with the All Blacks on Monday morning, named in the team Monday afternoon, pulling on The Jersey and playing against Australian Capital Territory on Wednesday.

"It all happened in a hell of a rush, I can tell you," Kreft said. "When I got to Sydney a couple of blokes came up to me and said, 'You're the man we want' and they drove me across the tarmac to another plane and told me to go.

"It was great arriving in Canberra because just about the whole team was there at the airport to greet me. That was a really nice touch and made me feel part of it right from the start."

Kreft didn't expect to play in the match in Canberra but the forward strength was so depleted by injury that coach Fred Allen didn't have a choice.

"So in I went," Kreft said. "We won 44–0 but the conditions were atrocious. Snow and rain and slush. Just like playing at home really."

Kreft's callup was so rushed he had no All Black gear but fellow prop Alister Hopkinson for some reason had his 1967 All Black blazer with him and loaned it to Kreft. "He was about my size so it fitted okay but don't ask me why he had his 1967 blazer with him . . . perhaps he was planning on raffling it. That would have been just like 'Hoppy'."

Tony Kreft played four matches on the tour, including the last test, won 19–18 by a penalty try in the last two minutes. Remarkably for a prop, he scored two tries in his four matches.

Tony Kreft.

'SELECT COMMITTEE' IN '24

The night before the Invincibles left on their historic tour in 1924, there were two contrasting functions in Wellington. One was a parliamentary farewell to the team at which the expected platitudes were spoken and toasts drunk, the other also had a parliamentary aspect to it but was much less convivial.

While the All Blacks were being farewelled at Parliament, the selection of the team was the subject of heated debate a few hundred metres away at a specially called meeting of the New Zealand union's management committee.

And central to the debate were Prime Minister William Massey and senior cabinet minister and Massey's heir presumptive, Gordon Coates. (He became prime minister in May the following year.)

Most of the All Blacks who were going to Britain had been on a brief visit to Australia where they had played four matches for one loss, then lost to Auckland and beat Manawatu-Horowhenua

when they got home.

Their performances were not overwhelmingly impressive and after the Auckland loss, the 1905 hooker George Tyler condemned them in the *New Zealand Herald*. "The weakest team New Zealand has ever had — weak in the scrums, weak on defence and lacking in pace sums up the present All Black team," he wrote.

That set a few Auckland minds to thinking as well as that of Ernie Little, a member of the Rugby Union who had managed the team on the brief trip to Australia.

Little proposed that an extra player be added and he specifically suggested Auckland halfback Don Wright because, he said, the form of the chosen halfback, Jimmy Mill, had been disappointing.

Not much unusual in that, although no modern All Black manager would dare advise — not →

The Invincibles, the 1924–25 All Blacks.

publicly anyway — the selectors who they should pick. What was unusual was that Little and others took their concerns to Massey and Coates.

Coates, who was the MP for Kaipara, then spoke to the chairman of the union, Stan Dean (who was also manager of the team to Britain), supporting the Auckland suggestion and said that if Wright's selection depended on extra funds being made available, he was sure the people of Auckland would stick their hands in their pockets.

Dean told the chairman of the selectors, Ted McKenzie, about this political interference and McKenzie — whose exact words were not recorded, probably fortunately — said he was happy with the team as it was and it wouldn't be changing.

Dean called a meeting of the management committee to discuss Coates' entreaties and it decided to let things stand as they were. That meeting was on a Saturday night and McKenzie couldn't get to it, but he did show up at the next meeting two nights later on the eve of the team's departure.

Discussion was heated, to say the least. In its report the next day, *The Dominion* said: "the most strained relations that have existed for many years in the controlling body of the New Zealand rugby game were evident".

The paper carried an almost verbatim report of the meeting, the committee having rejected a suggestion that it be held in private. "I want it in the open," McKenzie said. "I want the people of New Zealand to see how things have been carried on."

Because Dean had gone off to the parliamentary farewell, Wellington administrator Dolph Kitto took over the chair and began by saying: "Surely we are not going to let outsiders influence us?"

Edgar Wyllie, the union treasurer, said the Saturday meeting had been called "because we recognised that there was a very urgent appeal coming from the north and representations had been made to the prime minister".

Kitto asked at whose instigation the meeting had been called and Wyllie replied: "Mr Coates and the prime minister."

Kitto: "What have Mr Coates and the prime minister got to do with it?"

McKenzie: "They may be good at politics, but they may have to improve themselves at football."

That was when things got a bit heated and the harassed *Dominion* reporter inserted into his copy: "At this stage the members were speaking very rapidly in interjection and became difficult to interpret."

McKenzie at some stage talked about there being a "pull" from Auckland and later muttered about "this hole in the corner business".

Belatedly, the committee asked the press not to report a discussion about what was said between Coates and Dean. The reporters, though they remained present, obliged.

By the end, the committee expressed its confidence in the team as chosen.

Also expressing confidence in it was one of the men who wanted it changed, the prime minister. "They are out to defend the honour of New Zealand," he told the parliamentary farewell, "and we who are left behind will watch their progress with the greatest anxiety. As to whether they win or lose, or how they will take it, they will remember the sentiment of the writer who said, 'It is not that you are beaten in the fight that counts, it is how did you fight and why?'"

As it happened, they weren't beaten at all. So much for the weakest team.

———— ❖ ————

STAND BY FOR SYDNEY, ANTON

❧ Anton Oliver was looking forward to a good flight home. No more training for a while, no immediate match for which to prepare, just 20 or so hours of travelling and the luxury of his own bed at the end of it.

And if the cabin crew with the drink cart kept trundling by, why a man — even if he was only 18 — would be a fool not to take advantage of it. After all, he reckoned he deserved a drink or two.

It was July 1995 and the first southern hemisphere Colts tournament had just finished in

Anton Oliver, second from the left, being embraced by Glen Osborne after the All Blacks' win in Sydney in 1995.

Argentina and the young New Zealanders had won it well, beating Argentina, South Africa and Australia all in the space of a week.

The day after the tournament in Buenos Aires, Oliver was helping with the packing of the team gear and getting it onto the bus for the trip to the airport. He went to the room of the manager, Mike Banks, to ask if anything else needed doing.

"Ah Anton," Banks said, "I've got some news for you. Norm Hewitt's been injured and you've been called into the All Blacks. You'll be joining them as soon as we get home."

Hewitt had been the reserve hooker for the test against Australia in Auckland but couldn't make the trip to Sydney for the return test a week later.

So much for the carefree flight home. So much for returning to Dunedin to play in the club final the following weekend (in which Dunedin, captained by the Colts captain, Taine Randell, beat Oliver's University A).

"It was all mind-numbingly overwhelming," Oliver said. "One minute I'm looking forward to a few drinks on the way home, the next I'm in the All Blacks. It was all a bit of a quantum leap. I thought, if I'd thought of it at all, that I was miles away from getting in the All Blacks. Hell, I was only 18 and it was only my second or third season as a hooker."

So it was a sober, reflective flight home. Back at Auckland Airport, while the Colts farewelled each →

RECEIVING THE CALL

other and promised to stay in touch, Oliver was whisked off to the All Blacks' base camp of so many years, the Poenamo at Takapuna. From the bosom of the tyros of New Zealand rugby, Oliver went straight to the lair of the veterans: he roomed with Richard Loe the first night, then with Michael Jones when the team got to Sydney.

Oliver hardly knew any of his new team-mates, some not at all. His only previous acquaintance with Loe was playing alongside him in the inter-island match earlier that year in Dunedin.

Jonah Lomu, already the best-known name in world rugby even though he was in only his second year as an All Black, made a point of sitting with Oliver on the first bus trip. "He just did it to be friendly and put me at ease, knowing how I'd be feeling," Oliver said. "I really appreciated that."

There hadn't been time to get Oliver a full issue of All Black gear, so he wore his Colts blazer and team-mate Mike Brewer, who worked for Canterbury International at the time, rustled up some clothing.

If the circumstances of joining the All Blacks were bizarre, what was to follow came almost in the realm of fantasyland.

This was the time when the whispers were running hot about the threat from the World Rugby Corporation, when players were secretly negotiating their futures, when the New Zealand union dispatched Brian Lochore and Jock Hobbs to Sydney to try to keep the All Blacks in the fold, when the Wallabies and All Blacks thought they were playing their last tests, when the whole of the rugby world was in the greatest turmoil it had ever faced.

This was all news and new to Oliver.

"I distinctly remember being in Sydney," Oliver said, "and the All Blacks were walking along a beach and one of them spotted Lochore in the distance and said, 'Shit, there's Lochore'."

This was the same Lochore, revered man of New Zealand rugby, who had been the campaign manager at the World Cup in South Africa the month before, who had nursed and encouraged the players to the peaks they had reached. Now, he was on the other side.

"I didn't have a clue what was going on," Oliver said, "but it was obvious that a lot was. No one told me anything though because I was the new boy."

The test was played and won, the 100th test between New Zealand and Australia. It should have been a time for celebration and commemoration. It should have been a time when the players of today mixed with the players of yesterday, the torchbearers of their eras. But it wasn't. Instead, it was a time of intrigue and recrimination.

"After the test when we were still in the dressing room, Walter Little and Frank Bunce sat me down and told me what was happening. I was staggered. I was thinking, 'Whoa but hang on, this is the All Blacks. What do you mean, go and play somewhere else? What do you mean, bugger the Rugby Union? How can you say that? How can you play rugby without the Rugby Union?'"

Then came the infamous bus trip to the opulence of a house in inner Sydney where the merits of WRC were spelt out to the All Blacks. Oliver was with them, sampling the hors d'oeuvres when Sean Fitzpatrick went to him and asked him to leave. Oliver had not played for the All Blacks, therefore he was not wanted.

"I went outside and played basketball with the house owner's kids for a while because the bus had gone on some tiki tour round the suburbs to find a place to turn around," Oliver said. "When it returned and I got back on, Meads was livid."

Colin Meads, the mighty Pinetree, was the All Black manager and he was angry because the All Blacks should have been at the lavish dinner that had been set up to mark the 100th test.

Eventually, the players trooped out of the house and were delivered to the dinner. "There were all these great players from the past there and all their wives and the current players all had their wives and partners there, and I felt totally out of it. There was all this intrigue going on and there were muttered comments from some of the older guys. Fortunately, my father was there and I sat with him. If Dad hadn't been there, I think I would have just got up and walked out. I didn't feel a part of it at all.

"As far as introductions to the All Blacks go, I

reckon mine would have been one of the weirdest."

Oliver became a "real" All Black the following year, making his debut against Eastern Province in Port Elizabeth, the same opponents and the same ground that marked father Frank's debut 20 years before.

WE'RE NOT TAKING THE MICK

No place echoed more to the gasps of surprise and the cries of joy that accompanied the announcement of All Black teams than the room at Athletic Park that was variously described as the function room, the social room or the dungeon.

Thus it was the scene in the early evening of Saturday, 9 September 1967, while men, glass of beer in one hand, a sausage roll or a piece of battered tarakihi in the other and jug of beer planted firmly and protectively at the feet, waited for the three selectors to finish their task.

Players in the final trials that had finished nearly two hours before stood and chatted with an affected air of studied nonchalance that belied the question burning their brain and the apprehension that gripped their gut.

At the doorway, someone signalled. It was time.

The chairman of the New Zealand union, Tom Morrison, a man who as a player, a selector and an administrator was well versed in such occasions, gave the nod to his fellow members of the NZRFU council and they, everyone well knew, had to approve the team before it was made public.

The councillors left to meet the selectors, Fred Allen, Ivan Vodanovich and Les George, in a disused dressing room that served as the selection room. There was a hush as the councillors filed out, then the hubbub returned as the air of expectancy heightened.

Two minutes . . . three minutes . . . the councillors returned, the three selectors stood together in the only doorway, Morrison climbed the steps. No one needed to call for silence. Everyone knew silence was needed.

Mick Williment, who had a line through his name.

Morrison began: "The New Zealand rugby football team to tour the United Kingdom is as follows: . . . WF McCormick, Canterbury . . ."

Morrison read the names fast, too fast, and many were lost or not picked up amid the clamour.

He read the team again, this time more slowly.

Realisation dawned and there seemed to be a collective gasp. Where was Mick Williment? No Williment, one of the two fullbacks in the afternoon's main trial and an assured goalkicker for nine tests?

Williment the name was not there. Williment the man was there, sidling up to McCormick and saying, "Fergie, my deepest congratulations . . ."

A stunned McCormick, according to an *Evening Post* report, croaked back: "Mick, it should have been you."

Later, McCormick recalled in his biography written by Wellington journalist Alex Veysey: "I was conscious of Mick Williment at my side,

French centre Jean Trillo attempts to thwart Fergie McCormick in the second test against France in 1968. The other All Blacks are Chris Laidlaw and Earle Kirton.

grasping my hand . . . I felt sorry for him. I told him he was unlucky. Then everyone was round and it was bedlam . . . someone kept filling my glass and I kept emptying it . . . I was excited, so bloody elated . . ."

Williment, dignified man that he was, went to as many of the chosen ones as he could reach and congratulated them, hiding his own disappointment behind his smiling best wishes for others.

It may have been as early as that night, it may have been the next day, but a rumour soon started doing the rounds, the well-oiled rugby bush telegraph working as well as it ever had.

The selectors got it wrong, the rumour went. They'd jotted down 31 names on their piece of paper instead of the required 30. Morrison counted them up when the councillors went to approve the team and Allen

had to put a line through one of them. Whose name attracted the black line?

Was it the Auckland prop, Barry Thomas? Was it the Wellington flanker, Tom Lister? Was it Bruce Watt of Canterbury? Was it Williment? Someone else?

Speculation continued for years until Allen publicly confirmed, with reluctance, that it was Williment.

As a footnote to this story, the referee of the main trial that day, Allan Taylor of Canterbury, muttered to McCormick as he lined up a conversion attempt late in the game: "Kick this Fergie, and you'll get a trip to Britain."

McCormick didn't kick the goal, but he did gain the greater prize.

McCormick played in all four tests on the 1967 team's unbeaten tour and played a total of 43 matches for New Zealand, including 16 tests. He scored a record 24 points against Wales in 1969.

Williment was not chosen to play for the All Blacks again. He'd played in nine tests between 1964 and 1967, scoring 70 points.

GIVING A RIGHT ARM

A sacrifice, we should have learnt in school, is something with several meanings. It could be a ritual killing that offers up the victim to a god (not much call for that these days) and the victim itself becomes the sacrifice; it has a religious connotation still in some churches; in commerce a sacrifice could be something sold for less than it's worth just for the sake of getting rid of it.

And a sacrifice is giving up something of value for something that is even more important or worthy.

Here we bring in the All Blacks. Sacrifice is a word that has been bandied about regarding All Black history, almost since Samuel Sleigh first hit on the idea of taking a team of New Zealanders to New South Wales to show them how rugby really should be played.

Sacrifice in rugby is a two-way street. There has been (and probably still is) the player who would sacrifice just about anything to be an All Black; and there is the player who would sacrifice being an All Black to keep his job or to keep his family or to keep something else held dear.

They cover the spectrum of the One Thousand, from the first would-be All Black captain who decided his job was more important than playing rugby for his country (and if he could have known what later significance being an All Black would have had, would he have made the same decision or would he have told his boss to shove it?), to players today who along the road to All Blackdom have to sacrifice something.

They cover the remarkable story of Dick ("Red") Conway who lopped off a finger so he could continue to be an All Black to John Major who was sacked by his uncle because he was needed at work rather than away playing footy, to any number of them who have gone on tours not knowing where their next pound or dollar was coming from.

Sacrifice is not putting too grand a word or meaning on the desire to be an All Black (or the decision not to be one). This is not offering up virgins to the gods of rugby, it simply means that All Blacks throughout history have at some stage had to make a choice: their money or their sport, their family or their sport, a career or their sport, a wild social life or their sport, any number of alternatives.

Their decisions have, for better or for ill, shaped the rest of their lives. If a player put all considerations aside to become an All Black, and did so, an All Black forever he will be. When he dies, there'll be at least a couple of paragraphs in newspapers, usually headed, "Former All Black dies". If a player decides other factors are more important than being an All Black, he's not only in the minority but his notice of death will in all probability be confined to the paid advertisements at the back of the paper where the births and marriages are also recorded.

The All Black is an All Black and whatever else he does, he remains an All Black. Therein lies another sacrifice. Goodbye (at least during the playing days) to a private life, goodbye to going down to the pub for a few quiet drinks with the mates, goodbye to shopping without being stared and pointed at, goodbye to walking down the street without attracting stares and autograph seekers, goodbye to a life of anonymity. It's the non-All Blacks who have that and, in all likelihood, wonder until the end of their days if they made the right decision.

And if, God forbid, the All Black at some stage gets himself into trouble with the law or gains notoriety in some other way, it'll be the fact he was an All Black that will be pointed out first. Like it or lump it, All Blacks forego the escape clauses of life the rest of us can and occasionally do use; they must forever set the standards. Sir Richard Wild, Chief Justice and ardent rugby follower (and player), was the guest speaker at the New Zealand union's 75th anniversary dinner in 1967. "We must remember," he said, "fame brings responsibility and the All Black at the top does well to remember that he carries in his hands tremendous power for good or ill. He owes it to the game that brings him fame to set a standard of sensible, disciplined living and loyalty to the game."

It is a sacrifice of no mean standing, this undertaking to be an exemplar for all that is good in life. The regard New Zealanders have for All Blacks, the height of the pedestal on which they have been historically placed, demands of players who have been examples in one field of endeavour to be examples in fields far beyond their prowess as players. It is a heavy burden for young men and only as the young become old, and the competitive nature of the rugby player becomes mellowed, that the burden is carried more lightly.

It is possible to snort and scoff at the start of the 21st century about modern All Blacks making sacrifices and about them having burdens of responsibility. They're all well paid, probably among the top 10 per cent of earners in the country, so why shouldn't they shoulder a bit of responsibility? Why shouldn't they have to do a bit extra for the lavish amounts showered upon them, not to mention all the perks of the job that go with being an All Black? It's a harsh and demanding world that requires of All Blacks standards and responsibilities that we don't require of any number of other people, often in much more responsible positions.

It is indicative of the standing that All Blacks have that while they are the object of praise and idolatry, they are also quickly condemned and criticised. When they lose, certainly, because that goes with the territory of being an All Black and it has always been that way, but the condemnation and criticism can go way beyond their performances on the field. Such is the price of being an All Black.

Modern All Blacks are far more exposed to the whims of the public than any of their predecessors ever were, they're called on to do far more away from the rugby paddock. And since they're fulltime rugby players and the cream of professional sportsmen in New Zealand, that is only right and proper. But they are entitled to time off from their jobs like everyone else, they're entitled to go home at the end of their working day and flop down in front of the television set or whatever it is that people do in the privacy of their own homes. That is sometimes forgotten. All Blacks should not be 24-hour automatons yet sometimes that's how they feel. Just one more training session, one more interview, one more this, one more that, it'll only take five minutes.

Scorn is piled upon any player bold enough to say that the season's too long and that they need a break. Yet it's difficult to think of any other sport in which such demands are put on the physical and mental resources of its adherents for so long a season. Well, they're paid, aren't they? Yes, they're paid, but dollars in the bank don't lessen the impact on the body of 100 tackles or 100 scrums, of 80 minutes of hard physical endeavour for about 30 of the 52 weeks in a year, interspersed with training sessions which are almost as hard for most of the other weeks. Dollars in the bank don't make the muscles any more durable or the bones any less brittle.

New Zealanders make demands of All Blacks that they don't make of anyone else, not of people in other sports, not of business people, not of politicians, not of other people earning public money, not of anyone.

There are sacrifices in representing New Zealand at any sport. The cyclist who has to pay his own way to wear a New Zealand jersey at a world championships, the rower who has to give up her job for the constant hours of practice necessary to reach the top, the cricketer who lives out of hotels and suitcases in order to ply his trade; all make sacrifices in the pursuit of their endeavours. What makes the All Blacks different, historically and not in a money sense, is the demands placed upon them. The cyclist can go away and come back and only few will know that he even rode, never mind where he finished. The rower could be at a regatta somewhere without New Zealand knowing or caring. The cricketer wins some, loses some, draws a few, and it's accepted as the lot of the cricketer. But not the All Blacks. Wherever they are, whoever they're playing, there's constant attention and continual demands for them to win. For New Zealanders, nothing less will do and for the All Blacks as well, nothing less will do.

Players quit their jobs to further their careers or to go on tours, schoolteachers go on half-pay, some other occupations are lucky enough to go on full pay, others are unlucky enough to go on none. There was a time when employers indulged All Blacks, when it was seen to be doing a national service to have an All Black on the payroll and give him a sinecure so he had time to train and play. Sometimes the employers were former All Blacks themselves, sometimes there was benevolence on the board that allowed All Blacks to be carried. Sometimes All Blacks were set up in businesses by wealthy benefactors who were also avid rugby followers and knew well the meaning of All Black success to the nation. Those days are long gone, were gone even before professionalism removed the burden from the employer.

There is another type of sacrifice that All Blacks make (or have made) that

PHOTOSPORT

It is a heavy burden for young men . . . Tony Brown and Justin Marshall during the World Cup in 1999.

GIVING A RIGHT ARM

New Zealand Rugby Museum

Barney Armit.

surely is worthy of more study by people learned in such things. That is what seems to be an unusually high incidence of health problems, usually associated with joints, among former All Blacks compared with others of the same age who have led more sedentary lives. Maybe it's something some would-be orthopaedic surgeon could study and categorise for a medical journal. But it seems, from a layperson's point of view, that a disproportionate number of former All Blacks have had to undergo knee or hip replacements, some at unusually young ages, or in later life have had corrective surgery on troublesome knees that wasn't available when they were playing. Such things are another cost, i.e. sacrifice, of being an All Black.

Two All Blacks gave their lives for rugby. The first was an Otago player, Barney Armit, who died as a result of a tackle by another All Black, Alf Bayly, in an Otago–Taranaki match in 1899. The two had been team-mates on the 1897 All Black tour of Australia.

Early in the second half of the Otago–Taranaki match, Armit ran with the ball about a metre in from touch and had only Bayly to beat. Armit swerved back infield in an unsuccessful attempt to evade Bayly. In the words of the Otago captain, Jimmy Duncan, "Bayly then tackled him. He tackled him low in the usual style but Armit jumped from the ground. Bayly then naturally caught him lower down. He caught him by the calves of the legs and threw him. If Armit had not jumped, Bayly would have caught him above the knees. That was legitimate playing. I saw Armit fall. He fell right on his neck."

Armit lay motionless on the ground and play was held up while he was taken from the field to hospital. He told doctors he could feel nothing below his shoulders. A cervical vertebra had been dislocated and the spinal cord crushed. An operation fixed the dislocation but nothing could fix the snapped spinal cord and Armit lay wasting away in hospital for 11 weeks before he died.

As he lay dying, he exonerated Bayly. In a deposition to a justice of the peace, Armit said: "Bayly played the game. I don't think Alf would do it intentionally. I sincerely believe it was an accident. Bayly and I were friendly during the progress of the game. He just picked me up and let me drop. He tackled me in the ordinary way a man would to put another down."

But others were not so sure.

In a full reporting of the inquest in the *Otago Witness,* Duncan, a police sergeant, the referee and a touch judge all put the incident down to being one of those things, but Armit's brother Robert and a doctor at the match both gave a different view.

Both felt that Bayly had deliberately upended Armit in the tackle. The doctor, Robert Burns, said Bayly flung Armit to the ground at an angle of 45 degrees "head foremost, with the same violent action that one would impel a bayonet into an enemy".

The inquest ruled Armit had died accidentally but Burns and an uncle of Armit's, a Mr Miller, appealed to the Otago Rugby Union. "The constitution of that court and its proceedings seemed carefully designed," they said, "to stifle the truth and the verdict had been carefully led up to during Armit's protracted illness by persistent repetitions of false reports of the occurrence."

The Otago union quickly sidestepped any involvement. It would be

Nicky Allen (in front)
with his partner in the
victorious 1980 test
against Wales,
Dave Loveridge.

"altogether outside the province" of the union to interfere, it said.

Thousands lined Dunedin's streets as Armit's funeral cortege went from his family home in the suburb of Kaikorai to the Southern Cemetery overlooking Carisbrook. Among the many wreaths delivered to Armit's mother was one from Bayly.

The other All Black to give his life for rugby was Nicky Allen who, despite playing just two tests, was generally regarded as one of the most talented first five-eighths to play for New Zealand. One of his two tests was the centenary match against Wales in 1980, in which he gave a faultless display, according to one of his team-mates, Andy Haden.

"In combining with Dave Loveridge, Nicky was at his brilliant best, the catalyst around which developed the best backline that has represented New Zealand in the past 15 years or possibly ever," Haden wrote in a tribute to Allen in 1984. "Bill Osborne, Bruce Robertson, Stu Wilson, Bernie Fraser and Doug Rollerson would agree in one voice. Nicky was at least their equal, though sadly, but for a fleeting never-to-be-forgotten moment."

Allen stayed in Britain after the 1980 tour and played club rugby there until a knee injury seemed to have ended his career. He was able to return to play briefly for Auckland in 1983 before he continued his rugby in New South Wales. It was while playing for Port Kembla in a competition final against Kiama that Allen's head struck the ground when tackled.

He never regained consciousness and died in a Wollongong hospital nine days later.

The two world wars claimed several All Blacks, who made what was called the supreme sacrifice. In each of the war cemeteries that dot the landscape of northern France and Belgium there is a Stone of Remembrance, on which are carved the words from the Book of Ecclesiastes, "Their names liveth for evermore".

GIVING A RIGHT ARM

PALENSKI COLLECTION

ABOVE: Fred Lucas of the Invincibles lays a wreath on behalf of the Ponsonby club on the grave of Originals captain Dave Gallaher in Belgium.

RIGHT: The All Black captain in France in 2000, Todd Blackadder, also pays tribute to the fallen.

PHOTOSPORT

There are hundreds of such cemeteries, there are hundreds of thousands of names. Thousands of them are the names of New Zealanders, for the most part young men — men not dissimilar to young New Zealanders generations later who go to France to play rugby.

Some of those who died during the horrendous battles of the First World War were also rugby players, among them 13 who had been All Blacks. Rugby players were also included among the French catastrophic roll call of war dead. Of the New Zealand and French teams that first met on the international rugby field on New Year's Day 1906, the dividend of death was within a few years neatly divided — two All Blacks and two French players died in the war.

One of the All Blacks was the captain, Dave Gallaher. After he stopped playing, he became an All Black selector and when war came, though he was more than 40 years old, he once more answered his country's call. He lived for New Zealand and he died for New Zealand, one of the victims of the horror called Passchendaele.

His name has lived on, though, through his position as captain of the Original All Blacks, through his other contributions to rugby and to New Zealand and now through the Dave Gallaher Cup for tests between New Zealand and France, which was played for the first time in Paris in 2000.

It was fitting that the first contest for the cup was played on 11 November, Armistice Day in France and Remembrance Day in New Zealand, the day that marked the end of the First World War — the time when, at the 11th hour of the 11th day of the 11th month in 1918, the guns fell silent.

That moment was too late for thousands of New Zealanders. It was too late for All Black prop Ernest Dodd, killed a month before; it was too late for another All Black forward, Jimmy Ridland, killed just six days before the end of "the war to end all wars". Dodd and Ridland were both members of the New Zealand Rifle Brigade, a unit that is perhaps better remembered in France than it is in New Zealand.

It was the brigade which, in the last New Zealand action of the war, liberated the ancient French town of Le Quesnoy. It was and is a distinctive town, a 10th-century fortress built on high ground and surrounded by ramparts. It was held by Germans and was full of French civilians.

The easy way to have captured Le Quesnoy would have been by artillery bombardment. But that would have put at risk the French civilians and the historic town. So the Rifle Brigade, with the Canterbury and Otago Regiments in the van, mounted a more difficult and circuitous attack by outflanking the Germans and eventually moving in behind a technically difficult creeping barrage followed by a daring scaling of the ramparts. It succeeded and the French have never forgotten the consideration shown by the New Zealanders. Anzac Day continues to be marked in Le Quesnoy every year as a perpetual expression of French gratitude.

The All Blacks at various times have visited Gallaher's grave in Belgium and the 2000 team went both there and to Le Quesnoy.

The 13 All Blacks who died in the First World War (with their place of death in parentheses) were Jim Baird (France), Bobby Black (France), "Norkey" Dewar (Gallipoli), Ernest Dodd (France), "Doolan" Downing (Gallipoli), Dave Gallaher (Belgium), Eric Harper (Palestine), Jim McNeece (Belgium), Jimmy Ridland (France), George Sellars (Belgium), Reg Taylor (Belgium), "Jum" Turtill (France) and Frank Wilson (France).

Those killed in the Second World War were Bill Carson (at sea,

Mediterranean), Don Cobden (English Channel), Jack Harris (Italy), George Hart (Italy), Cyril Pepper (New Zealand, from wounds), Arthur Wesney (Libya) and Jim Wynyard (El Alamein).

Sacrifice comes in many guises. Among them were the players who, through ill luck or personal choice, were chosen for the All Blacks but never became All Blacks. For the rugby player, there surely can't be any more galling status: selected but did not play.

Many in that unfortunate category were from the 19th century and couldn't get time off from their work for such fripperies as a rugby tour. Had the All Blacks then had the status they subsequently acquired, it's reasonable to assume that the stay-at-home players would have given heaven and earth a bit more of a shove to make the tour. It's also reasonable to assume that their employers would have looked more kindly on the requests for time off if they could have known there was some status in employing an All Black.

Not all of the absences in that period were because of work. Bob Whiteside, a dashing Auckland wing also noted as a cricketer and track athlete, was chosen for the first tour in 1884 but he withdrew after the organiser, Samuel Sleigh, told him he wouldn't be paid for playing rugby for his country.

Max Grierson, a law student in Auckland, was selected for the first test against South Africa in 1921 but when he was told the chosen ones had to be at a 10-day camp in Dunedin before the test, he decided his university studies came first. He opted out of playing against New South Wales later the same year for the same reason. His dedication to his work clearly paid off because he became a noted barrister and solicitor and founded his own law firm.

Another lawyer of a later generation, Greg Denholm, also put his practice first when he twice refused call-ups to the All Blacks — the first to go to South Africa in 1976 as a replacement for the injured Brad Johnstone and the second in 1977 when he made himself unavailable for the tour of France. His was a strange career. Undoubtedly among the best props in New Zealand in the 70s and a stalwart of Auckland teams, he was never chosen for a home test and he was never required for an All Black trial.

There have been some genuinely unlucky players denied All Black status by a cruel fate. Ross Fraser, a Taranaki blindside flanker, was chosen for the All Blacks to play Argentina in 1979 but the selectors didn't know that, when they chose their team, Fraser had a broken leg. He'd broken it in a Taranaki–Counties match the day the team was chosen. Fraser was not sought by the national selectors again.

The All Black team came into the same category as the team in Argentina three years before. It was a second-string lineup chosen to play unofficial tests against Argentina, unofficial because Argentina wasn't a member of the International Rugby Board. The All Blacks though were still deemed by New Zealand union chairman Ces Blazey to be full New Zealand representatives, as had been their predecessors in 1976.

Also in the desperately unlucky category was Otago fullback David Halligan, who was picked for his All Black debut in the first test against Scotland in 1981. He strained a thigh muscle at training on the Thursday before the match and the following day, when he realised it was no better and he couldn't do justice to himself, he withdrew from the team. Halligan played for Otago the following year and also played for the New Zealand Juniors and New Zealand Universities, but, like Fraser, was not again wanted by the All Black selectors.

'PINETREE' OUT . . . ON A LIMB

∽ No All Black arm could have been more written about, spoken about, speculated about, commented on than the left upper limb of Colin Meads in South Africa in 1970.

How was it broken? How long would he be out for? Should he stay or should he go? Questions, questions, questions about what Meads called "the damned arm".

Damned it may have been, broken it most certainly was.

The most celebrated break in All Black history was to the ulna bone in Meads' left arm — one of the two bones in the forearm. An X-ray showed a clean snap about seven centimetres north of where the radius and the ulna form the wrist joint.

It happened in a midweek game against Eastern Transvaal at a place called Springs, a place known in rugby history only because that was where Meads broke an arm. The auguries weren't good right from the start of the match.

For a start, Meads had not received the normal telegram of best wishes from his wife, Verna. She'd gone off to a Waitete club match in Te Kuiti and by the time she'd realised she hadn't sent it, it was too late. Anyway, she figured, Colin never thanked her for them. But he still appreciated them and looked forward to them. But this time, there was nothing.

Terry McLean, that indefatigable recorder of the important and the trivial on All Black tours for nearly 40 years, wrote solemnly that Meads was the second All Black onto the field on the fateful day, 8 July, behind his captain, Brian Lochore. So what? So Meads for all but one other match in his career to that point always ran out last. The other match was against Scotland in 1967, the day the great Pinetree became just the second player to be ordered off in a test.

The Pinetree limb was rent asunder after six minutes of play (or seven, or eight, depending on which report is read). He went down in a ruck with his 101 kg weight on the arm and somehow a Transvaal boot found him.

Colin Meads against Northern Transvaal toward the end of the 1970 tour of South Africa.

Twenty or so minutes later, Meads went to the touchline for treatment and with a diffident suggestion that he leave the field. Lochore agreed he should leave. A doctor, whose name has not been recorded for posterity, advised Meads to get the arm strapped and play on. It was and he did.

Only after the game when he was taken to hospital and the X-ray taken was the real extent of the damage known. Medical opinion about when he could resume playing was widely divergent and at one point, Meads considered going home. But the All Black coach, Ivan Vodanovich, would have none of that and said he and the boys wanted him to stay and play . . . however long it took.

The first test came and went. All Black loss. The second test came and went. All Black win. All the while Meads did what he could for training with one arm in plaster and otherwise watched in frustration his team-mates. →

GIVING A RIGHT ARM

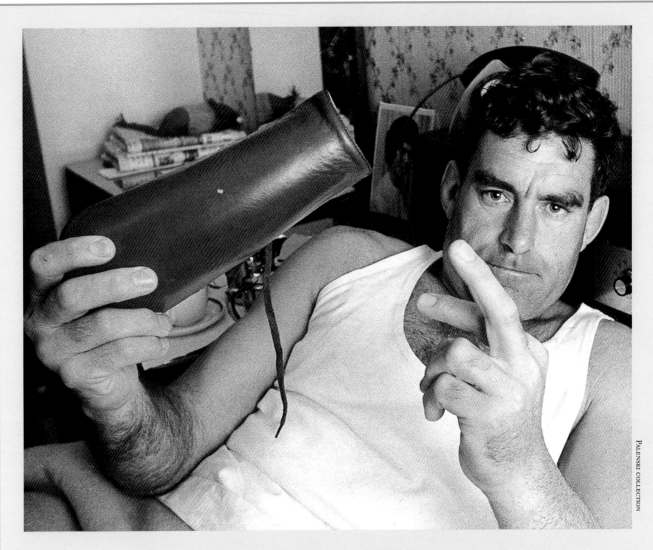

Colin Meads with the specially-made protector for his arm.

Eight matches came and went before Meads again took his place in the team, leading the All Blacks against South-Western Districts at George, a match notable for nothing other than the return of the Tree.

He'd had a leather guard fashioned to wear as protection for the forearm and that in itself created a measure of controversy, with a couple of suggestions that Meads could use it as a weapon. (Not that Meads ever needed anything other than the accoutrements with which he was born.) Meads then played each of the next five games to ensure he was back to full match fitness for the critical third test.

But was the arm back to full match fitness? Evidently not. "Frankly," Meads recalled, "I do not think I should have played in the third test. . . the arm was not right and I knew it.

"The week leading up to the test was arm, arm, arm instead of rugby, rugby, rugby. . . Would I be the first man in history to play a test with a broken arm?" Apparently so.

"I was so conscious of it that I played accordingly," he said. "Apart from the lineouts, I did not play well at all. Afterward I felt I had let the team down by playing."

Only Meads ever got away with accusing Meads of letting the team down.

CAMPBELL'S QUANDARY —
JOB OR JOURNEY?

∽ Sacrifice can be a two-edged sword. Some players have sacrificed jobs and other personal considerations to be an All Black. But others have taken the opposite view and sacrificed being an All Black for various reasons, usually on the score of job security.

George Campbell, a Wellington forward, not only turned down the chance to play for New Zealand, but also walked away from the chance of being New Zealand's first captain.

And he regretted it for the rest of his life.

Campbell played for Wellington from 1875 until 1884 and was one of the players originally nominated for the first New Zealand team, which was privately organised by a Dunedin businessman, Samuel Sleigh, and the secretary of the Canterbury union, William Millton.

Campbell worked for the government's Audit Department and applied to the auditor-general for leave without pay for the length of time that the team would be in Australia.

The application was refused.

"I toed the line, accepted the refusal and never went to Australia; never in fact became an All Black," Campbell was later quoted as saying.

"Although I went in 1893 as manager of the New Zealand team, I regretted it all my life that I had missed the tour as a player."

Co-organiser Millton became the first captain.

Campbell served three separate terms as president of the New Zealand union and in addition to managing the 1893 team in Australia, the first under the auspices of the New Zealand union, he also followed the Original All Blacks on their epic tour of 1905–06.

He advanced through the ranks of the Audit Department to serve as Auditor-General.

Ironically, he was in that position in 1924 when a department cadet, Arthur Carman, applied for leave without pay to follow the All Blacks to Britain in 1924–25 as a freelance journalist.

Campbell refused the application, so Carman

NEW ZEALAND RUGBY MUSEUM

George Campbell, who turned down the chance to play for New Zealand but who become an influential man in early New Zealand rugby. He was president of the NZRFU for three terms, a national selector for two years and manager of the first official team, in 1893 to Australia. The trick photography appears to show how Campbell had rugby under his wing.

resigned. Campbell then tore the resignation up, granted the application, and told Carman: "I wish I had the guts you've got."

Carman was later co-founder and editor of the *New Zealand Rugby Almanack* and *New Zealand Cricket Almanack*.

GIVING A RIGHT ARM

IF YOU CAN'T BEAT 'EM, POISON 'EM!

❧ The story of the All Blacks having food poisoning before the World Cup final in South Africa in 1995 is well known, how if the final had been on the Friday rather than the Saturday there may not have been 15 fit players. And how a meal in the hotel was blamed and how fingers were pointed in shady directions.

Almost as sensational, and almost as well known, was an earlier poisoning episode in Australia in 1980, when the All Blacks on the eve of the deciding third test were in varying states of collapse and some of them unable to see out the game the following day.

Then too, fingers were pointed in shady directions, especially by Stu Wilson and Bernie Fraser who called the poisoning deliberate and said it was something to do with a betting plunge.

Their accusation, four years after the event, may also have had something to do with getting publicity for their book, *Ebony and Ivory*.

In both cases, the World Cup final and the test in Australia, the All Blacks lost.

Less well known, with less calamitous effects and without accompanying accusations, was another poisoning scare.

When the Invincibles arrived in Liverpool for the ninth match of their tour, some of the players were feeling a bit crook. They reckoned it must have been some fish they ate in their previous hotel, in Birmingham, but captain Cliff Porter thought it was just the effects of a tonic powder they'd bought at a chemist's.

Whatever it was, it excited the local reporters. Within the restrained newspaper design of the time, the All Blacks' "poisoning" was treated as big news. The Liverpool *Post* got a little carried away. "Sensational Incident Of Their Visit to Merseyside", it said. "Fifteen men seized by illness". "Mysterious Ailment Suspected to be Ptomaine Poisoning".

The players laughed it off, though there was no doubt there was illness. "A number of us were not

feeling too well," lock Read Masters wrote, "and several changes had to be made in our team to play Cheshire while quite half of those who did take part in the match were suffering from the effects of the illness."

Overstated it may have been, but wing forward Jim Parker and manager Stan Dean had to spend two days in bed and couldn't travel with the rest of the team when it left Liverpool for Sunderland on the Monday after the match.

That time, though, there was no loss to attribute to poisoning, deliberate or otherwise. The ailing All Blacks beat Cheshire 18–5.

ABOVE: Finger pointers Bernie Fraser and Stu Wilson ham it up.
OPPOSITE: How the *Liverpool Post* reported the "sensational incident".

Sensational Incident Of Their Visit To Merseyside.

FIFTEEN MEN SEIZED BY ILLNESS

Mysterious Ailment Suspected To Be Ptomaine Poisoning.

SUBSTITUTES IN TEAM AGAINST CHESHIRE.

There has been an extraordinary incident in connection with the visit of the New Zealand Rugby team to Merseyside.

Eight members of the famous "All Black" team, which is due to play against Cheshire at Birkenhead Park this afternoon, are suffering from an illness believed to be ptomaine poisoning.

Fortunately capable substitutes were ready to take the place of the affected men chosen to play to-day.

Altogether fifteen men were concerned, the worst symptoms being shown by J.H.Parker, one of the forward, and by one of the officials.

The New Zealanders themselves belittle the matter, and assert, laughingly, that two or three of their players are not very well through over-eating. One prominent member even declared that there had been no poisoning at all.

GIVING A RIGHT ARM

GIVING A RIGHT FINGER —
RED CONWAY

❧ Many New Zealand men would give a right arm to play for the All Blacks, so it's said, quite overlooking the inconvenient assumption that the All Black selectors may not be too interested in a one-armed enthusiast.

So giving a right arm is probably a wasted gesture, however heroically sacrificial it may be.

But what about giving a finger off a right hand? That's a different story. There is a precedent for it.

Richard James Conway, known variously then and now as Dick or Red and a man for whom the phrase "fiery flanker" could have been coined, was faced with a choice before he went to South Africa with the All Blacks in 1960: lop off a finger and you can go,

Dick Conway scores against Transvaal in 1960. By then, he'd discarded the special glove he wore as protection.

keep it and you probably won't play much more footy.

For a man as committed to rugby as Conway was, it was Hobson's choice. Off went the finger and off he went to South Africa.

The story of the damned digit had its origins on the softball diamond. Conway was a catcher and one of the occupational hazards of such a job is getting the ball in the hand that doesn't wear the glove.

"You get a foul tip sometimes and it flies off and then it sometimes hits the bare hand. Well, that happened to me and the ball whacked into the third finger of my right hand and it was all swollen."

A doctor said it was just sprained and Conway had the finger in a splint for a couple of weeks. Back behind the batter, another foul tip, another whack into the right hand, and the offending finger was hurt again.

This time it was X-rayed and the break was clearly shown, the jagged ends of bone

overlapping. It was reset but when the break mended, the finger had a permanent kink.

"The specialist told me he didn't think it would last when I played footy again," Conway recalled. "It would break again, have to be reset again and we'd go through the whole process."

This was late summer 1960 and the All Black tour of South Africa was looming and Conway, having tasted life as an All Black against the Lions in 1959, didn't fancy anything that might jeopardise his chances of going.

Sure enough, someone trod on the affected hand in a club match and the finger broke again.

Conway had it reset and soldiered on but when the team for South Africa was named and he was in it, he decided it was time something permanent was done.

He had it amputated in the time between the final trial and leaving for South Africa. "The specialist said it was a simple enough operation and that I'd be back playing again in a few weeks," Conway said. "I still could have gone to South Africa with the finger but if it had broken again I would have had to go through the whole process again and miss too much footy. So I reckoned getting it taken off was the best option."

So off it came and his landlady in Dunedin at the time, the mother of Otago hooker Ian Stevens and halfback Alan, made him a mitt so he could still play while it healed.

"It proved to be no problem at all," Conway said. "We played in Australia on the way to South Africa and I wore the mitt in those games but by the time the tour proper started I was as right as rain."

And was it a sacrifice just to get in the All Blacks? "Well, I suppose it was, but it wasn't any big deal. But then, players didn't get to go to South Africa very often in those days, not like now, and I didn't want anything to upset my chances."

Conway played in three of the tests in South Africa but wasn't required for the All Blacks again until the next time they played the Springboks, in 1965, and he played in all four tests.

He finally gave first-class rugby away in 1968 after 157 games, first with Otago, then a year with

Waikato and his last six years with his native Bay of Plenty. "I certainly wouldn't have played for that long if the finger hadn't come off," he said.

GRASS GREENER AT HOME FOR CABINETMAKER CLEM

Clem Green found himself in the middle of controversy when he was chosen for the All Blacks' tour of Australia in 1914.

The four national selectors, headed by the Originals' captain, Dave Gallaher, opted for Green from Buller and a Canterbury man, Henry Taylor, as the two halfbacks.

This caused enormous fuss because it left no room for the player regarded as by far the best halfback in New Zealand, Teddy Roberts, who it seemed had been outplayed by Taylor in the inter-island match that had been used as the final trial.

Green didn't even get on the field in the interisland match, but was still chosen for the All Blacks.

Not even *The Press* in Christchurch agreed with Taylor's selection. Nothing he'd done, the usually parochial paper's rugby writer said, could justify his selection. "Granted the fact that he played a fine game on Saturday in the inter-island match, this one performance does not entitle him to his place," he wrote.

Doubtless, *The Press* man went on, Green would end up playing second fiddle to Taylor on tour.

It's funny how things turn out sometimes.

Green pulled out of the tour because he was worried how his wife and four children would fare without his income as a cabinetmaker. He thus unselfishly entered the ranks of the selected but did not play.

Green's withdrawal led to a recall for the unwanted Roberts, who played in the three tests of the tour and Taylor, the most criticised of the selections, ended up playing on a wing.

TRAINSPOTTING BOTHER FOR JACK OF ALL TRADES

꙳ No All Black surely could have been punished for wanting to do an extra bit for his team. But one was.

Jack Finlay, such a versatile footballer that he played first-class matches in such varied positions as five-eighth, loose forward, prop and hooker, played in just one test — the first after the Second World War, against Australia in Dunedin in 1946.

The All Blacks won it well, 31–8, and Finlay scored one of New Zealand's seven tries, but he wanted to make a greater impression in the second test, a fortnight later in Auckland.

So he caught a train to Auckland a day earlier than the rest of the team so he could get in a bit of extra practice.

"I really went up to Auckland on my own account a day early because I really wanted to play well in Auckland," he said.

Flooding in the King Country blocked the Main Trunk, so passengers were put on buses for part of the journey. Finlay's bus pulled into the Taumarunui railway station to allow the passengers a refreshment stop and Finlay sprinted down the platform, anxious to avoid the throng in the refreshment room.

"I was running down the platform and a chap in the railway pushed out one of those half windows and it hit me in the eye," Finlay said.

The gash was so bad he had to pull out of the test.

"I was going to get out on a high note and that was that," he said. "Or try to get on a high note, one should say."

Finlay, who was vice-captain of the famed 2NZEF army team, retired from rugby at the end of 1946. He was later a North Island and New Zealand selector.

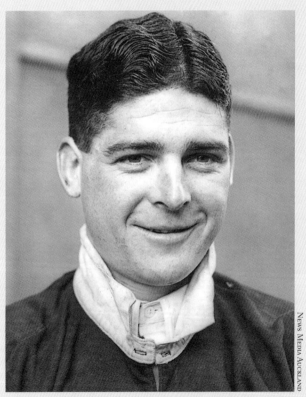

Jack Finlay, laid low by his own diligence.

ACROBAT ALLEN'S BRUSH WITH THE LAW

꙳ Nicky Allen, who had a fleetingly brilliant career with the All Blacks and who died as the result of a tackle in a rugby match, was known for his free spirit and love of life.

A team-mate of his, Andy Haden, once related how Allen was stopped by a traffic cop in Auckland.

"The officer asked him to explain his somewhat erratic driving, suggesting it may have been due to the influence of alcohol," Haden said. "Nicky promptly exhibited a perfect handstand and walked upside down around the car and followed that with a few flips and back somersaults before redressing himself in front of the officer with this question: 'Would I be drunk if I could do that?'"

"You'd have to be drunk to attempt it," was the officer's dry reply.

TEST MORNING

A year or two ago at one of those grounds that double as a rugby and a cricket venue, a rugby team was preparing for training while the national cricket team was preparing for a test match.

The ground was the cricketers'. The rugby players were there just to change and move off to another ground for their training.

Sounds carried through the batts-less walls of the dressing rooms. From the direction of the cricketers' room, the rugby players could hear sounds of hilarity, a card game was evidently in progress and a ghetto blaster was noisily doing the job for which it was designed.

"You wouldn't think they were about to play a test, would you?" one rugby player remarked to another.

This is not to criticise how the national cricketers prepare for a match. Each team does what works for it. Each team has different methods and procedures. The point is one of comparison, the point of difference. Noise seemed not to bother the cricketers. Noise is a silent factor for rugby players when they prepare for a test.

For All Blacks, test day is a combination of traditional rituals, individual tastes; the hours leading up to the test are times for reflection and mental preparation; times when players think about their own roles in matches.

Teams have prepared in different ways in different eras but the constant theme has been the same: an air of purpose pervades the All Black space as the collective resolve heightens, but still there is room for individual foibles.

Let's just take a typical test day from the modern era and let's assume it's real modern and that it's a night test.

It's the night before. The trainings are done, the signing sessions (balls, jerseys, T-shirts, books — anything imaginable that will take a pen or a Vivid) are done, the sponsor obligations are done, the media

A constant chore for All Blacks.

PETER BUSH

interviews are done. Tickets have been dispatched to relatives and friends with promises to catch up after the game. The kickers have been to the ground for another pre-test ritual. The All Blacks close ranks. Now is the time that gives rise to such tags as "unsmiling giants", the unfortunate phrase foisted on Ian Kirkpatrick's All Blacks of 1972–73. Some teams, and some players within the All Blacks, can be relaxed and cheery, talking to all and sundry almost right up to kickoff, but it's not the way of the All Black collective. When the outside world shuts down for the All Blacks, the atmosphere thickens, tension rises. Such conversations as these are are disjointed and brief, the talk usually is only the talk of necessity.

Before dinner, the players gather in the team room, usually a hotel function room set aside for the express purpose of being the All Blacks' inner sanctum, the portals of which are crossed only by the All Blacks and their management and by hotel staff tiptoeing in and out with food or drinks. The team room is a place for the players to relax away from their rooms (which can get pretty crowded with two large bodies, two smaller beds and an Everest of gear), to watch videos, to play board games or cards, to sit around and chew the fat. Or, to use the most modern All Blacks' argot, to chill out. But the leisurely ways are behind the players now. The team room takes on the same serious purpose as the players themselves. It is for the final mental preparations for the test.

This is the time for the captain's meeting. The coaches are there

The 1999 World Cup All Blacks sort through their gear.

initially, perhaps using a video of the previous match to make a few points, perhaps going over some strategies that were walked through and then run through at training during the week. The coaches leave and in the room remain only the players named for the match, the starting 15 and the reserves. The captain takes over. He'll talk about the attitude that's required, sometimes he'll touch on some aspect of what it is to be an All Black, of what the jersey must mean to the players. "If you don't think you're good enough to be here, you shouldn't be." "All Blacks never give up." "This jersey means a hell of a lot to a great many people and we're not going to let them down." Those sorts of phrases are used. The captain will talk about specifics — he may ask one of the flankers to talk about what can be expected from the opposition flankers; he may ask one of the jumpers to talk about how they'll overcome the problems in the lineouts in the previous match. The senior players, those who've been there before, those to whom naturally the younger ones look to not so much for advice but as an example, sometimes have a say. The captain's meeting doesn't usually last long. Three or four minutes sometimes, maybe 10 minutes sometimes. Ten minutes tops.

The players then file out and down to the dining room. The quietness has begun. If it's a big hotel, and they usually are, the players are able to eat away from other diners, away from possible distractions. The food has been predetermined. There's no picking and choosing from menus, no interplay with dining room staff. The players sit where there's a seat. There has been the occasional problem in the past with players sitting in cliques, based usually on geography or on longevity in the team, but when it happens it's discouraged. There's little conversation during the meal and certainly none of the banter expected of young males in a group together. The time for that was earlier in the week. There's time now only to look forward. When players finish, they get up and go. There's little lingering, no polite waiting until everyone's finished. Some will grab some fruit to take with them. Some may take some extra bread or a jug of water or flavoured milk. Perhaps a couple of players in linked playing positions may have a low-voiced conversation, going over old ground. If they run into someone they know in the dining room or elsewhere in the hotel as they make their way to their rooms or the team room, the conversation is brief. It's amazing how many New Zealanders in particular appreciate the pre-match ritual and don't try to intrude on the players. "All the best for tomorrow guys," is about all that's spoken to them. "Cheers mate," is usually the solemn reply.

There was a time when players would go to the bar the night before the match. Not for some rip-roaring session, merely to have two or three quiet drinks. One All Black of the 70s made it a ritual to sit propped up at the end of the bar, sipping and smoking on his own, lost in his own contemplation. Not anymore. Drinking no. Smoking a definite no. Contemplation's OK.

All that takes a player to the bar is if he needs something and that's where some of the team officials may be. But even the officials are there for only a brief period. The cloud of concentration and yes, some apprehension, descends on all who are involved with the team.

As the night goes on, some players may be in the team room watching a video or having a rub or getting treatment from the physiotherapist or doctor; often the rub or the treatment becomes a placebo — it's more for psychological reassurance than any physiological or anatomical need. Other players are in rooms, either their own or a team-mate's, watching the inevitable video or maybe something that's on television, something light that requires no concentration or depth of understanding. The television is on for sound and light, for comfort and company. Maybe in some rooms there's music on the radio or a CD player and, again, it's background to the main event, thinking about what's to come. Some players may lie on their beds or lounge in a chair in the team room and read but, again, nothing that taxes the mind too much. All Blacks have been known to have read two or three chapters and then have to reread them a couple of days later because they couldn't remember what they'd read. Few All Black coaches or managers have imposed curfews, there's no prescribed lights out. The players know what's required. Most of them are in bed between 10 and 11.

It's a night match and the All Blacks are encouraged to sleep in. It's a long day when there's a test at night. Far better for them if it was an afternoon match as they all used to be, then all the preparation and waiting gets compressed into four or five hours. With a night match, it spins out to six or seven hours.

Breakfast is a moveable feast. Some players are there by 8, others by 10, some not at all. There's no compulsion. There's no rush either. Breakfast, like dinner the night before, is mostly quiet. Players come, players go, few words are spoken.

Back in their rooms, there may be a newspaper to flick through (and the wise, experienced ones skip the writing about the match) and there are preparations to be made. Boots are cleaned or recleaned, laces replaced, sprigs inspected, adjusted, replaced, inspected again, adjusted again, maybe even replaced again. The packing of the gear bag is done according to a mental checklist. Then checked again and again. Some players pack their bags early, some leave it until later. Some constantly check to see they've got everything they need. They've heard the stories about players getting to the ground to find they've left their boots behind, or headgear, or anything.

The morning passes slowly. The forwards have a meeting and that usually consists of going out to the carpark or somewhere else that's handy and spacious for a few lineouts. It's not that they need the practice or that they are changing the calls or the methods they've practised all week and in all the preceding weeks. It's become a ritual, it's something to do, it's getting the feel of the ball, it's moving around, it's interaction with the men upon whom each will be dependent that night.

The backs too have a meeting and the halfback may fire the ball out to the first five-eighth, or there might be some desultory interpassing, and there'll be some talk, but again it's going over old well-trodden ground, experiencing the comfort of the familiar.

They go back to the team room or their own rooms. Every television set is turned on and while players may seem to be looking at them, no one's

OPPOSITE: A test morning ritual, All Blacks practising lineouts. This is Hud Rickit, Murray Mexted and Graham Mourie in the carpark of the Southern Cross Hotel in Dunedin before the 1981 Scotland test.

PETER BUSH

TEST MORNING

watching. Or at least no one's taking in what they're watching. Time to recheck the gear. Time to get out the number ones and make sure there's a respectably clean No 1 shirt to wear or that the tie's not too crumpled after being in the bottom of the suitcase since the last match. Clean the dress shoes if they need it. Clean the boots whether they need it or not. Check the sprigs. Get the tracksuit out. If it's going to be a cold night, get out the stadium jacket or whatever the team issue of the moment is.

Since it's a night match, lunch sometimes gets bypassed although there are sandwiches and fruit available. Sometimes there's a team outing — into the bus and off to play mini-golf or 10-pin bowls or something just to fill in time. Only an hour or so then back to the hotel.

Another hour or two to fill in. Some players try to sleep. Some players watch TV or read and nod off anyway. Roomies talk to roomies, sometimes about the game, sometimes about some shared experience but they're the types of conversations in which two people are talking but no one's really listening.

The pre-match meal comes around. For a day test, that used to be brunch around 11 or 11.30. Now it's a mid-afternoon meal and invariably the fare is prescribed by dietitians. Poached eggs, baked beans or canned spaghetti, maybe some pasta dish, wholemeal bread, mashed spuds. The steak, eggs and chips of pre-match meals of long ago are now just memories.

It's even quieter now, the tension higher. Some players whistle or hum subconsciously. Even the compulsive talkers in the team, and there usually are some, are quieter. Some players go to the team room to be strapped by the physio or doctor, strapping for ankles as a preventative measure, specialised strapping for troublesome areas for some players such as shoulders or knees.

Back to the rooms, this time for the last time before the match. This is the time to get ready, to get into the designated dress of the day, usually number ones which means suit and tie or blazer and tie, or the team tracksuit, whatever's been decided by the dress committee in conjunction with the team management. Check the gearbag again. Check the things that get forgotten such as shampoo, deodorant, comb or brush. Check the time. Check it again. Roomie asks roomie what the time is.

All Blacks like to arrive at a ground an hour before kick-off. The timing of the final team meeting therefore is determined by how long it will take the bus to get to the ground. Sometimes it's a five-minute trip, sometimes longer. Half an hour is usually tops and that's probably only in London or Paris. If the trip to the ground takes longer than that, the team's choice of hotel was wrong or the bus driver got lost (and that's happened).

Players file into the team room for the last pre-match meeting. The team room's been cleaned up by hotel staff. The food's been taken away, games put where they belong, massage and treatment tables folded, the television definitely off and out of the way. Seats have been arranged in audience fashion.

The All Blacks arrive in ones and twos, dropping their gearbag inside the door and taking a seat. Sitting quietly. No conversation other than whispered necessities. Faces are pensive. Some players are nervous, some relaxed. Players arrive in plenty of time. No one wants to be last and, worst of all, no one wants to be late.

The coach or coaches walk in. Again, not a word. The coach will sit and look around at the players. He'll know when they're all there, he'll know if someone's missing. When he's satisfied all are present, he'll stand and begin his final talk. It's usually brief and to the point. It's all been said before. The players know what is required of them. If they don't, it's way, way too late. The coach may want to just reassure some, he may want to cajole others. He may want to remind them of some points. The message may just be of a general nature. It's delivered in measured tones. It's not a harangue anymore. There's no shouting and swearing and no demands for players to charge through brick walls. Those days are well gone.

It ends, invariably, with "OK, let's go." Or sometimes, in the famed last words of American murderer Gary Gilmour before his execution, "Let's do it." Players get up, head for the door and pick up their gearbags on the way. They walk down the hotel corridor and out through the foyer to the waiting bus. Not a word is said. Bags are usually given to the driver and some willing assistants who stow them in the compartments underneath. Players file onto the bus and take their seats that have been determined over the season or over the years by their time in the team. The longest-serving head for the back seat. The captain sits almost at the front, not too many rows back from the coaches, manager and medical staff who have the front seats.

Silent and concentrating, All Blacks arrive at a test venue an hour away from kick-off.

It's still quiet. The driver, having overseen the loading, climbs into his seat and looks to the manager for confirmation that it's time to roll. Even the driver knows that silence now is golden. The radio or the tape deck or the television set on other bus trips are on and loud. On the bus trip to the ground, they stay off. Some players though have their own methods of concentration and on their ears will be clamped headphones or earpieces for their Walkmans. It is music intended to soothe not so much a savage beast as an apprehensive young man.

Some bus trips are smooth and painless. Some are to be endured. They're the ones that go through interminable traffic lights which, by sod's law, are all red when approached. They're the ones that get stuck in match day traffic. The best ones are when there's a police escort, especially in France or Argentina, when the escorts have their sirens going and woebetide any motorist who dares impede the raucous progress. Raucous outside with sirens wailing and the hee-haw sound of police klaxons, but still quiet inside the bus. There may be the occasional whispered sentence, but generally the players' faces are like those of the American presidents carved on Mt Rushmore: stony and immobile, seeing but unseeing.

As the ground nears, the traffic increases and so too do the people heading for the test, spilling out onto the roads. When they see the bus approaching, some give a thumbs up, some raise a cheer and some raise a jeer. It all comes down to tribal allegiance, ancient and human.

The bus manouevres into position. For most test grounds, it's out in the street. At Twickenham, the bus lumbers into the posh carpark and passes the Rovers and Jags and BMWs where spectators eat their chicken legs and sip their wine before the match. Wherever it is, the players have to run some sort of human gauntlet to get to their dressing room. Whether the reception is friendly, indifferent or just politely curious, the players ignore it all. Having retrieved their gearbags from the underside of the bus, they walk purposefully for their haven.

It's all ritual, this pre-match stuff. The players go to their designated places in the dressing room. It's according to numbers. Fifteen next to 14, 13 to 12 and so on. After the loosehead prop, No 1, come the reserves, 16, 17, etc.

Most dump their gearbags and head out the tunnel onto the ground. They walk around, they test the wind, they test the firmness of the surface, all with that seeing but unseeing look so graphically described by soldiers in Vietnam as the thousand-yard stare. The opposition can be there at the same time, but rarely is a word exchanged. There may be a perfunctory handshake for an opponent who's also a friend or even a relative, but any other niceties are left for later. The coach and captain usually stand together, looking at one end and then the other; sometimes they'll involve the goalkicker in their conversation.

Back into the dressing room. Players get into shorts and T-shirts and sometimes runners to go through their warm-up routines, far more organised and scientific than the old running on the spot and half-hearted stretches. Sometimes they wear boots and warm up on the ground itself; it just depends on what's available or what's allowed.

PALENSKI COLLECTION

While some pre-test rituals remain as they have always been, others have changed. At top, All Blacks survey the ground before the third test against the Lions in 1971. From left, Lyn Davis, Howard Joseph, Alex Wyllie (obscured), Brian Lochore, Sid Going, Colin Meads, Richie Guy and coach Ivan Vodanovich. At right, it's all a bit different. Robin Brooke leads the team around the ground.

PHOTOSPORT

TEST MORNING

The patron of the New Zealand union, Sir David Beattie, hands out specially-made caps before the first of the centenary tests in 1992. He's shaking hands with Va'aiga Tuigamala with John Kirwan on the right and captain Sean Fitzpatrick on the left.

The warm-ups completed, the players dress for battle. Some have their personal little quirks. Right boot first, left boot first. Lucky underpants. Some need last-minute strapping, the locks wind the tape round their heads to ward off that unique rugby condition, auricular haemotoma, otherwise known as cauliflower ears. Increasingly, they wear headgear now that it's fashionable again.

The referee's been and gone after inspecting sprigs, another of rugby's rituals. He's also supervised the toss, bringing the captains together briefly for the only words that are spoken between them pre-match, "heads" or "tails".

The coaches move among the players, a quiet word here, a pat there. Then they leave for their places in the stand. The reserves, decked out in their tracksuits and with blankets if it's cold, also leave for their place of waiting. As game time gets ever nearer, the dressing room gradually empties to leave just the players. The medical staff, their work done for now, leave to take up their touchline vigil. The manager takes up station outside the dressing room door, match ball in hand, there to synchronise timing with the match manager, television and the opposition.

The captain moves among the players in the dressing room, reminding, urging, encouraging. Some players idly toss a ball about, some sit with head in hands, someone inevitably is in the toilet.

The manager puts his head in the door and says quietly, "Two minutes."

The players are all on their feet now. They come together in a huddle, arms around shoulders. The captain says a few more words. One or other of the senior players may utter a key word such as "discipline" or "tackle" or a particular word they've chosen as shared motivation for the day.

One last quick trip to the toilet. It's a nervous time for the most nerveless.

The dressing room door opens again, wider this time. The manager stands with ball held out. "Good luck guys."

The captain takes the ball and heads for the tunnel, preceded by a television cameraman scuttling backwards and followed by his players in an order they've chosen for themselves — some like to run out second, some last, some second-last — or in an order they've been thrust.

As they emerge from the tunnel into the light of night, they break into a run. The captain passes to whoever's nearest, someone else sweeps down and grabs a handful of grass, someone else stretches hamstrings one more time, someone else looks around, taking in the crowd and the roar.

They line up for the anthems. Thoughts on the game, on what they have to do, on who they're playing for, during the opposition anthem. More intense thoughts during their own. Some grasp the silver fern on their left breast. Some sing. The intensity of the moment almost shuts out all thought.

As the last bars fade away, as television crews and photographers and

**And now the anthems:
Taine Randell, Justin Marshall,
Andrew Mehrtens and
Kees Meeuws.**

TEST MORNING

Ross Wiggins

musicians get out of the way, it's out to the middle. Line up again. Line up for that most New Zealand of match beginnings. "*Ka rite . . . !*" The haka. It's a challenge to the opposition, it's a pride in New Zealand and in the All Blacks, and it's a way of releasing some of the built-up tension.

There are still some nerves. There's still some wondering. Most of all there's concentration and determination. The time is now. The referee's whistle shrills, the kicker moves. This is what it's all for.

The morning routine can also include the distribution of the match jerseys. Whether a player is about to play his first test or whether he's played many and can barely remember his second (all All Blacks remember their first), the moment is the same: one of solemnity, one of pride.

The manager has the jerseys in his room and one by one the players are called and handed the appropriate jersey, the manager wishes them luck and hands are shaken.

The routine differs from time to time and differed in a big and significant way in 1995 when the All Blacks were in Paris. They'd lost the first test in Toulouse which, coming after losses in Christchurch and Auckland the year

Brian Lochore leads out the All Blacks in South Africa in 1970.

OPPOSITE PAGE: Now there's only the match to come. Taine Randell leads the All Blacks in the climax of the haka.

TEST MORNING

Caption (left column):

Test jerseys are prepared for handing out in Argentina in 1991 by manager John Sturgeon, doctor John Mayhew and coach Alex Wyllie.

before, gave France an unprecedented three in a row against the All Blacks. A fourth win was almost unimaginable.

The Paris test was also the last for the All Black coach, Laurie Mains. For 33 tests since the series against the World XV marking the New Zealand union centenary in 1992, Mains had guided the All Blacks. He had been there in good times and bad. The good was a win in what might be called the reunion test in South Africa in 1992, a series victory over the British Isles in 1993, victory over South Africa at home in 1994, the stunning performances at the World Cup in 1995 which was followed by two emphatic wins over Australia, the second of them marking a century of tests between the two. The bad included one loss to the Lions in Wellington and losses to Australia and France.

Mains had been there also in a time of great transition and turmoil for rugby. He was there as a player and a coach in the amateur days and he was there at the end of the amateur days and was the first All Black coach of the professional era. In Paris, it was all coming to an end for him.

Mains had been an All Black for 15 matches and four tests between 1971 and 1976 and was terribly proud that he was one of the One Thousand (although it wasn't that many then). This pride showed on test days when he was the coach because Mains chose to wear the tie that only All Blacks who have played tests are entitled to wear. He was passionate about rugby, even more passionate about the collective body that is known as the All Blacks.

There was the usual tension on test match morning (and for Mains on some test mornings, the word tension was an understatement), but there was also sadness. Sadness that he was leaving behind the best job in world rugby — some others would say the best job in sport, perhaps others the best job period — sadness that he was leaving behind the whole travelling road show that is the All Blacks, sadness that no longer would he be able to choose players and take satisfaction in their development and success. But there would have been relief too, the relief that all his predecessors (well, most of them, the ones who chose the day of their departure) would have felt when stepping away from a job in which they're damned if they do and damned if they don't, a job in which the credit goes to the team for a win but the blame is dumped on the coach for a loss. Relief that the phone wouldn't ring as much, there'd be no crisis piled upon crisis to deal with, your name wouldn't be in 72-point type in the papers in the morning and eventually, perhaps, you'd be able to lead a semi-normal life and do things such as go out to dinner or to a pub without strangers telling you who should (or should not) be in the All Blacks.

So Mains, in this strange mixed mood of tension for what the afternoon held and sadness for what he was leaving and relief for what he was heading for, called the players to the team room in the Paris hotel. It was an odd call for players to receive. It was too early for a team talk, the wrong time for any other form of team meeting.

PALENSKI COLLECTION

Laurie Mains, tense but with relief in sight, before his final test in Paris in 1995.

He talked to the players about the past four years, what they'd meant to him, and he traced the good times and the bad times although collectively they would qualify for that memorable phrase coined by Charles Dickens, "It was the best of times." (No need to follow with the next six Dickens words.)

It was an emotive Mains and the players knew they were hearing something special. What followed was even more special. The day's test jerseys were neatly folded on a table beside Mains and he called up each player individually to receive his. It was a solemn occasion . . . Glen Osborne, Jonah Lomu, Frank Bunce, Walter Little, Eric Rush, Simon Culhane . . . so it went on, a roll call of the chosen.

As Mains handed the jersey to each player, he made a personal comment. Each was tailored to the individual. Mains wouldn't say after that day's match — when his tenure ended with an emphatic victory, the All Blacks' last appearance at the atmospheric Parc des Princes — what he'd said to any of them. They were personal comments and should remain private, he said. He stuck to that line the following year in his book, *Laurie Mains.*

Whatever he said, it had an effect on the players. Their performance that afternoon was a collective effort "for Laurie" and they showed it by the manner

A rare photo of an All Black team talk. The expressions of Kel Tremain, Ken Gray, Sid Going and Fred Allen tell the story.

of their play and by carrying him off the field. And when players such as Craig Dowd or Ian Jones or debutant Justin Marshall were asked by journalists about the game, they talked not of beating France, but of the inspiration they drew from Mains that morning.

The time before a test, for perhaps 24 hours and even up to 48 at times, is the time for the players and management only. It is not a time for outriders, especially not for journalists. They are around, especially when on tour and they're bunked down in the same hotel as the team, but it's a rule that doesn't need to be spoken that the players are off-limits.

And the team meeting? It would be unthinkable, even unimaginable, to let a journalist into one of them on test day. But it has happened.

It occurred in Australia in 1968 when Alex Veysey, who was writing for *The Dominion* in Wellington, asked to sit in on the meeting so he could report how the infamous Needle prepared his team for a test. Fred Allen, the said Needle whose bark was much worse than his bite, readily agreed. He couldn't see anything wrong with it and anyway, Ronnie Dawson of Ireland, the onetime Irish and Lions captain, had sat in on one meeting the year before.

So Veysey sat as quiet as a mouse as Allen geed up his troops for the match,

then wrote what he heard and saw. It all seemed harmless enough.

Back in Wellington, though, the Rugby Union saw it as far from being harmless. Publicly, the men who ran rugby said little but privately they said much, including phrases such as "Who the blankety-blank-blank does Allen think he is?"

Allen, the most successful of all All Black coaches, was told by manager Duncan Ross that the boys at the union, august figures such as Tom Morrison, Jack Sullivan and Frank Kilby — all former All Blacks — were not happy and such a move should not be repeated.

Allen, who stepped down the following year, had thought for some time that the NZRFU chaps thought he was getting too big for his boots and latched on to the "public" team talk as just the stick they were looking for with which to beat him.

It wasn't the only time the reaction, or anticipated reaction, from Wellington played a part in a team talk being publicly written about.

When the All Backs were in Japan in 1987 — a funny sort of an All Black team that was a result of negotiations and compromise between the New Zealand and Japan unions — it was the first time John Hart had been coach of the national team. He and Alex Wyllie, fresh from their provincial successes with Auckland and Canterbury, had been assistants to Brian Lochore during the stunning 1987

The odd couple . . . John Hart and Alex Wyllie before a match.

TEST MORNING

World Cup campaign. Lochore decided against going to Japan and suggested that one of his assistants take the Colts at home and the other take the All Blacks in Japan. For all the supposed enmity between the two, it was a quick decision that Wyllie would have the Colts and Hart the All Blacks.

The final game of the Japanese tour, essentially a flag-waving exercise and not at all a real test of All Black skills, was against a President's XV which included such European luminaries as Gavin Hastings, Dean Richards, John Jeffrey and Phil Orr among others, Bill Campbell of Australia and former All Black midfielder Victor Simpson. Although a scratch combination, it was seen as the "test" of the tour and I asked Hart if I could tape his team talk.

He, I gathered, consulted a few players and agreed, providing I wasn't present and one of the non-players operated the tape recorder for me. Grant Fox, whose No 10 jersey had been taken by Frano Botica for the match (and who was replaced to allow Graeme Bachop to play at first five-eighth for a time), was designated Recorder of the Talk.

The intention, as Hart well knew, was for me to write about what he said for *The Dominion,* to give readers an idea of the motivational powers of a man who was then favourite to take over as All Black coach the following year.

The team talk was given, it was recorded, but before I could write a line, Hart asked me to hold off because he feared that the New Zealand union — which was soon to sit in judgment on the All Black coach applicants — would see it as a bit of Hart grandstanding and limelight-hogging ahead of the vote. When Hart came to me with his request (which I couldn't refuse anyway) I groaned and lamented another lost scoop. The other journalists in Japan of course fell about laughing and compensated by force-feeding me on sake.

But he was probably right. As he was to find many times throughout his career, both when he wanted the All Black job and when he had it, he had plenty of opponents who saw him as just a bit too clever, a bit too smarmy and manipulative; not at all a chip off the old All Black coach block. This view was particularly noticeable south of the Bombay Hills.

Fortunately, the stalled recording wasn't forever lost from All Black history. When Hart and writer Paul Thomas were working on the first Hart book, *Straight From the Hart,* Thomas came calling and asked if I just happened to have kept the tape. Not only did I have the tape, I had also laboriously transcribed it and what I think was a verbatim report of the team talk appeared in the book.

Given that Hart spoke off the cuff, although he had subject headings noted down, and given its length, it was a remarkable piece of public speaking. But Hart's gifts in that area also rebounded years later when some All Blacks complained that he spoke too much.

Much of the Tokyo talk related to the specifics of the game and to the All Blacks' opponents, but Hart also neatly brought some New Zealand history and sporting pride into it. The match was at the National Stadium in Tokyo and the All Blacks had beaten Japan there 106–4 just three days before. They'd had pointed out to them a plaque on the wall outside which recorded that was where Peter Snell had won the 800 and 1500 metres at the Olympics in 1964. This was the sort of motivation Hart wanted.

"He came here 23 years ago, seeking to establish himself as one of the greatest athletes of all time," Hart said. "He came here with doubts in his mind as a 25 year old, about the same as the average age of this team playing tonight, to try to

PETER BUSH

prove to himself that he had a quality and an excellence beyond the opposition. The rest is history. . . Tonight there are many similarities although the opposition isn't the best in the world. We came here searching for quality, excellence of performance. We came here with some doubts as to whether we could achieve the style and the quality we looked for. We've achieved much but what we achieve will be based on the final verdict . . ."

Hart even remarked that Snell returned to be voted Sportsman of the Year for 1964 and that the All Blacks had the chance that year for the same award for the first time.

They won the game handsomely enough, 38–9, and they, being the World Cup All Blacks, also won the Sportsman of the Year.

In their build-up to big matches, the All Blacks sometimes seize on a specific word, a word that gets repeated and repeated as the match nears and it's intended as both motivation and a reminder of some quality that is needed in the game.

The All Blacks played Wales in 1980 as the centrepiece to the Welsh union's centenary and the word for that match was balance. "Have you got your balance?" one player would ask another. It was balance between enjoying the tour and achieving what they set out to achieve, the balance between too much and not enough, the balance between going over the top and staying focused on the job that awaited at the Arms Park.

So successful was the phrase — the All Blacks won 23–3 — that it carried through to the dinner and the revelry after the test. The old Welsh guy who weaved an unsteady path out of the dinner, after perhaps reminiscing about the days when Wales really did beat the All Blacks, looked a little bemused when an All Black standing by the door looked at him and asked, "Have you got your balance?"

"I'm OK, I haven't had much," the old guy replied, surprised an All Black should be so solicitous of his welfare.

In Cardiff, it was a victorious night that followed a pensive, contemplative morning. In Cardiff, London, Auckland, Sydney, wherever . . . in 1980, 1903, any year, it is a winning formula.

The All Blacks against Wales in 1980 had their balance. Dave Loveridge to Doug Rollerson to Graham Mourie.

FANATACISM IN '56 . . .
AND A MAN NAMED JONES

Every test, any All Black and any New Zealander for that matter would say, is important. But some can assume a greater importance and significance than others.

Few could have had the tension, such a grip on rugby and such a clutch on the hearts of all New Zealanders of the fourth test of the epic series in 1956 against South Africa.

The All Blacks were two-one up with one to play; they couldn't lose the series, but one test win would give New Zealand victory over South Africa in a series for the first time.

It would ease the increasingly distant memories of the tied series of 1921, the aggrieved echoes of another tied series, in South Africa in 1928, the humiliation of the loss in New Zealand in 1937 and the recent bitterness of the four-nil loss of 1949.

The series of tests of 1956 had the fervour and intensity of feeling of a religious crusade; it became something more than a series of rugby matches: it was a desperate wish by a nation to express its national identity, to restore its pride in its own rugby.

The All Blacks were under enormous pressure to do the will of a country. One of them was Peter Jones, a flanker from the far north of New Zealand. He had first been an All Black on the 1953–54 tour of Britain, played again against Australia in 1955, and had been reintroduced as one of the several changes after the second test against South Africa was lost.

In a television interview in the late 1980s, Jones recalled how he and his team-mates felt on the morning of 1 September 1956: the day of the fourth test.

"You woke up about three in the morning," he said, "and you were saying, 'Can it be done or can't it?' because that was the final test. So you thought, 'No, you've got to sleep'. So you went to sleep and you woke up early again and started preparing.

"When you went to breakfast everybody was silent and then, as the morning wore on, you felt a great calm."

The All Blacks were quartered in the Station Hotel (now the Auckland City Hotel) on Anzac Avenue, just along the road from league headquarters, Carlaw Park, and below the Domain. Eden Park, the scene of the afternoon's encounter, was a hill and a dream away.

"We just had a very light lunch and things started to build and build and that atmosphere in that little room down below in the Station Hotel was just electrifying," Jones said. "I remember the great Tom Morrison, members of the council, they all stood with us. It was everybody in the New Zealand union and the players . . . and we knew what to expect. People were there to see you do the job . . . as the day wore on, you realised it was do or die."

Jones remembered that he thought during the morning about the Springboks, about how he'd watched them and listened to them during their tour, about how he'd decided they had to be dominated. "If you let them get on top of you, you can forget it . . . I thought you've got to keep the whip on them right from the word go and the harder you crack the whip, then they'll fade . . ."

And that's what happened. New Zealand 11, South Africa 5.

The only All Black try that day was scored by Jones, who seized on a ball after a lineout five minutes into the second half and charged about 30 metres to the line at the Sandringham Road end of the ground.

The game won, the series won, history righted, New Zealanders wanted to hear from the men who had carried the day. Jones was slumped in the dressing room, spent, relieved. The crowd chanted for him and another hero of the hour, Kevin Skinner, draped an All Black blazer over Jones's sweating, exhausted shoulders. "Come on Jonesy," Skinner said.

So up into the stand Jones went, there to be confronted by a microphone. "I didn't even think of what I was going to say and I just said, 'I'm absolutely buggered' and I was. Everything had gone out of me. Everything that I'd built up the two days before the test, I just felt there was nothing left — it was all gone."

One of the heroes of 1956, Peter Jones, during the series.

The test, the win, the series and Jones' after-match comment remains forever in New Zealand memories.

In the innocent, staid ways of the day, Jones' comment was a shock. Such words then were not uttered over the public airwaves, not printed in newspapers. It entered New Zealand — not just rugby — folklore in the same manner as Ed Hillary's comment of three years before, "We knocked the bastard off."

Which is precisely what the All Blacks had just done and Jones's comment was occasion for New Zealand smiles to be just that little wider.

Peter Jones (full name: Peter Frederick Hilton-Jones) played 37 matches for the All Blacks (including 11 tests) and scored 20 tries. He last played for the All Blacks in 1960 — also against South Africa. Jones died in 1994, aged 62.

Practical joker Massa Johnston with another Original, Charlie Seeling.

PALENSKI COLLECTION

ORIGINALS' SIN — OR JUST A PRACTICAL JOKE

∾ Not all match mornings are spent in sombre contemplation of the battles that the afternoon will bring.

The Originals had a private dining room at their hotel in Gloucester and the day before their match there, the 10th of the tour, they were sitting around opening mail.

"Hello boys," cried the Otago flanker, Massa Johnston, "I've got a letter from a girl called Zoe asking for my hatband."

(The 1905 team dress uniform included a straw boater that had a black hatband bearing a silver

fern. They were evidently highly prized souvenirs.)

"So have I," said another player, recalled Billy Wallace in a series of reminiscences he wrote for the New Zealand *Sportsman* newspaper in 1932.

"And so have I," chorused another.

Wallace said that seven or eight players, including himself, all received the same letter from the enterprising Zoe.

But one player — unidentified — sat forlornly in the dining room and said, "No girls ever write to me."

Thompson, according to Wallace, decided to

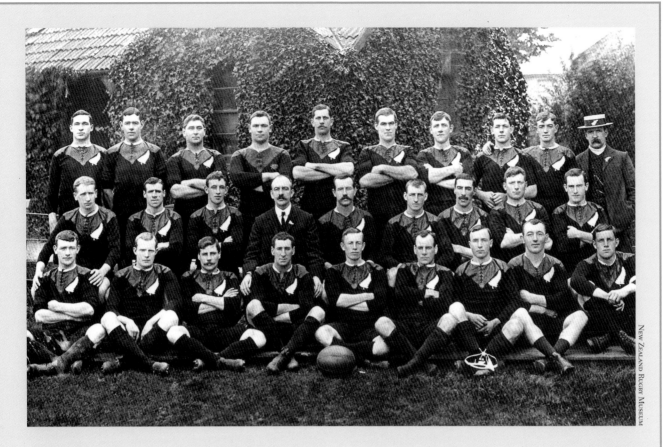

New Zealand Rugby Museum

relieve his team-mate's melancholy and got one of the hotel waitresses to write a quick note to the unloved player who, in Wallace's words, was not a lady-killer.

The waitress' letter suggested that she and the player meet the next morning, the morning of the match, at 11 o'clock.

"We watched him very eagerly next morning at the breakfast table and saw him get the letter, open it with a smile of satisfaction, and put it quietly away in his pocket," Wallace wrote. "He said nothing to us and stole quietly away at about 10.30.

"Of course we let him get well away and then strolled up the street, and there he was, waiting at the appointed place.

"'What oh,' we cried out, 'what are you doing here?'

"'Take your hook out of it,' he sang out, 'I'm expecting an heiress here shortly.'"

Wallace records they left the player to his

Dedicated, ruthless and efficient on the field, the Originals showed they also know how to relax and have fun off it. This was the formal photo taken of them at Newton Abbott in Devon before their first match.

anticipatory vigil, but returned about half an hour later. He was still waiting.

"Plenty of time yet," he told the others. "Ladies are never very punctual, you know."

An hour later the player returned to the hotel, crestfallen that his romantic rendezvous had not come to pass.

The players still didn't let on that he'd been the victim of a practical joke, but Johnston did enlist the aid of the waitress again to write another note, expressing regret that she'd been unavoidably detained but that she hoped she'd be able to meet him later in the tour.

Wallace did not record how the let-down would-be Lothario performed in the match that afternoon, which the All Blacks won 44–0.

TEST MORNING

LOCHORE'S CALL-UP AS LATE AS IT GETS

❧ Some test mornings are not all straightforward, the players all primed and ready and following familiar rituals. Just ask Brian Lochore.

On the morning of 4 January 1964, the day of the All Blacks' test against England at Twickenham, Lochore had arranged to play squash. He knew he wasn't involved in the afternoon's match so said see you later to room-mate Keith Nelson and headed off, squash racket under his arm.

He got as far as the hotel lift when captain Wilson Whineray saw him and asked him where he was going.

"I'm going off to play squash," Lochore replied.

Whineray looked at him. "I wonder if you'd just go back to your room," he said, "you might be needed."

Flanker Waka Nathan had injured his jaw in the previous match against Llanelli and while he'd been selected in the test team, there was still doubt about him.

Lochore knew this but figured that Nelson, his room-mate, was the likely one to be called in if the need arose. Nelson had, after all, played two tests at No 8 against Australia in 1962 and Lochore had no test experience other than being a reserve against England in New Zealand the year before. Nelson had trained at No 8 with the test team in Nathan's place.

"I got back to our room," Lochore recalled, "and Keith was on the phone to his parents back home and I could hear them saying, 'Well, are you playing?' and Keith said, 'Well, if Waka is not playing I'll be playing, I've been practising.'"

Nelson finished his call, looked at Lochore and asked why he was back so soon. Lochore told him what Whineray had said then the phone rang.

It was the manager, Frank Kilby. And it was for Lochore. "You'll be playing," Kilby said. Nathan had had to withdraw because his jaw had been confirmed as being broken.

Lochore replied: "I've got a bit of the flu or something."

Kilby: "You'll get over that".

Kilby then put the phone down and Lochore turned to Nelson and told him the news — glad news for Lochore, sad for Nelson.

"It was really hard on him," Lochore recalled. "I think it was fairly hard on me also, having to lift myself without having thought about the game at all, from 10 o'clock in the morning until 2 in the afternoon to play in that test."

Kel Tremain, No 8 in the previous test, moved to Nathan's place on the side of the scrum and Lochore went to No 8 for his first test.

ALL NIGHT 'CAMPERS' STUNNED TREMAIN

❧ Though the All Blacks have a well-worn routine before big matches, tried and proven over many tests and many tours, there are always exceptions.

The great All Black flanker, Kel Tremain, once told the story of how he left the team's hotel in Wellington on the eve of his first test because he'd heard that people were queuing up at the gates and would be camping out all night.

It was the night before the second test against the Lions in 1959 and Tremain had been called into the team to replace Rex Pickering, who had been in the team that won the first test 18–17 thanks to Don Clarke a month before.

"I wouldn't believe that people would queue up all night to watch me play rugby," Tremain recalled. "So I went up there to count a couple of thousand people lined up to watch me play."

Tremain did the same thing two years later on the eve of the second test against France — that was the test played in such a gale that the ocean liner *Canberra* weighed anchor off the heads because it was too dangerous to enter harbour. The gale had hit the night before.

Brian Lochore and team-mates on Twickenham before his first test, a test he didn't expect to be playing. With him are Earle Kirton, Mac Herewini, Wilson Whineray, Kel Tremain, Colin Meads and Jules Le Lievre.

TEST MORNING

"It was such terrible weather," Tremain said. "I remember going by car or taxi up to Athletic Park about 9 o'clock at night just to see how many stupid people were out in the rain waiting to see the test the next day."

Not as many as for the Lions, but there were still hundreds.

"The next morning you just couldn't believe it and I think most of us thought the thing would be called off," Tremain said.

A test called off? Never. The All Blacks arrived and again their pre-match routine was different.

"You always have a look at the ground before the game," he said. "It wasn't the ground we looked at, it was the Millard Stand. It was moving something like, to us, about 10 or 12 feet every time the wind blew. She blew 12 feet up toward the centre of Wellington — the wind stopped and she sort of fell back into place again. It was pretty scary.

"You could see that a dozen or 20 people were game enough to get up on top there. They must have been half full of the suds. I can remember my dad afterward — he was walking to Athletic Park, up the hill and the wind caught his hat — he reckons the last he saw of it it was going past Somes Island."

When Angus McLeod met Andy MacDonald

⌐ Players prepare themselves for test matches in different ways.

Bruce McLeod, the hooker known to his teammates as Angus who played 24 tests between 1964 and 1970, once related a story for *Rugby News* about differing preparations before the second test against South Africa in Dunedin in 1965.

The All Blacks were sitting in the stand watching the curtainraiser and McLeod was alongside Colin Meads. "I always liked to sit next to Colin on such occasions," McLeod said, "it

gave me a sort of reassurance."

The curtainraiser was Otago B against North Otago and while test players look at such matches while they're waiting for their own, there's a difference between looking and seeing.

As is often the way with players before a test, McLeod was nervous and went down under the stand to the toilet.

"Just as I got there I bumped into the Springboks' king-size prop, Andy MacDonald, coming out. He was stripped and had grease around his ears and eyebrows. It was quite a confrontation. Neither of us spoke. We just stood there glaring at each other for about 10 to 15 seconds."

McLeod returned to his seat in the stand and said to Meads, "Hell, Pinetree, those jokers are ready!"

Meads, McLeod said, turned to him and fixed him with a granite gaze: "Angus, I'm bloody ready too."

The All Blacks won the test 13–0 (and McLeod scored a try).

NEWS MEDIA AUCKLAND

Bruce McLeod.

WHAT THE
ALL BLACKS MEAN

At a grave risk to the public health and welfare of reopening old wounds, there seemed no better example in recent times of what the All Blacks mean to New Zealand than the World Cup in 1999 or, rather, the aftermath of the cup.

Or are they even old wounds? Are they still fresh with just a thin veneer of scar tissue, liable to be breached at the slightest provocation? Such questions are not rhetorical and the answers are immediately obvious to any New Zealander who has followed rugby with even a desultory interest.

The figurative scars of matches lost and campaigns vanquished are borne forever, a cicatrice of memories that comes flooding back whenever trigger words or dates are mentioned: 1937, 1949, 1971, 1991, 1999 . . .

It is indicative of the New Zealand rugby psyche and of the All Blacks' enduring excellence that it is the memory of defeats rather than the recollection of victories that show the depth of feeling there is for the All Blacks. They're expected to win and when they do, it is only right and proper and such wins get filed away in the sections of the memory banks where the pleasant, expected things lie.

But when they lose, oh dear, when they lose, the memory goes into a dark place where it stays, alongside grudges which never die, alongside injustices which are never righted, alongside wrongs which are never forgiven.

The World Cup of 1999 was the time of the ugly New Zealander, a time of accusation and disgust, of unreasoned words and behaviour, of deep, grievous hurt.

No one, the All Blacks of 1999 were fond of saying, hurt more than they did after the semi-final loss to France. Perhaps not hurt more, but just as much.

The reaction to that loss, for all its intemperance and intolerance, reflected what New Zealand thought of the All Blacks and what the All Blacks mean to New Zealand. The All Blacks were beaten in a semi-final. After losing the following match, the play-off against South Africa, they ended up fourth in the tournament after Australia, France and South Africa. Some countries, had they made the semi-finals, would have declared national holidays and rugby in such places would never have wanted for government or sponsors' money again. Had Wales made the semi-finals, Graham Henry would have been declared King Henry the Ninth (only the ninth because the previous eight had earlier been allocated). Had Scotland made the semi-finals, Bonnie Prince Charlie himself wouldn't have got a greater reception north of Hadrian's Wall. Had England made the semi-finals, the rest of the world would still be hearing about it.

Put it another way. When Australia, World Cup winners in 1991, failed in 1995 in South Africa, their coach was Bob Dwyer. Though he didn't continue as the Wallaby coach, his reputation and standing were barely diminished, and deservedly so.

Yet New Zealanders are harsher judges when it comes to rugby and, particularly, to the All Blacks. Not for us the emotional contradiction of celebrating a loss, at least not by the All Blacks. Not for us the lap of honour to thank the loyal fans while the scoreboard is still showing that the All Blacks came second. And not for us thinking that just making the semi-finals is OK. That's for lesser rugby beings.

New Zealanders have been conditioned to thinking in terms of rugby success almost since 1905 even though there have been some lean periods. And if ever New Zealanders were conditioned almost beyond reason to expect victory, it was in 1999. This was not the fault of the All Blacks themselves, neither was it the fault of the principal coach, John Hart, or of his various assistants. Let's get this straight so there's no misunderstanding. It was the conditioning of the New Zealand attitude that was not the fault of the players or the coach. The losses were their fault, because who else could take the blame, but the conditioning of the public, an unreasoned and unreasonable expectation that the All Blacks only had to show up in Britain to bring the cup home, could not be laid at the team's door.

It could though be laid in various directions. The news media, always a convenient whipping boy (or girl), could take some blame for creating or at least reflecting an expectant environment. Rugby followers themselves, those whose minds were conditioned, could also take some blame. The New Zealand Rugby Union, the greatest beneficiary had the cup been won, could take some blame. And the marketers and the advertising agencies who whipped up promotional campaigns could take some blame. All contributed to the expectation that the All Blacks would win. And New Zealanders, usually knowledgeable about rugby and not gullible, were taken in, were conned.

Too many didn't read the signs that were there to be read and many, as a result, suffered. None suffered more than the All Black coach, none bore a greater burden. Yet he wasn't on the field, not for the losses to South Africa and France, and not for the wins. Neither did he approve of some of the marketing excesses that contributed subliminally to the great New Zealand expectation. He railed against, to no avail, the monstrosity of the mural of the front row that was plastered across an Air New Zealand aircraft. That is not the New Zealand way and no New Zealander in his right mind would have allowed such a stupidly arrogant contrivance. But it was there and it contributed, however indirectly, to the public expectation.

So France beat the All Blacks in the semi-final and a nation was mortified, outraged, disgusted.

And a nation that had allowed itself to be conditioned, to be conned, struck back. It struck back in hurtful, undignified, unjustified ways, it struck out against rugby people in a manner that not even the most reviled criminals, the most despised politicians, ever know.

After Hart came back to Auckland to face a press conference, with sad and

**Prop Kees Meeuws leaves the
field after the 1999 World Cup
semi-final loss to France.**

WHAT THE ALL BLACKS MEAN

RUGBY WORLD CUP 1999 | RYGBI CWPAN Y BYD 1999

Captain Taine Randell and coach John Hart at a World Cup press conference.

despairing dignity, it is well known that he went to Addington to watch the horse in which he owns a share, Holmes DG, run. Hart was shouted at, abused, spat on. The horse had beer cans thrown at it. Hart's family did not escape the abuse.

Thereafter, Hart kept his silence, publicly anyway, and thereafter, Hart was lost to rugby. In a rugby context, he went into a self-exile. This was the same John Hart who two and three years before had barely lost a test match, who was coach of the first All Black team to win a series in South Africa, who was regarded as one of the finest — some said the finest — rugby brains in the country.

No one would have sensibly claimed he was perfect, no one could say he did not make errors of judgment with selections or with methods, but what All Black coach has not?

If his subsequent treatment showed how fickle and shallow public adulation can be, it also showed in the most graphic ways possible how much the All Blacks meant to New Zealand. New Zealanders were hurt that their All Blacks lost and they irrationally struck back.

Rod Macqueen, who coached the Australians who won the cup, was appalled at what he saw and heard. It was bad for a country, he said in a television interview 18 months after the cup, when so much depends on winning and losing. But that is what the All Blacks have brought to New Zealand: an expectation of success and nothing less will do. It is to the great credit of All Blacks over the years that they have been able to sustain their record of excellence while bearing such a burden of expectation. As professionalism has helped close the playing standard with some countries, as familiarity with some opponents has bred the comfort of understanding, the All Blacks face a greater task in the future of maintaining their edge and their record. The edge may already be lost. It would be an understanding, caring public that acknowledges the shape of the rugby world has changed and that while the All Blacks should still win more than they lose, and while they will still earn the respect if not the awe of opponents, eras of domination may be a thing of the past.

What a contrast there was in perception and reaction with the previous World Cup, in South Africa in 1995, when the All Blacks lost in the extra time final of kicks to the Springboks. That came into the realm of an acceptable loss because there was some satisfaction in the general acknowledgement that the All Blacks were the best team at the tournament that had played the most entertaining rugby. There was also the retrospective knowledge of the food poisoning that left so many of the players debilitated and the results of the tournament were soon washed from the forefront of minds by the changes that swept rugby over the following weeks.

But a crucial factor in the reaction was that the level of expectation was not as great. New Zealanders hoped, as they always do, that the All Blacks would win, but the feeling then was not as it was in 1999. In 1995, the All Blacks were so laid back they were almost invisible in the lead-up to the cup and in the first few matches. No television commercials paraded the All Blacks as unbeatable superstars, no billboards proclaimed their greatness, no aeroplanes were disfigured by their images. The All Blacks almost slipped into South Africa unnoticed and, under the cool guidance of Brian Lochore, quietly went about their business. Public expectation therefore was not built up to anything like the degree it was in 1999 when the higher New Zealand hopes were raised, the further they had to fall.

The first World Cup, in New Zealand and Australia in 1987, underlined in a different way what the All Blacks mean to New Zealand. This was the time they won back the universal support that had been broken down by the bitter years of the debate over playing against South Africa when it was still under the apartheid system. There's no way of quantifying such things, but there's no doubt that support for rugby — and therefore the All Blacks — fell away during the 80s in the aftermath of the insanity of the 1981 tour and the obsession some New Zealand rugby people had with maintaining links with South Africa when the rest of the world shunned the country. Rugby itself was split in the 1985–86 period after the enforced cancellation of the tour to South Africa in 1985 and its subsequent replacement the following year by the All Blacks going instead as the Cavaliers. That was the "unauthorised tour" as the New Zealand union chairman, Ces Blazey, described it, but the "rebel All Blacks" as they became known. When they were back playing against Australia and a tour of France, there were divisions within the All Black camp itself.

The World Cup became the resurrection and restoration of All Black rugby. There was unity again with a smiling face as the All Blacks, under Lochore, Hart and Alex Wyllie, took the playing of the game to a higher plane and showed that they alone understood the peculiar demands of a World Cup. It was perhaps fortuitous for the All Blacks' image that the chosen cup captain, Andy Dalton, was injured and couldn't play and the All Blacks were led instead by David Kirk, who had spurned the Cavaliers trip the year before. Kirk was, in the memorable

Peter Bush

The Whetton twins Alan and Gary with the World Cup that cheered not only the All Blacks, but all New Zealand.

phrase of Russ Thomas, who had succeeded Blazey as chairman, the type of "boy" young women swooned over and every older woman would love as a son.

Confirmation that all New Zealand was behind the All Blacks was most emphatically delivered to the All Blacks the day of the final when they left their hotel on the North Shore and headed for Eden Park. A crowd of about 500 was outside the hotel to cheer them on and as the bus went over the bridge and round the edge of inner Auckland, people waved and shouted best wishes. It was a nation alive with interest in and passion for the All Blacks. These were their boys who would do battle that afternoon.

As Lochore recalled, "I needn't have bothered with a team talk. The people of New Zealand were saying it all. It was there for all to see and hear. The players knew. They were playing for the people outside the hotel, the people in the streets, the people outside the park, the people inside, the people at home watching on television. They were playing for all New Zealanders everywhere."

The All Blacks were the representatives of the people and they, All Blacks and people, were as one.

Opposite Page: One of the great men of New Zealand rugby, Brian Lochore, is grim-faced before the 1995 World Cup final.

That curious, changeable thing, the mood of the people, is said to be determined by among other things the success of the All Blacks. In the aftermath of the 1999 World Cup, this theme was explored by academics, psychologists and even political strategists because 1999 happened also to be election year. Though differing by degree, most opinions were united on one constant: that the fortunes

of the All Blacks do to a large degree determine how we feel about ourselves individually and as a nation.

Since politics increasingly is more about image and appearance than it is about substance and policies, such intangibles as the mood of the nation are important. If the All Blacks had won the World Cup in 1999, the theory went, we would have been a happier nation and would, therefore, have been more inclined to think that everything was rosy in our particular garden and the National government would have been returned. But with the cup lost and a nation distraught, Labour and its coalition partners breezed in. Would the cup have made such a significant difference to the governance of a nation? Can the performances of the All Blacks bring down governments? The compelling view was that they can be a significant contributing factor.

Politicians haven't been slow to coat-tail onto sporting successes, knowing it's better for their images to be associated with times of happiness than times of despair. That wily old prime minister of Britain in the 60s and 70s, Harold Wilson, happily remarked often enough that the highpoint of his term of office was when England won the soccer World Cup in 1966. Bob Hawke when he was Australian prime minister always had the happy knack of showing up at winning sporting moments, most notably when the Australians won the America's Cup in 1983. Jim Bolger also wasn't averse when he was New Zealand prime minister to beaming alongside winning All Blacks.

Prime Minister Jim Bolger gets alongside winning All Blacks Richard Loe and Paul Henderson in 1992.

After the dark days of early November 1999 an economist was asked if the All Blacks losing could really affect business confidence, or did it just seem that way. His reply was revealing and simplistically put so that no one needed a business degree from Harvard to keep pace. If a prospective businessman, he said, was weighing up whether to invest in another business or an expansion of his own, he was more likely to decide to go ahead in moments of high public self-esteem rather than in times of national self-doubt. Regardless of more formal economic indicators, the rush of nationalism that a significant All Black victory would bring — or an America's Cup win or a major triumph at the Olympics such as Peter Snell and Murray Halberg winning on the same day — would probably tip the scales for the businessman in the direction of increased investment.

On a smaller, more practical scale, the success or otherwise of All Black teams certainly affects the business community in the area in which they're playing. Even their mere presence in a city adds quantifiably to turnover and therefore profitability. A University of Otago study showed that in 1997 when the Bledisloe Cup test was played in Dunedin, the two days of activity brought an added $17 million of economic activity to the city.

The hospitality industry is an immediate beneficiary of All Black success. Any bar or restaurant owner in a New Zealand city where the All Blacks play will declare that business booms the night of a victory but is much less vibrant if they've lost. People throng the streets and the bars to celebrate victory, but they're in no mood to do so to reflect on defeat.

The temporary boost of an America's Cup regatta aside, no other New Zealand sports team can have such a direct effect on the economy and, by extension, on the livelihoods of people.

The New Zealand Rugby Football Union showed in its annual report for the calendar year 2000 that its income was $76 million, up from $62 million the previous year. It had total assets of $48 million. Just a sports governing body it may be, but it is the size of a medium-size successful business with a direct responsibility for its employees and contractors, a direct responsibility to the 27 provincial unions and an indirect responsibility that affects thousands of New Zealanders.

It was ever thus: 2001 or 1901, just adjust for economies of scale. For all the changes in the world, for all the great inventions of the 20th century that changed our lives forever, for all the diverse pursuits and interests now available, for all the efforts to channel New Zealanders' thoughts into something more meaningful than mere sport and the winning and losing, rugby and the All Blacks in particular remain as much the national barometer as they ever were.

John Mulgan wrote his noted semi-biographical *Report On Experience* during the Second World War and reflected on growing up in New Zealand in a more innocent age. "Rugby football was the best of all our pleasures: it was religion and desire and fulfilment all in one," he wrote. "Most New Zealanders can look back on some game which they played to win and whose issues then seemed to them a good deal more important than a lot that has happened since.

"This phenomenon is greatly deprecated by a lot of thinkers who feel that an exaggerated attention to games gives the young a wrong sense of values. This may well be true, and if it is true, the majority of New Zealanders have a wrong sense of values for the whole of their lives."

If that was true of New Zealanders more than 50 years ago, it's no less true of

New Zealanders still. It certainly wasn't less true in 1949 when the All Blacks lost four tests in South Africa while at the same time a second All Black team lost two tests to Australia. And it wasn't less true when the South African losses of 1949 and 1937 were avenged, though not expunged from memories, by the fanatical crusade of 1956.

Nor was it any less true during other series won and series lost, and during the World Cups from 1987 to 1999.

Mulgan was writing about New Zealand and New Zealanders, but are we that unique on the polyglot world stage, are we the only country in which our moods and our hopes and dreams are pinned, sometimes irrationally, on the success of sports teams? Of course we're not.

We snigger into our cornflakes when we read of riots in the streets because an Italian soccer team has lost, we gloat when soccer's so-called supporters go on their rioting rampages in Europe, we're aghast when we hear some Colombian soccer follower shot his television and then his wife because his team lost. For all our reverence for and obsession with the All Blacks, we're not at that stage. In reality, we're no different from sports followers in any number of countries, no different from the Aussies and their cricket team or their various footy teams, no different from the Americans and their passion for the big four of professional sports, football, baseball, ice hockey and basketball, no different from millions of Asians and Europeans who dote on handball, a sport about which New Zealanders know almost nothing.

If there is a point of difference, it is one of expectation. Soccer teams draw and lose, baseballers play so many games in a season that to expect an unbeaten run is to expect the impossible (an expectation though, that is not unfamiliar to sports followers), the fortunes of sport fluctuate for all.

But we, tucked away in our little corner of excellence, don't expect the All Blacks to lose. There's not much in the world that we're the best at, not much even that we can be the best at, so the All Blacks are savoured all the more. They're our source of national pride, they're our flagbearer, they're our signal to the rest of the world that says we can be the best at something. Consistently.

And when they're not the best in the world, we wonder about ourselves, about our place in the world. When the All Blacks win, all is well with the world. When they don't, and especially when the losses come too regularly, life in New Zealand becomes a question.

PETER BUSH

Tucked away in their little corner of excellence, All Black fans don't expect their team to lose.

OPPOSITE PAGE: The Bledisloe Cup, here held aloft by Sean Fitzpatrick, generates a significant economic boost for cities where cup are held.

WHAT THE ALL BLACKS MEAN

Pember Reeves —
The Invincibles' Poet

The test dinner is one of rugby's traditions, if not as honoured now as it once was. It is a time when the two teams within a couple of hours of the end of the match have to get into their best bib and tucker and troop off to a dinner they would probably rather do without.

It is a time for administrators, past and present, for the referees and touch judges, for a few notables from the past and even, on occasion, a few carefully screened journalists.

It is a time of formality, the level of formality determined usually by where it is. In New Zealand test dinners are rarely formal affairs, at which dinner suits and bowties must be worn. In Britain, it is rare that such fancy attire is not required.

It is a time for drinking, eating and listening to speeches and sometimes, if the first has overtaken the second and if the third sounds as if they will outlast them all, it is a time for ribaldry: a bit of bun-throwing, a bit of tie-snipping, a bit of pocket-ripping, boys will be boys stuff.

A test dinner is not a time for writing poetry.

Not ordinarily anyway, but such was the way one of the notables, a distinguished New Zealander, William Pember Reeves, occupied himself at the test dinner after the All Blacks' defeat of England in 1925 — the 28th and last match that earned them the right to be known forever as the Invincibles.

The dinner was in the Café Royal, one of the more upper of the upper-middle class establishments in the London of the 1920s. It was the most formal of dinners, the All Blacks in their dinner suits made for the purpose, cigarettes and cigars broken out only after the royal toast which was right and proper, the port passed from left to right as it must be.

As the speeches carried on, by various notables but none more notable than the All Black captain, Cliff Porter, and the England captain, Wavell Wakefield, Reeves must have sat writing his poem.

A ticket to the Invincibles' test against England and the menu from the post-test dinner at the Café Royal.

Rugby Football Union

N

DINNER.

In Honour of the New Zealand XV.

AT THE

CAFÉ ROYAL,

ON

SATURDAY, 3rd JANUARY 1925

Chairman : W. E. DONNE, Esq., Prest., R.F.U.

J. Richardson, Esq.   W. W. Wakefield, Esq.
Capt. of the New Zealand XV.   Capt. of the English XV.

New Zealand Rugby Museum

He could write, of that there was no doubt. He'd been a politician, historian, New Zealand's first high commissioner in Britain, and he was also noted as a writer, a skill that was honed when working for his father on the *Lyttelton Times*.

It's known the poem was written during the dinner because he signed it, dated it, timed it: William Pember Reeves, 3rd January 1925, 10pm.

He called it *The Last of the Twenty-eight*, a reference to the number of All Black matches.

He wrote of his enthusiasm for the match:
Thirty-five years on the march have swung
Since I could try to play,
Yet one old fellow today grew young,
I was a boy today,
Shouting at scrimmages stark and stern,
Cheering the triumph great
Of the sinewy sons of the Silver Fern
In the Last of the Twenty-Eight.

He wrote of the sending off of Cyril Brownlie:
'Twas a bath of misery, all allow,
When the hurricane loosed its breath,
And the storm above and the slime below
Were mingled on black Blackheath;
But the tightest corner of corners tight
Came after the word of fate
Left fourteen fighting a fifteen's fight
In the tussle for Twenty-Eight.

He wrote how the All Blacks out-thought England:
"A fine machine" — so the scribes repeat
"Machine"! but when all is said,
The All Black plays with his hand and feet,
But the All Black wins with his head.
Thews and sinews and brawn to boot
Had in that hour been vain,
Had not dexterous hand and outspeeding foot
Been steered by the ready brain.

And he gloried in their victory:
Weave them a crown, for they gained it there,
Winning achievement's aim,
Twine them a wreath of the fern they wear,

Famed, since they gave it fame.
For the forest leaves that our champions earn
Tell best of the glory great
Of the conquering sons of the Silver Fern,
And the Last of the Twenty-Eight.

Only in Ireland, Spike

It's not just New Zealanders for whom the All Blacks are special. The eccentric Spike Milligan (above), as revered as a Goon as Brian Lochore was as an All Black, once wrote for the *Guardian* in Britain of his love for the game. He explained how he was very anxious to see the All Blacks play Ireland at Lansdowne Road but could not get a ticket.

": . . I went over to Dublin because I knew there were bound to be touts outside the ground. So I went around saying, 'Anybody got a ticket? Anybody got a ticket?'

"This woman came over to me and said, 'Yes, I've got a ticket.' I said, 'Well, how much?' And she said: 'Two hundred pounds.' I said: 'Two hundred pounds? For that amount of money I could get the most beautiful woman in Dublin.' To which she replied: 'Ah yes, but she certainly would not give you 45 [sic] minutes each way with a wonderful brass band playing in the middle'."

A WONDERFUL PHRASE, BUT WAS IT REALLY GARETH'S?

ᔓ There is something about the blackness of an All Black jersey which sends a shudder through your heart.

So wrote the great Welsh halfback, Gareth Edwards, in his first book, *Gareth, an autobiography*, published in 1978.

It was a phrase that neatly summed up the opponent's view of the All Blacks and was a phrase that Lion Nathan borrowed for a Steinlager promotion and one that has been quoted and requoted by journalists through the years.

Did Edwards coin such a memorable phrase? As an articulate Welshman — almost a tautology, that — he may have, but the phrase is more likely to have come from the fertile brain of Tony Lewis, Edwards' partner in rhyme, journalist, broadcaster, onetime captain of the England cricket team and more latterly, president of MCC.

The lilting Welsh accents of both Edwards and Lewis almost leap out of the page as the description continues: "Fifteen of them look dark and sinful; eight snorting bulls and seven black panthers. It takes a second or two to tell yourself that they're only human. It takes a success or two of your own before you know they are saying the same about you." (Would Colin Meads really have said such stuff about any opponents?)

Edwards (Lewis) wrote the colour of the jersey betrayed the All Blacks' attitude to rugby.

"It is as hard as flint," he wrote. "They are raised as boys to compete and no preparation of the mind or body is too tough. The game is part of their body and bone. No one teaches them about failure."

Not against Wales anyway, not since 1953.

A master himself, Gareth Edwards recognised the All Blacks' mastery.

THE ALL BLACK FAMILY

During April of 1992, the New Zealand Rugby Football Union celebrated its centenary. It was a grand occasion and a moveable feast. To mark the centenary, the All Blacks played three tests against a World XV chosen by one of the greatest of All Blacks, Brian Lochore, and after each test in Christchurch, Wellington and Auckland there were centenary dinners.

They were nights for wallowing in the past, for remembering players of other years and other eras and for swapping yarns, telling tales and catching up with old mates.

Peter Wild, a member of the New Zealand union council, had been secretary of a special centennial committee and among his duties he'd tracked down the whereabouts of as many former All Blacks as he could, and there were many of them.

He confessed he missed a few and conceded defeat on just one, Keith Murdoch.

Each was invited to one of the three dinners, the one they attended being their choice.

They were also nights of recognition. "Put on a bit of weight, haven't you?" was a common phrase at each of the three dinners. And so was the more complimentary, "Jeez, you haven't changed a bit." Followed by the expected response, "Lost a bit of hair, got a bit thicker round the middle."

There were also moments of poignant silence as player recognised player, giant hand reached out for giant hand and, without a word being said, the two would then join in bearhug embrace. There was also a tear or two.

There were lots of "old bastards" and reminiscing about "good bastards".

The years fell away as tours and games were recalled and relived, incidents on the field and off were replayed and laughed about and, as the beer and wine flowed, the tales became taller, the talk louder, the most repeated phrases, "D'ya remember . . ." and "Whatever happened to old . . .?"

It was the freemasonry of All Blackdom in full flow. Each of the dinners was like 30 or 40 team reunions all happening at once, but the generations and the years were transcended. One older All Black would tell a younger one what it was like in his day, then the younger one would recount to the older one what it was like in his day. The days, the matches, the tours, they all merged in the

Jock Richardson was 93 and the oldest All Black when he attended NZRFU centenary dinners in Wellington and Auckland in 1992.

The only triple treat of All Blacks — Ned Barry, grandson Liam and son Kevin . . .

cameraderie of the moments and the shared endeavours.

For they had one thing in common, these men. They had all been All Blacks. They had all had conferred upon them the highest honour New Zealand rugby — New Zealand sport — could bestow. They had the shared accolade of having worn the silver fern on the left breast of The Jersey, some of them for years and many matches, some of them fleetingly but all of them of the same status: All Black.

Whatever else they did in life, whatever their successes or failures, whatever their later standing, they each had All Blackdom as their common factor.

It is a fraternity likened to men coming home from war. They can talk to others about what it was like, about what happened, about the near misses and the lucky breaks, about the action and the inaction, but only another who has also been in a war can truly understand, can really comprehend what it was like.

A former governor-general, Sir David Beattie, himself a rugby player good enough to play for New Zealand Services in Britain during the Second World War, spoke at a dinner in 1987 to honour the All Blacks who won the first World Cup. He too reached for the war analogy and he told the players that at the end of the North African campaign in 1943, Field Marshal Bernard Montgomery told his assembled soldiers, "Whatever else you do in life, your proudest boast will be that you once marched with the Eighth Army."

Your proudest boast, Beattie told the All Blacks, will be that you were part of the team that won the first World Cup.

At the centenary dinners, it was old friends and old comrades, but it was also fathers and sons, brothers and brothers. In Auckland, Ned and Kevin Barry proudly walked in together, father and son, with no way of knowing that another generation of the Barry family, Liam, would be an All Black within a year — the only three-generation All Blacks. At the Auckland dinner also were the brothers Clarke, Ian and Don, the twin brothers Whetton, Gary and Alan (and Gary played that afternoon for the World XV against his former team-mates). There were also the Fitzpatricks, Sean the captain of the team that beat the World XV, and Brian the father who had toured Britain with the 1953–54 All Blacks.

Such scenes were repeated at the other dinners . . . the Mexteds father and son, the Deans brothers, the Jaffray brothers, the Stuart brothers, the Daltons father and son.

They were the blood ties and blood, we're told, is thicker than water. But it must be a particularly viscous water that flows through generations of All Blacks because they are all part of one big family, a family of history and tradition and shared endeavour on the rugby paddock, of shared times and status off it.

OPPOSITE PAGE . . . and the only All Black twins, Alan and Gary Whetton.

Chris Laidlaw, one of the best of All Black halfbacks, achieved much else in his life beyond gracing the All Blacks for 20 tests. Rhodes scholar, diplomat, adviser to politicians, an MP himself, race relations conciliator . . . his has been

THE JERSEY

THE ALL BLACK FAMILY

KENJI ITO

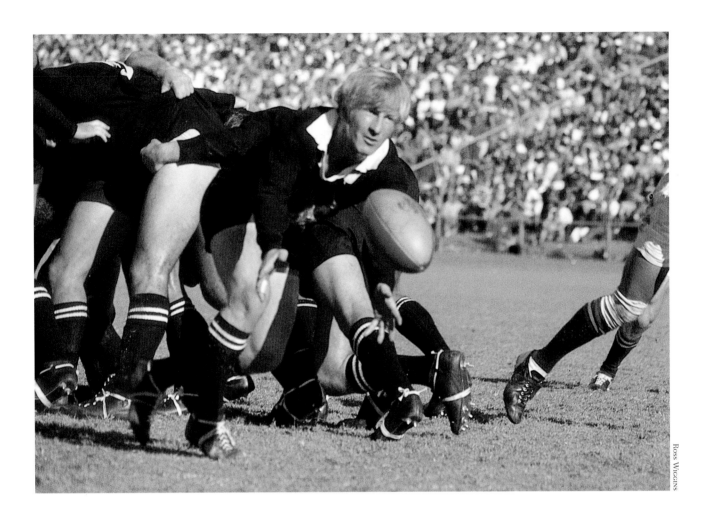

The multi-faceted Chris Laidlaw doing what he was best known for, on this occasion in South Africa in 1970.

a full life. He once complained that whatever else he did, whatever other accomplishments went his way, he was forever being introduced as "former All Black" Chris Laidlaw. But even with Laidlaw, who could be the master of the droll, there was a sense that it wasn't really a complaint at all and that there was a great deal of pride and satisfaction in his sustained attainment of the status to which all young New Zealand males would like to aspire. In Laidlaw's time and in his environment, sometimes it may not have been fashionable for him to be known too loudly as an All Black, but the deep sense of achievement and satisfaction would have been there nevertheless. The kinship would also have been there, the closeness to men who were so unlike him in so many other ways, the closeness that shared desires and shared achievements bring.

It has been a characteristic of the All Blacks, this cross-pollination of interests, types, intellects, races and a host of other differences. Any All Black team, from the first to the most recent, has essentially been a cross-section of New Zealand society itself, drawing together men of difference but with a shared passion for playing rugby and moulding them into a team united in purpose. That has historically been more apparent in New Zealand rugby than in any other country, except perhaps Wales, and therein may lie one of the secrets of New Zealand's sustained success. British and Australian rugby was essentially based on private schools and higher learning and to a large extent still is; South African rugby

while it brought together the Afrikaans and the English was a white man's sport, and, in terms of total population, it still is. Only in New Zealand was rugby truly egalitarian, the lawyer packing down with the labourer, the well-heeled working out moves with the perennially poor, the Pakeha with the Maori or, more recently, with the Samoan or Tongan or Fijian; a butcher, baker and candlestick maker of personal and ethnic diversity.

In All Blackdom of course, this all changed forever in 1995 when the outdated amateur regulations were dropped. Social distinctions, as unremarkable as they were within the All Blacks, were also dropped and all became rugby players. Some for a time clung to other jobs and some pursued tertiary education to prepare for their lives after rugby, but they became young men who all did the same job for roughly the same hours for a level of pay they could have only fantasised about a year earlier.

The camaraderie between All Blacks, whatever their status and whatever their era, continued off the paddock and long after their playing days were over. Bob Deans, the All Black of 1905 who became best known for a try he wasn't awarded, came from a wealthy Canterbury family and his quiet generosity towards his team-mates, some of whom struggled to budget with the three shillings a day they were paid and with no other money to back them up, has been recorded often enough.

The personal and ethnic diversity of the All Blacks as represented by Pakeha Ian Jones, Niuean Frank Bunce, Pakeha Sean Fitzpatrick and Maori Zinzan Brooke.

THE ALL BLACK FAMILY

Other All Blacks have helped each other through difficult financial times or in other ways. When a former All Black was too proud to ask, the word got around and he'd be "looked after", to use one of the great euphemisms of the days of amateur rugby. This was the phrase used too when All Blacks heading for an overseas tour would be given a farewell by their local club and in addition to the presentation of a travelling rug or clock or something, they'd also be handed an envelope. On later opening, the player found it held the proceeds of a whip-round by club members to ensure that the All Black wouldn't go short.

One player who wasn't at any of the 1992 centenary dinners was Jamie Hendrie, a Scottish-Australian who'd been called in at short notice to play for the All Blacks in Perth in 1970 when Sid Going couldn't play because it was a Sunday match. The All Blacks, who were on their way to South Africa, played two matches that day: Chris Laidlaw was halfback in one and Hendrie in the other. (Wing Bruce Hunter, incidentally, made history that day by playing two games for the All Blacks in the one day).

Hendrie wasn't at any of the centenary dinners because he hadn't been invited. His name somehow must have missed the eagle-eye attention of Peter Wild. But Hendrie didn't need a dinner to remind him of his day as an All Black. "I'm probably the least known All Black of all time," he said, "and it sometimes seems difficult for even me to believe."

Hendrie was a medical student at the time and has since plied his doctoring trade in Australia, most recently living and working in Melbourne where rugby is not a priority sport and not one of the great conversations at social gatherings. "Sometimes though the conversation gets around to sport and people might ask me what I played in my younger days and when I tell them, their jaw sort of drops," he said. Hendrie has not maintained contact with any of the All Blacks with whom he played but he does admit to the odd pang whenever he sees the All Blacks. He went to both tests the All Blacks have played in Melbourne and though he wanted Australia to win because Australia is his adopted home, he admitted to a residual attachment to the All Blacks. "When they play anyone else other than Australia, of course I'm always on the All Blacks' side," he said.

Another not at the dinner was a player Wild tried to trace but couldn't, Keith Murdoch. Wild was in good company. Many have tried to trace Murdoch and many have failed. His is one of the tragic stories of the All Blacks and his last captain, Ian Kirkpatrick, still admits to sadness and regret when he recalls how Murdoch was treated.

Murdoch ran foul of not so much an officious security guard (whom he bopped) in the Angel Hotel in Cardiff, but of a high-handed British reaction and a precipitate decision by New Zealand union chairman Jack Sullivan to bring Murdoch home. Murdoch's team-mates in 1972-73 still feel deeply about their self-exiled comrade who, it has to be assumed, felt so much shame at being sent home from an All Black tour that he quit the journey in Singapore and has lived outside of New Zealand ever since. He has slipped back quietly into New Zealand from time to time but never spoken a word publicly and never attempted to explain his side of events in Wales in December 1972.

Murdoch was not the ogre he'd been painted. Much of the painting had been done by journalists, especially in Britain where he was tagged a wild man, but team-mates swore by him as a gentle giant. The coach in South Africa in 1970, Ivan Vodanovich, always regarded Murdoch as the ideal team man and one who made

OPPOSITE PAGE: The long journey home that didn't quite make it home. Keith Murdoch at Euston Station in London after being expelled from the 1972-73 tour.

The All Black family

The other side of Keith Murdoch — hamming it up in South Africa in 1970 and in Queensland in 1992.

more effort than most when assigned the menial daily chores which are the lot of the team duty boy. The stories of Murdoch's strength are part of rugby's folklore. One All Black, puny by comparison, was said to have been on his hands and knees in a hotel room one day searching for something he'd dropped. Murdoch walked in and upon inquiring about the missing object, stood between the room's twin beds and lifted both at once so his team-mate could retrieve the lost item.

There is also the often-told story, which is evidently not apocryphal, of Murdoch offering a hand to a mate whose car had broken down. "Do you want a tow, mate?" Murdoch was said to have asked. "Yeah, that'd be great," said the mate. Whereupon Murdoch hopped into his car, grabbed the towrope in one hand and drove off, dragging the car uphill.

That was one form of strength, the physical kind. Murdoch displayed the other kind, strength of character, with his decision not to return to New Zealand.

There are some unwritten rules for the family of All Blackdom. One is that no All Black should ever criticise any All Black team or individual, although that rule has been transgressed more in recent years as former players have become television commentators and newspaper columnists. When the All Black team was in Japan in 1987, Andy Haden was strongly critical of the team and of the tour, labelling the whole exercise a farce, and was taken to task by some of his former colleagues.

Another unwritten rule is that no All Black should play against the All Blacks. It's not the done thing, goes the rule. Perhaps not, but plenty have. Also in Japan in 1987, the All Blacks resented Victor Simpson fronting up in an Asian Barbarians team against them although one of them, Gary Whetton, five years later played for the World XV against the All Blacks. At least one New Zealander, Nolan Fell,

OPPOSITE PAGE: It's not the done thing to play against your own, though plenty have. Gary Whetton plays for the World XV at Eden Park in 1992.

THE ALL BLACK FAMILY

Photosport

News Media Auckland

Brian Lochore and Colin Meads appear in white against black. This was for a President's XV in 1973 in two matches widely regarded as farewells for Meads. The bandaged All Black is Andy Haden.

refused to play against his countrymen when he was chosen for Scotland in 1905 but there are many examples of players who have felt otherwise. Even the man commonly regarded as the greatest of All Blacks, Colin Meads, played his two farewell matches in 1973 against the team he had graced for so long. But Meads, being Meads, admitted to feeling "not quite right" about playing.

In the professional era, as players and coaches ply their trades wherever they can, it's much more common. Even a former All Black player and coach, Alex Wyllie, had no qualms about coaching Argentina against the All Blacks though another former coach, Laurie Mains, vowed he would never coach a national team against the side he formerly controlled.

A bane of an All Black's life is the "heavy", the well-meaning but often boring official or rugby hanger-on who buttonholes players at functions and gives them unsolicited the benefit of his wisdom about how the team is playing, what they should have done, what they still could do and who should be in the team. Such men are usually blazered, pot-bellied and boozed, in no particular order. All Blacks have to stand and listen politely, though they did used to have a signal to team-mates that they needed rescuing. If the bore droned on too long, the player would pull on an ear lobe, a signal to a team-mate to come and get him away with some concocted story.

Every All Black has known such people, but if the heavy is a former All Black, even if he is giving earnest advice harking back from "his day", the current All Black is more respectful and tolerant. "If we know he was an All Black, it makes a difference," one current All Black explained. "It doesn't make him any more interesting or his views any more valid, but the fact he was an All Black just puts him in a different category and one that we'll listen to out of courtesy and respect for him having been an All Black."

Being different men leading different lives in different places, not all All Blacks stay in touch when their playing days are over. But the bonds, though stretched, seldom break.

Some of the times when they get back together are organised, such as reunions, and some are much sadder occasions. When the All Black of 1967 to 1970, Alister Hopkinson, died in 1999, just about every All Black with whom he'd played was at his funeral. They came from seemingly everywhere to Christchurch, just to farewell "Hoppy".

So it was too when an All Black from a slightly earlier era, Kel Tremain, died and his funeral was held at Taradale. As the strains of the great Welsh anthem, Land of My Fathers, sounded around and outside the church, there was hardly a dry eye. All Blacks feel keenly their losses. So do they the losses of their team-mates.

NEWS MEDIA AUCKLAND

Kel Tremain, whose death in 1992 plunged All Blackdom into mourning.

All Black teams have not always been heartwarming examples of harmony, which is only to be expected when there are up to 30 young men (or 36 for a time) living together for weeks on end. Though they have a common purpose and goal, and though they all share the gift of talent as a rugby player, they are still individuals. It's inevitable that at times some don't get on, though any animosity or indifference is subjugated by the greater good of the team when on the field. All Blacks rely implicitly and instinctively, or should be able to, on their team-mates doing the right thing at the right time and being in the right place when on the field.

There was said to be disharmony among players in the 20s when a North-South split evidently developed. There was apparently something similar in the late 80s and early 90s when the highly successful All Black team of that period was dominated by Auckland players but they were captained by a North Harbour player, Wayne Shelford.

There had also been disharmony earlier in the 80s when the two factions of the Cavaliers who went to South Africa in 1986 and the players who stayed home got back together for tests against Australia and France. By the third test against Australia, after the All Blacks, without the Cavaliers, had lost the first by a point then, with the Cavaliers, won the second by a point, there was a simmering resentment between the two groups.

"I thought I was dealing just with rugby players but there was more to it than that," coach Brian Lochore later recorded. "Some players had their own agendas. Nothing was ever reported directly to me but it was evident there was quite strong feeling between some of the players. I had to remind them that

United on the field and off it, Josh Kronfeld and Jeff Wilson.

they were all All Blacks in the same team and that they were playing for their country together."

Lochore conceded there had been spats between players but felt they had no effect on how the team performed on the field. A tour of France at the end of that year helped repair what rifts there were within the team and, within six months, a united All Blacks won the first World Cup.

Disharmony reared again in 1995 when Jeff Wilson and Josh Kronfeld broke ranks with the rest of the All Blacks and signed with the New Zealand union rather than with the breakaway World Rugby Corporation. Some players were said to be furious with the two, whose move ultimately forced the rest of the team to also sign with the New Zealand union. One of them, Zinzan Brooke, made a public remark about catching Wilson or Kronfeld at the bottom of a ruck but he later laughed it off as a joke. Joke it may have been, but there was no doubt feelings were running high among the All Blacks at the time.

Such times are rare and are the exceptions rather than the rule. All Blacks, through their shared endeavours and their reliance on one another, become generally a happy band of brothers, to borrow an expression from Shakespeare, and the friendships formed on tours last for the rest of their lives.

FROM ONE HARD MAN TO ANOTHER

ꝏ Frank Oliver, an All Black lock between 1976 and 1981 and captain in the series against Australia in 1978, was always reckoned to be one of the hard men of New Zealand rugby. So hard he had the universally known nickname of "Filth".

He could be gruff and pungently pointed in words as well as actions, on and off the field.

It took another hard All Black forward, his son Anton, to reduce him almost to tears.

Frank turned 50 on Christmas Eve 1998 and Anton had given considerable thought about a gift for his father on such an auspicious milestone.

He rang Frank's wife Jane and asked if Frank's first test jersey could be surreptitiously whisked away from wherever Frank had stored it. Jane found a pile of old jerseys in the hot water cupboard and established, through some artful questioning, which jersey was the right one.

"She sent it to me," Anton recalled, "and because it had been in the hot water cupboard it had shrunk and looked like it could have fitted a 10 year old."

The younger Oliver then retrieved his first test jersey from its resting place. He went to the public library in Blenheim to find the date and venue of Frank's first test then he took both jerseys to a picture framer's and had them mounted together.

Under the older jersey it gave the match and date, New Zealand v South Africa, Johannesburg, September 18, 1976; and under the newer jersey it gave the match and date of Anton's first test, New Zealand v Fiji, Albany, June 14, 1997.

The Olivers father and son with the framed jerseys.

OLIVER COLLECTION

THE ALL BLACK FAMILY

Two jerseys in the one frame is a bulky object and Anton took it with him when he flew to Auckland from Blenheim, and then caught a bus from Auckland to Thames. Frank picked him up at Thames and drove to Pauanui Beach, where Frank and Jane were spending Christmas.

On Christmas Eve, when Frank turned 50, Anton handed his gift over. "It was quite emotional," Anton said. "You could feel the electricity and tell that Frank was pretty moved by it. He wasn't moved to tears but they weren't far off.

"There were six or seven people there and they were all pretty moved but then they all broke up with laughter when I said to Dad, 'The only thing I ask is that when you're six feet under I get it back'."

Frank and Anton are one of 15 father-son combinations to have played for New Zealand. Frank, who was the founding coach of the Hurricanes and then coached the Auckland Blues, also coached New Zealand Under 19 in 1994 when Anton was captain.

STRAIN ON EARLY RUGBY SAFARI

∾ Not all All Blacks have been the closest of mates. From the mists of time comes the story of a coolness between two of the greatest players in New Zealand rugby history, Maurice Brownlie and Mark Nicholls.

They were captain and vice-captain on the tour of South Africa in 1928 and both served on the tour selection committee, which also included manager Bill Hornig, five-eighth Neil McGregor and loose forward Ron Stewart.

Nicholls, possessed of a shrewd rugby brain and with physical attributes to match, had been playing test rugby since 1921 and would have been a first choice by most armchair selectors, but he wasn't wanted for the first three tests.

His selection was stymied by McGregor and Stewart, whom Nicholls later said exerted a sinister South Island influence. There had been bad blood, he said, from the Invincibles' tour four years earlier which had included Brownlie, Nicholls, McGregor and Stewart.

The All Blacks went to Cape Town for the fourth test in 1928 one down in the series. The last test, Nicholls wrote, would be the most vital played in New Zealand rugby history.

And he wanted to be a part of it.

Nicholls, in an unpublished manuscript, made this point when talking about his selection for the fourth test after missing out on the first three: "I am not suggesting that the selectors were wrong in not selecting me. The point that I am making is that when they did select me in the last and vital test of the tour they gave me 80 minutes of one match to prove that my previous six years of international playing was not a mistake on the part of the previous various New Zealand selectors."

Nicholls related that when the All Blacks were walking out on to Newlands, Brownlie told him he'd won the toss and asked him which way he thought they should play. Nicholls said they should play with the wind.

"This was the first time that Morry had asked me my opinion on a decision he had to make," Nicholls wrote, "and I was very pleased when he decided to play with the wind as he invariably played against it if he won the toss."

During the second half, with the All Blacks up 9–5 (including two penalties from Nicholls), they were given a defensive penalty.

Nicholls recalled: "I picked the ball up and walked over to take the kick when Morry said to me, 'Who's captain of this team?' I replied 'You are' and immediately passed the ball to him."

Later, after another penalty, Nicholls said he was moving toward the ball when Stewart said to Brownlie, "For — sake, leave him alone" and Brownlie walked away, leaving Nicholls to pick the ball up and kick for touch.

**Not always the closest of mates, Mark Nicholls (above) and
Maurice Brownlie (right).**

The All Blacks won 13–5 to square the series,
with the previously unwanted Nicholls scoring 10
of the points.

Brownlie's captaincy in South Africa had often
been criticised and Terry McLean in *Rugby
Legends* quoted centre Toby Sheen as saying:
"That bastard. I hated his guts. He was a bastard
of a man. He was no more a captain than my
backside."

Brownlie was also said to have been indifferent
to journalists on the tour, one of whom was Syd
Nicholls, a brother of Mark's. "I don't think Morry's
attitude," hooker Jim Burrows was quoted as
saying, "did us or him any good whatever."

For all Brownlie's critics, there was no doubting
his ability as a player and, as a captain, the drawn
series in South Africa was something that All Black
captains who followed him couldn't do until 1996.

THE ALL BLACK FAMILY

Everyone loved Bob

∽ Bob Deans will forever be known in New Zealand rugby history as the centre who got across the line against Wales in 1905 but whose try was disallowed and Wales went on to become the only side to beat the Originals.

What is less well known about Deans was the esteem in which he was held by his team-mates.

"To know Bob was to love him," one of his team-mates, Billy Wallace, wrote.

Deans died three years after the tour, at the age of 24, from appendicitis.

"The Grim Reaper struck him down in the full

An artist's rather fanciful impression of Bob Deans "scoring" against Wales in 1905.

PALENSKI COLLECTION

pride of his manhood and left us all lamenting," Wallace said. "It is difficult for me to pay a sufficient tribute to such a sportsman as Bob."

Deans' grandfather was one of the original settlers in Canterbury in 1843 and the family farmed large tracts of land. He was the epitome of the well-bred son of a wealthy family.

Many of the Originals smoked, Deans did not; most of them drank, Deans did not. He was also a devout churchgoer. Many of the All Blacks were almost constantly broke: their three shillings a day didn't get them far and they had no wages or other means to fall back on. Deans quietly helped many of them out.

Wallace once told a story of how one of the players crept into Deans' hotel room and "borrowed" his expensive gold watch and a sovereign case containing a few coins, fully intending to give them back when Deans — as all assumed he would — complained they had been stolen.

But no further word was said.

After a few days of silence, vice-captain Billy Stead went to Deans and said, "Didn't you lose something at Leicester?"

"Yes I did," Deans replied. "I lost my watch and chain and sovereign case."

Stead then handed them over, saying it had been a joke and asking why nothing had been said.

"Well," Deans replied, "when I looked at the two housemaids I could see by their faces that they were honest girls and I knew no member of the team would take it so I thought I would say nothing about it."

It was a small incident, Wallace wrote, "but it will perhaps show the generous nature of the great-hearted Bob and perhaps my readers will understand just why we loved him so much."

Rob Deans, the All Black fullback from 1983 to 1985 and later the Canterbury and Crusaders coach, and brother Bruce, All Black halfback from 1987 to 1989, were great-nephews of Bob Deans.

Carl's priceless wardrobe

Prop Carl Hoeft has a wardrobe that he reckons needs a lock because it contains the most valuable items he owns – his All Black test jerseys.

Hoeft, who had played 20 tests by the end of 2000, still has 15 of his test jerseys and he has them hanging together in the wardrobe along with a collection of other international jerseys plus others that mean much to him.

"They're so important to me," he says, "more important than anything else I own."

Another Hoeft pride and joy is a classic 1967 Chevrolet Impala but even that doesn't rank with the jerseys.

"The car's not quite there," he says, "though it's one of my favourite possessions."

Hoeft says he thought of getting special insurance for his jerseys but reckoned that nothing could compensate if they were ever lost. "They mean much more than money," he says.

Hoeft's collection of international jerseys — including one from the World Cup semi-final against France "because you need reminders of things like that" — were swapped when All Blacks were given two test jerseys, one to swap and one to keep.

"Now we just get the one," he says, "and that's much better because it's so special."

Hoeft doesn't have his first test jersey though — that went to his father.

Carl Hoeft with his unique lineup of jerseys.

CRAIG BAXTER

THE ALL BLACK FAMILY

GALLAHER'S GALLIC GESTURE

Imagine the All Blacks getting a few points up in a test against France and the All Black captain telling his players to ease off and let France score.

Can't imagine it?

It happened.

The Originals' test at the Parc des Princes on New Year's Day 1906 was a first for France and became almost an exhibition.

The French captain, Henri Armand, conceded the toss before the game, saying that Dave Gallaher as the guest of France should choose ends and kick off. Gallaher repaid the compliment by choosing to play into the wind and rain.

When the first scrum was ordered, the All Blacks went down in their well-ordered way but the French stood around and watched. It was only after a bit of fractured French and English that the All Blacks realised the French didn't know how to pack down in a scrum and they waited for the All Blacks to go down first so they could see what to do.

By halftime, the All Blacks led 18–3.

Just after halftime, Billy Wallace recorded, Gallaher called his team together and told them to ease off so the French could score again. They did, through a try and a conversion, then the All Blacks put their feet back on the accelerator and scored another six tries.

"They were lacking in the finer points of the game," Wallace wrote of the French, "but they were by no means the worst team we met. With a little coaching they would have made a formidable side for they had physique and pace and enthusiasm."

Wallace also recorded that the French were strong tacklers. "They certainly knew how to bring their men down and they bowled us over like skittles. Most of them were military men and with typical French politeness they would dump us well and truly and then help us to our feet again."

Gallaher and Armand, Wallace said, swapped jerseys after the game and were like brothers together.

Originals captain Dave Gallaher prepares to throw into a lineout.

Less than 12 years later, Gallaher gave his life in the defence of France and Armand, who lived until 1967, visited his grave at the Nine Elms War Cemetery in Flanders soon after the First World War ended.

ROYAL REMEMBRANCES

New Zealand Rugby Museum

It's not just team-mates who stay in the memories and on the friendship list of All Blacks.

So do some opponents.

One of them was a Russian émigré prince, Alex Obolensky (above), who scored two tries in England's 13–0 win against Jack Manchester's All Blacks at Twickenham in 1935.

Both were in the first half, the first a fairly orthodox affair at the end of a backline move and the second a try written about for years later as one of the greatest for England. He went in off his wing and ran about 40 metres to score, evading →

tacklers as he went, on the opposite wing.

Obolensky joined the British Royal Air Force in 1939 and was killed the following year in a training flight accident.

Among the wreaths at his funeral was one marked: "From the 1935–36 All Blacks."

THORNEY QUESTION

∽ The unwritten rule that former All Blacks don't criticise those who follow them in the black jersey has often been bent in more recent years as an increasing number of former players have become commentators or columnists about the game.

One of the first All Blacks to replace the jersey with a microphone was the versatile and lively back in 10 tests between 1967 and 1970, Grahame Thorne.

Thorne, in an interview, once acknowledged the unwritten law, but said his credibility as a broadcaster was on the line and he had to call things the way he saw them.

"Not to do so would not be being true to yourself," he said. "When I was broadcasting any test match, I tried to be positive. I tried to bring out the positive things of the game, not the mistakes but the good play of the player beating the tackle. Not the dropped passes but the good takes."

Thorne said he didn't need to name players who did something completely stupid because they and everyone else knew.

"The one thing I wouldn't take on television," he said, "was foul play and I don't care who did it. You name the guy and say that is not on."

Grahame Thorne on the attack in the fourth test against South Africa in 1970, a test the All Blacks needed to win to square the series. But despite a magnificent fightback in the second half, they lost 20—17 and the series was lost 3—1.

ROSS WIGGINS

ONE FROM THE HEART

ᴄ✎ When halfback Mark Donaldson was on tour with the All Blacks for the first time, in France in 1977, his greatest supporter, father Bill, had a serious heart attack.

Bill, who had played for Manawatu and New Zealand Universities and had nurtured his son's career, was told he'd need a triple bypass. But the procedure was then in its infancy and Bill told medical staff he'd take his chances with drugs.

As soon as Mark was back from France, he went to his father's hospital room and dropped on his bed the All Black jersey he wore in the first test in Toulouse – unwashed, still with mud and dried sweat on it. Father and son exchanged only a few words and Mark left. "I'd never been much on hospitals and besides, actions speak louder than words," Mark recalled.

Whether it was the medication, whether it was Bill's determination or whether it was the healing powers of the All Black jersey, Bill continues to enjoy a full and active life – and still has The Jersey, still unwashed. "What with foot and mouth and everything, I doubt I'd get away with bringing home a jersey like that today," Mark said.

Bill and Mark Donaldson listening to the announcement of the All Black team to tour France in 1977, the first time Mark's name was called. The announcement was in Palmerston North after Manawatu's final Ranfurly Shield defence of the year, against Otago.

News Media Auckland

Tried, but not tested

Carlos Paz is a delightful little resort town in the hinterland of Argentina about an hour's drive from the less delightful major city, Cordoba. The All Blacks of 1976, the first New Zealand team to go to Argentina, played in Cordoba but stayed in Carlos Paz.

They went there by military aircraft the day after disposing of a combined Buenos Aires team in the Argentine capital and, in a bar the night of the game, some of the players talked about their status.

They weren't real All Blacks, some of them said. They were, after all, the second best 30 players in New Zealand that year after the top 30 had gone to South Africa. Some of them mentioned evident confusion within the New Zealand union about what precisely the team should be called. Initially, when the tour was first announced earlier in the year, the union secretary at the time,

The 1976 All Blacks who went to Argentina.

PHOTOSPORT

Jack Jeffs, said they would be known as "a New Zealand XV", ie, not All Blacks. A couple of months later when the team was chosen, its manager Ron Don, a member of the union council and therefore in effect one of Jeffs' employers, said the team was in every way an official New Zealand team.

"They're as much All Blacks as the team in South Africa was," Don said.

They played Argentina in two tests but the matches weren't official tests, not because of any lingering doubts about the All Blacks' status but because Argentina were not then a member of the International Rugby Board and the official view was that full tests could be only between IRB member countries.

So little wonder there was some confusion among the players.

Their coach, Jack Gleeson, hadn't been in the bar where the conversations took place but during the morning flying from Buenos Aires to Cordoba and then on by bus to Carlos Paz, he heard about the gist of them.

The players' rooms weren't ready when the team arrived at the Gran Lourdes Hotel de Turismo so Gleeson took the opportunity to ram a message home.

There was no room in which the team could meet so Gleeson, Don and captain Graham Mourie stood on half a dozen stairs that led from the foyer to the dining room. The players sat and stood in the foyer where they could find room.

"I've heard," Gleeson began, "that some of you reckon you're not real All Blacks. Well, that's bullshit. If you don't think you're All Blacks there's no place for you here and I'm sure Ron [Don] can organise an early flight home for you."

Gleeson said he regarded himself as the All Black coach, Don was the All Black manager and Mourie was the All Black captain.

It was an impassioned speech, one with feeling and delivered at times with anger. At one point, Gleeson reached down into a bag at his feet and pulled out an All Black jersey. "What's this?" he asked. "You know very well what this is. It's an All Black jersey and it's got a silver fern on it — look!"

Gleeson then traced a finger round the silver fern and held the jersey up so all players could see it. "This is what you wear when you play. Are you still going to tell me you're not real All Blacks? I could think of hundreds of players back in New Zealand who would do anything to be here in your places. You're All Blacks all right, you dress as All Blacks, you train as All Blacks and as far as I'm concerned, you'll play as All Blacks. You represent New Zealand rugby every bit as much as the guys who were in South Africa did."

Gleeson also told them that if the team that went to South Africa in May had been able to be chosen on form in 1976, many of the players in Argentina would have been in it. But the selectors — of whom he was one — had to base much of their decisions on form in 1975.

He also told them that the Lions would be in New Zealand within six months and that some of the Argentine All Blacks would be playing against them in the tests. "Some of the All Blacks in South Africa will have retired, some will have lost form and you're the guys who will be replacing them," he said. "So let's cut out this crap about not being real All Blacks and play on the rest of this tour knowing that you're All Blacks and bring credit to New Zealand and to New Zealand rugby."

Gleeson's chosen one as captain, Graham Mourie.

PETER BUSH

TRIED, BUT NOT TESTED

Welsh wing Clive Rees finds himself trapped by Andy Haden in the 1978 test. Haden used the Argentine tour two years earlier to revive his career.

Mourie, standing alongside Gleeson, was asked his view. He was succinct: "I'm representing New Zealand, that's the main thing isn't it?"

Gleeson had nipped a crisis in confidence, an identity crisis, in the bud and the All Blacks were unbeaten on their tour, which included two wins over the Argentine national side which was then a powerful force and which, a week before the tour, had lost to Wales by only a point. And that was when Wales were strong too.

Among the All Blacks in Argentina, other than Mourie who went on to become one of the greatest of All Black captains, were Andy Haden, who consolidated a slow start to his All Black career by playing more than 100 games and becoming one of the finest of locks, and Stu Wilson, another of the greats of New Zealand rugby. There were others, such as the two hookers, Peter Sloane and John Black, who went on to play tests.

Haden in fact used the Argentine tour to get his career going again. He'd been in Ian Kirkpatrick's team that toured Britain in 1972–73 but he then spent two seasons in France and when he returned to New Zealand was not even chosen for the trials held to pick the team to go to South Africa. He got a trial only when one of the first-choice locks, Peter Whiting, was injured. Haden said that if he hadn't been chosen for the tour of Argentina, where after one match Gleeson likened his performance to Colin Meads at his best, he would probably have played out his career in France.

That tour of Argentina also provided a good example of the team spirit of All

Blacks which drives those who don't get selected for tests to support those who do. Though the two matches against Argentina weren't tests, the players treated them as if they were — as they should have. There were, therefore, the test players and the dirties, the name given to players who don't strip for matches.

Though the derivation of the term has never been pinned down, it seems likely to have originated in South Africa and could be a corruption of Voortrekkers, the Afrikaners who mounted the Great Trek away from the Cape Colony in the 19th century. "Voortrekkers" became "dirt-trackers" to signify those players who trained away from the main team and eventually the dirt-trackers became just dirties. Then there are dirties and dirty dirties. The dirties often mean the reserves, while the dirty dirties are those players who sit at games in their number ones.

In the unwritten rules of All Blackdom, it is the role of the dirties and dirty dirties to support those who are playing in the next match. They must be prepared to take their place if necessary, but they must also support them in any other way they can. On a tour, when squads tend to develop into test teams and non-test teams, it's the latter who are the dirties and they take great pride in their role and they see their games as being every bit as important as the tests.

So it was in Argentina in 1976. Unusually, there was one match after the last of the tests. It was in Mendoza in the foothills of the Andes and, being the last match and being after the tests, it had the potential to be a loss because the focus of the tour had already been achieved. No one likes add-on matches, they upset the tour rhythms.

The dirties were determined they would win their "test" too for the sake of the tour. One of them on this tour was Black, the Canterbury hooker, and he spoke for them all when he said, "The test men have won their series. We're going to do our bit by winning the last match."

They even organised a training run for themselves while the test players were still celebrating their win in the second test in Buenos Aires. And, true to their word, the dirties won the final match to preserve the team's unbeaten record.

For all the novelty of the All Blacks being in Argentina then, there had been many precedents of All Black teams not being the first-choice selections. There had been a game against New South Wales in 1921 when the main All Black team was locked in combat with the first South African team. There was also the much better known occasion in 1949 when an All Black team was beaten by Australia while the main All Black team was in South Africa. That led to the unique occurrence of the All Blacks losing two tests on the one day — 3 September 1949, a fateful day for All Black rugby if ever there was one. Beaten 11–6 by Australia in Wellington and then beaten 9–3 by South Africa in Durban.

The "second" All Blacks, beaten by Australia, were captained by the great Northland centre, Johnny Smith — a Maori and therefore not considered for South Africa — and their vice-captain was Bob Stuart, who later captained the All Blacks in 1953–54, coached the forwards in 1956 and was a New Zealand union councillor from 1974 until 1989.

Stuart had played in the trials for the South Africa tour but missed out in selection to Peter Johnstone of Otago. The team that played Australia was the next best plus the Maoris who otherwise would have been almost automatic selections for South Africa. As well as Smith, Ben Couch and Vince Bevan would surely have been chosen.

Stuart recalled the "second" team being treated by the New Zealand union in

Peter Bush

John Gallagher in Japan in 1987.

every way as *the* New Zealand team, even though the first-choice 30 were in South Africa. "I don't think the status of the All Blacks was diminished in any way," he said. "We didn't pretend we were up to South Africa but we wouldn't have minded playing them."

The Australian team that year was exceptionally good and Stuart put it this way: "We were the third team and we went within an ace of beating the top team in Australia so there is that sort of negative satisfaction I guess."

There was also the 1987 tour of Japan by an All Black team that was a strange mixture of World Cup-winning players and others plucked out of provinces. The reasons for that were that New Zealand wanted to send a development team to Japan but the Japanese union — or rather, its head Shiggy Kono — wanted the full All Black team or nothing. Kono had his heart set on the first World Cup winners playing in Japan. Negotiation and compromise resulted in the final selection of the team, which seemed harsh on those seven or eight cup winners who didn't go. But good presumably for those players who hadn't been involved in the cup but who did go, especially for John Buchan, Robbie McLean and Paul Simonsson, for whom Japan was their only time as All Blacks.

It was that tour that led to the chairman of the New Zealand union then, Russ Thomas, saying that while it was an official New Zealand team, there was no such thing as the All Blacks as far as the union was concerned. That was just a nickname, he said.

Official or not, the All Blacks regarded themselves as All Blacks, just as the team in 1949 did, as did presumably, the team in 1921, as well as all the other teams chosen in similar circumstances.

In a totally different rugby environment, the All Blacks also played in Japan in 2000 en route to their tour of France and Italy. The players still wore the All Black jersey and were called the All Blacks, but it became a match of no official status because it wasn't played according to the laws of the game, i.e., both the All Blacks and their opposition, the so-called Pacific Barbarians, used more than the allowable number of replacements. The match thus didn't count as an All Black match and two players who hadn't played for New Zealand before, Bruce Reihana and Jason O'Halloran, had their debuts delayed until later in the tour. Reihana

Bruce Reihana with Jason O'Halloran in support against the Pacific Barbarians in 2000, a match that didn't count.

PHOTOSPORT

TRIED, BUT NOT TESTED

was chosen for two of the tests but O'Halloran's All Black career was delayed until 11 minutes from the end of the last test, against Italy.

All Black coach Wayne Smith used the match as preparation for the tour and he knew beforehand that if too many substitutes were used, the match would have no status. He acknowledged this and said the greater good of the team had to come first — meaning the preparation for the tour was more important than the All Black status of two individuals.

Ruling out matches from official status because laws relating to replacements, number of players or match duration were not adhered to is a tricky business. The match in Japan was an exception, as was also a match played by the New Zealand Barbarians in England in 1996 when the New Zealand team used more than the allowable number of replacements. In such cases, the breach is acknowledged as being for reasons of development or giving a match to players who otherwise wouldn't have one.

But there must have been matches in the past that could have been ruled out, but weren't because of a lack of records or because of a lack of vigilance on the part of match officials. When the All Blacks in 1976 played against Uruguay, for example, the local team changed three or four players at halftime when, strictly speaking, replacements should only have been made because of injury. While the New Zealand camp noticed the changes, the referee evidently did not or, if he did, he did nothing about it. The players could of course have been injured and thus legitimately replaced, but if they were it's stretching the imagination to believe that all gamely hung on until halftime. So that match, technically speaking, should not have qualified as an official All Black match.

Undoubtedly there would have been others, especially in the 19th century when laws were sometimes vague or even unknown, and when reports of matches were either brief or non-existent, leaving no evidence for posterity.

The professional era has brought great change to many aspects of All Blackdom, not least the number of matches other than tests that are played or, rather, not played. The compression of the season into "windows" for Super 12, internationals, NPC and northern hemisphere tests, plus the drive for test and television rights revenue at the expense of showing-the-flag matches, has brought an end to the old traditional tours and thus an end to matches that aren't tests.

The figures are revealing. Colin Meads, in his career that lasted from 1957 until 1971, played 133 matches for the All Blacks but less than half of them were tests (55). His total number of matches remains the record for the All Blacks, but his test record has long since been overtaken by eight players, with more likely to do so.

Another All Black centurion, Ian Kirkpatrick, played 113 matches but only 39 of them were tests. Andy Haden played 117 matches, 41 of which were tests.

Contrast those figures with some statistics from current players. Christian Cullen, whose All Black career dates from the first full year of professionalism, 1996, had played 53 matches to the end of 2000, 51 of which were tests. The figures for other modern All Blacks are comparatively similar. There are many who have not played in anything but a test. Norm Maxwell had by the end of 2000 played 20 times for the All Blacks and every one of them had been a test.

Coaches' figures show a similar imbalance. John Hart coached the All Blacks in 51 matches, of which 41 (80 per cent) were tests. His predecessor, Laurie Mains, coached the All Blacks in 62 matches and 34 of them were tests, just 55 per cent. Mains' overall win record as coach was 80.6 per cent, but Hart's was

PETER BUSH

78.4 per cent. The greater number of tests played is a factor often overlooked when comparing coaches' records and even the records of players.

Fred Allen, coach of the All Blacks during their winning 60s streak, ended with a win record of 97.3 per cent, by far the best of any All Black coach. But the great majority of his victories, plus those by the next most successful coaches Jack Gleeson, Neil McPhail and Alex Wyllie, were non-tests.

The end of the touring days, and it must be assumed they have pretty much ended, has meant that All Blacks have been chosen in recent years purely for their ability to fit into test sides. Either they're chosen for a specific position or they're chosen because of their ability to cover various roles as a reserve.

This obligatory selection policy (and it's not the selectors' fault that they're choosing only for test matches), means there's now less room — or even no room — for the players who became All Blacks who were primarily known as midweek players.

Without tours and therefore without the same chances to become All Blacks,

Colin Meads, who at 133, played more games for the All Blacks than anyone else, swaps jerseys with Lions captain Willie John McBride after his 55th and last test in 1971.

TRIED, BUT NOT TESTED

John Mitchell in action in England in 1993.

those players are mainly the type who now head for superannuation playing contracts in Japan or Europe, taking away from New Zealand a solid tier of experience and talent from just below the highest of the elite levels. By one count, there were about 400 New Zealanders with first-class playing experience plying their trade around the globe during 2001. That is a lot of top experience for New Zealand to lose from its game. It's a loss of experience, rugby knowledge and wisdom from provincial and club rugby as well.

The lack of tours also denies players such as Graeme Crossman and John Mitchell the opportunity of being All Blacks. One from the early 70s and one 20 years later, both were chosen for tours because of their high ability as players but also because of their perceived leadership qualities. Crossman in Australia in 1974 and in South Africa in 1976 was seen not just as the No 2 hooker to Tane Norton, but also as the stand-in captain for the midweek matches.

Similarly with Mitchell, who clearly was chosen for the 1993 tour of England and Scotland as much for his leadership qualities as for his play at No 8. This was confirmed early the following year when he was chosen as captain of a New Zealand Development team that went to Argentina. While the inclusion of Mitchell may have stretched the definition of "development", it was obvious he was selected because of his experience and his ability to meld together a team of relatively young players.

Both Crossman and Mitchell acknowledged and accepted their roles and filled them admirably, but their unofficial designation as midweek All Blacks didn't mean they couldn't have taken the step up to the tests if required.

Their pride in being All Blacks was no less because they were not test players. The story of Mitchell in Gateshead in England in 1993 has been published a couple of times now and illustrates just what being an All Black meant to him, and anyone who may have questioned his loyalties later when he was assistant coach of England ought to have been reminded of what happened. How Mitchell, who had been in the reserves for the afternoon's game against England A, sat in the bar at night still dressed fully in his number one uniform of All Black blazer and tie, long after his team-mates had changed and gone off into the Gateshead and Newcastle nights. And of how, when asked why he was sitting on his own, sipping solitary on a beer while dressed to the nines, he replied simply that being an All Black meant so much to him he wanted to take every opportunity of dressing as one.

It is entirely possible that in the modern era, men such as Crossman and Mitchell, and any number of others who played for the All Blacks but didn't play tests, wouldn't make it to the All Blacks at all.

Perhaps no one realised it at the time (well maybe not no one, men of such rugby knowledge as Brian Lochore, John Hart and Alex Wyllie did see it), but the 1987 World Cup was the first glimpse of the future. The cup was a novelty for all of the countries: some chose their squads as if they were going off on another tour. But not the three All Black selectors. They sat down in a variety of places, Pukekohe, Ashburton, New Plymouth, Hamilton and Whangarei, and settled on the new approach. They saw the cup as clearly different from another tour. The All Blacks to win the cup would have to win six test matches in succession, an average of one a week. They pencilled in their likely first XV, their test team, then wrote in the names of other players who could fill in if necessary because of injury and who could be in the reserves to cover areas such as loose forwards, inside backs etc. It was an early dawn of the era that later came upon New Zealand rugby.

JOHN RUBYTHON

Graeme Crossman, chosen for his leadership qualities, plays in South Africa in 1976.

TRIED, BUT NOT TESTED

Destined never to 'beet' the 'boks

꙳ Beet Algar, a Wellington five-eighth or wing both before and after the First World War, played six times for New Zealand but never in a test match. Not being chosen for a test was, he said in an interview shortly before his death in 1989, the only disappointment of his career. It wasn't just a simple case of non-selection, however.

Algar was chosen as first emergency for the All Blacks for the first test against South Africa in Dunedin in 1921 but since reserves — or emergencies as they were known — then couldn't take the field, he refused to travel from Wellington to Dunedin to merely watch the match.

A week later, when the All Black selectors were

The formal photo of the enlarged New Zealand party for the scoreless test against South Africa in Wellington in 1921:
Back row, from left: Pat Coira (masseur), Jim Taylor (masseur), "Nap" Kingstone, Mark Nicholls, Dick Fogarty, Bill Duncan, Dorrie Leslie (trainer), Alex McDonald (coach).
Middle row: Moke Belliss, Charles Fletcher, Keith Siddells, Alf West, Andrew McLean, James Moffitt, George Nicholson (selector), Jim Donald, Jock Richardson, John Turnbull.
Front row: Donald Stuart (selector), Beet Algar, Karl Ifwerson, Ginger Nicholls, Jack Steel, William Fea, "Jockey" Ford, Teddy Roberts (captain), Alf Griffiths (manager and selector).

considering their team for the second test in Auckland, Algar was asked if he would go there if he was named as an emergency.

No, he said.

"So they came to me before the third test and said, 'Will you go into training at Days Bay if you are guaranteed in the team?' and I said, 'Yes'."

Nothing went smoothly for Algar, however.

A fortnight before the final test against the Springboks in Wellington, he was chosen for the New Zealand team to play New South Wales in Christchurch. The All Blacks lost 0–17. "I ripped my ankle," Algar recalled. "We got beaten and I was the cause of them losing because I could only walk about the field.

"So when we came back [to Wellington] — my ankle healed in no time — we were over at Days Bay for two weeks. We came in to play a curtainraiser for a Wellington match for a run for the team and Alf Griffiths* [an All Black selector who was also, like Algar, a Poneke man] was keen for me to be in the test team. He said if you feel the ankle at all, you come off. Well, I came off. I didn't feel my ankle. I came off and who should I run into but Pat McEvedy, the union doctor. So I told him the tale and he didn't say anything. But the next Friday he came over to Days Bay to examine me and he said, 'You came off the paddock last week, didn't you?' And I said yes and he said, 'No buts, you're out'."

So ended Algar's chance to play a test.

Though known as "Beet", Algar's real name was Beethoven, giving him the most musical name of any All Black. "My mother was a composer," he said, "and she composed quite a lot of stuff but unfortunately she was an alcoholic. She was an alcoholic all her life and we were separated from her when I was about six years of age. I had a brother Haydn and very nearly had another brother named Mozart." Beet Algar died in 1989, aged 95.

Alf Griffiths, who played for Wellington in 1904 and 1905 and who was an All Black selector 1920–23, was the father of 1930s All Black Jack Griffiths.

THERE WAS NO PLACE FOR HOLMES

Bevan Holmes played 31 times for the All Blacks. He played in Australia, South Africa and Britain as well as in New Zealand in the black jersey with the silver fern.

But he never played in a test. No one's played more matches for the All Blacks without having been in a test than Holmes.

It doesn't worry him.

"I suppose when I think about it, it would have been something I'd liked to have done," he says, "but I've never really worried about it. Just playing for the All Blacks was pretty special for me."

Holmes was a No 8 from Northland who toured South Africa in 1970 and Britain on the 1972–73 tour as well as being on both All Black internal tours in 1972 and 1973.

"If I ever thought about playing in a test," he says, "it was along the lines that I'd always been pretty good at jumping up to the next level, right from my school days in Kaikohe. So a test match would have been the ultimate rung up the ladder and if the chance had come my way, I'd like to think I would have made the step up. But the chance never came."

Though Holmes could play on the side of the scrum as well, he was a specialist No 8. There was no surprise he wasn't chosen for a test in South Africa in 1970. The captain was also the No 8, Brian Lochore, and Holmes became one of three players in the squad of 30 not to play a test.

By the British tour of 1972–73, Alan Sutherland was established as the test No 8 though Alex Wyllie played the Scottish test there when Sutherland had the flu.

Holmes does have a regret about his time as an All Black, but it has nothing to do with his being consigned to the midweek matches.

"My one regret was that I would have liked to have seen more mentoring for the players coming through," he says. "Younger players or inexperienced players didn't get as much support as they should have. In our era, you just learned from experience." →

Bevan Holmes (right) with 1971 Lion Barry John and Grant Batty and Ian Stevens inspect Cardiff Arms Park in 1972.

He was also a little surprised by the quality of team talks in the All Blacks. "They were along the lines of 'Get out there and win, boys' and I expected something more than that," he says. "Of course, I'd been spoilt by having such a long involvement with Ted Griffin in Northland. We were very keen not to lose because of him. We wanted to make sure he smiled at us after a game. He demanded victory of us.

"I was surprised to a degree by the All Black team talks. Colin Meads and Brian Lochore were magnificent, but the team talks weren't what I was used to."

Griffin, a legendary coach in Northland, had predicted before the trials in 1970 that Holmes would be picked to go to South Africa. "He's got every attribute — strength, pace, physique and good hands — and his future is extremely bright," Griffin said.

Griffin had also promoted an earlier Northland loose forward, Peter Jones, and paid his own fare to get from Whangarei to Wellington for the trials in 1953 to ensure that Jones made the team. He did. "He was a great man for Northland rugby," Holmes agrees.

A POUND OF FLESH,
A FISTFUL OF DOLLARS

If by some magical process or if the properties of the Tardis could be transformed from fiction into reality and an All Black of earlier years could be transported into the All Blacks of today, eyes would be wide with wonder and mouths would be agape.

And what if the reverse could also apply, if an All Black of today could be whisked back in time to find himself leaning on the railing of a ship waving his relatives and sweetheart goodbye, not to see them again for three or four months?

The eyes would be wide not so much in wonder but in amazement.

The name of the game is the same for time travelling All Blacks of either direction, it's still rugby. Almost unrecognisable from one era to another, but rugby nevertheless. The Jersey is the same, almost. It's black and there's a silver fern, the only changes reflecting designers' foibles, different materials and the name of the manufacturer. Boots? Unrecognisable from one era to the next but still demonstrably footy boots, lowcut mostly for the backs and highcut for the forwards. The physical requirements have changed but fitness is a relative thing. The 1905 All Blacks were considered the fittest team there had been in their time and were as fit as they could make themselves. But they'd probably seem like sluggards today. For a start, it's been a long time since anyone smoked a pipe in an All Black dressing room and cigarettes haven't appeared for perhaps a decade. And besides, New Zealand male body types have changed enormously through the years as society's diets have changed. It's hard to imagine admittedly, but if somehow Andrew Mehrtens could flit back in time and become one of the 1924 All Blacks, the Invincibles, he'd be the third heaviest, weightier than them all except Maurice Brownlie and Ian Harvey.

Travel? All Blacks until 1953 when they went overseas went everywhere by ship, six weeks or more of a few jerks on deck (of the physical kind, that's not a description of the passengers), playing cards or singing round a piano in the saloon at night, trying to sleep in a narrow bunk while the ship rolls this way and that, pitches that way and this. When the first flying All Blacks, Bob Stuart's team to Britain in 1953–54, took off there were published concerns about how the flying would affect them and whether they could play within a week of landing.

Now, the All Blacks accumulate so many air points they'd need to spend the

All Blacks go through the various routines that were a feature of shipboard life as they headed off on tour in a more leisurely age.

first three years after retirement just redeeming them.

South Africa in former days was a distant land of a formidable foe that every All Black would have given his eye teeth (assuming he still had some) to see and to play but generations of fine All Blacks had been born at the wrong time and were destined never to get there.

Now, the All Blacks are there at least twice a year, sometimes three times. The exotic has become the routine.

But of all the changes, large and small, obvious and not so noticeable, the most significant has been money. All Blacks of days gone by never got enough of it, if they got any at all, and All Blacks of today get, well, enough to get by. All Blacks now show up in those rich lists that are occasionally compiled by using reasonable assumptions and guesswork that may be reasonable and may not be. Some All Blacks of other years could have qualified for a poor list.

It was the way it was. Rugby in Britain in its formative years set itself on a path of righteous (and snobbish) amateurism, shying away from the road of payment that its founding sibling, soccer, took and which later league also followed. Rugby, old chap, was the sport of the southern England upper middle class who had the wealth and the independent means to indulge in sport purely for its own sake. Money for playing sport was best left to the vulgar masses, with which rugby wanted nothing to do. While the proponents and protectors of the amateur ethos can rightly be denigrated for their elitism and for their pigheaded short-sightedness in stunting the development of rugby as a sport for all, it's difficult not to admire their persistence and their pervasive and persuasive influence. Somehow, they contrived and conspired to paint amateurism as something that was noble and pure and unsullied by mere money, and had it last for more than 100 years before finally those who suffered under its yoke cried "enough".

As a Welsh sports historian, Brian Dobbs, put it in 1973: "Is it not an odd phenomenon in our society that it is almost inevitably true that the men who have quite sufficient money of their own to live comfortably are also the ones to find activities carried out for fees or wages, sordid? There is nothing so effective as a private income in enabling one to take a moral stance. And moral stances taken against the new phenomenon of professional sport were legion throughout the late Victorian and Edwardian eras."

Amateurism, an indulgence for those who could afford it and a curse for those who couldn't, curiously transplanted itself from the landed gentry of southern England into all manner of places, including New Zealand. Since New Zealand adopted the game at an early stage, only 40 years after the establishment of formal government, and since the rugby roost was then ruled by England (as it would still dearly love to do), New Zealand had to fall in line with the decisions made by the English. The English, or more correctly the Rugby Football Union as it is grandly known, legislated for the world of rugby as it then was without knowing much, or anything, about countries other than its own for whom it was legislating.

Thus we had the amateurism rules laid down for well-heeled Englishmen applying equally to down-at-heel New Zealanders who just wanted a game of footy on a Saturday afternoon to be with their mates after slogging away all week

WHY DID THE ALL BLACKS WIN THE SECOND TEST?

BECAUSE THEY FED ON "SWAN" SAUSAGES BEFORE THE GAME AND AT HALF-TIME!

NOTE—The Shipment of "Swan" Sausages arrived too late for the First Test.

Endorsements aren't just a modern feature of an All Black's life. This enthusiasm for sausages came from the 1932 tour of Australia.

A POUND OF FLESH, A FISTFUL OF DOLLARS

on whatever it was that brought in their money.

One of the great early men of New Zealand rugby, Tom Ellison — the man who decided The Jersey should be black — saw through the hypocrisy and the inconsistency. When it was suggested in the late 1890s that a New Zealand team should tour "the old country", he had reservations.

"The idea is excellent," he wrote. "I see one difficulty only and that is getting the best men away without giving them some allowance over and above their actual hotel and travelling expenses — a difficulty due to the stringency of the laws as to professionalism. Personally, I think these laws were never intended to apply to extended tours abroad . . ."

He argued that to adhere to the English-framed laws on long tours that were not contemplated by the laws' framers would have the effect of players losing their jobs and, in some cases, their homes. "I think that in such cases the rules may well be relaxed to admit of compensation being allowed to players so forfeiting their pay; to deny them some compensation would be obviously unfair and tantamount to prohibiting them from going away at all."

Captains together. Highlanders, Otago and sometime All Black captain Taine Randell at the grave of the 1893 New Zealand captain, Tom Ellison, the man who decided The Jersey would be black.

Such a voice from the other side of the world was also a voice crying in the wilderness. No exceptions were made and "compensation" had become one of rugby's original dirty words after the split with the northern English counties that led eventually to the formation of league.

Some All Blacks certainly lost jobs through touring and some may also have lost their homes. All at some point would have lost money through their desire to play for their country. Some people in New Zealand sport still do lose money in the pursuit of national representation. Any number of athletes from so-called minor sports have to fork out for trips overseas even when they've been chosen in a national team. It's far from uncommon for a cyclist or an athlete or a softballer to receive a letter (or increasingly, an email) saying they've been selected for a team, congratulations are extended and then the next sentence hits them with the stinger: "You will be required to pay $5000 toward the cost of the trip."

All Blacks have never had to pay for the privilege, and neither should they have. The point here is that these other sports are and always have been on a hand-to-mouth existence and rely on quasi-government grants or the treadmill of raffles, house-painting and other money-raisers. Rugby has never had to do that. As the pre-eminent sport almost throughout its entire existence, it has seldom been short of a bob and in fact, for most of its history it's been relatively rich (relative to other sports) while its players until the last few years have been kept mainly poor.

The NZRFU had no qualms about paying the Original All Blacks three shillings a day expenses (they became known as three bob a day men) which were intended to cover such things as laundry, meals away from hotels, the odd beer or two, and sundry items such as writing paper and postage. But even that was too much for the staid old Corinthians of British rugby. The Scots in particular were incensed, their horror exacerbated by the fact they underestimated the Originals' crowd-pulling power and gave up the chance of earning a big gate for the test. The Scots hounded the New Zealanders for years afterward and even four years after the tour, tried to get the Originals declared professionals. They failed in that but with the support of Ireland, the International Rugby Board did resolve in 1909: "That the making of any allowance to players in cash in the opinion of the committee is contrary to the principles of amateur rugby football and in future no such allowance be made to any player."

New Zealand rugby, and particularly the old council of the New Zealand union, adopted almost a missionary zeal to the policing of the laws on professionalism, especially — ironically enough — the longer the 20th century wore on. When the whole issue should have long since been dead and buried in the 1970s and 80s, All Blacks were still being called to account for supposed transgressions of the amateur regulations. Graham Mourie took the honest way out and wrote to the chairman of the New Zealand union, Ces Blazey, in 1982 and said he'd received payment for his book, *Graham Mourie — Captain*. Under the 1880s attitude prevailing still in the 1980s, Mourie was declared a professional.

One of Mourie's contemporaries, Andy Haden, was the

For accepting the proceeds from this book, Graham Mourie was banished.

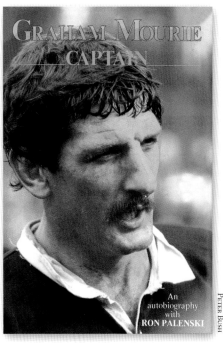

GRAHAM MOURIE CAPTAIN

An autobiography with RON PALENSKI

PETER BUSH

A POUND OF FLESH, A FISTFUL OF DOLLARS

subject of a full-blown inquiry into his supposed deeds and misdeeds, all because he'd written a book. But Haden, who in his All Black days was sometimes known as the Minister of Lurks and Perks because of his penchant for getting around the stuffy old rules, was able to say he was a professional writer and thus able legally to write a book. And he produced a bona fide press card from the daily French sports paper, *L'Equipe*, to prove it.

Even in the late 1980s when Russ Thomas was the chairman, still the occasional witchhunt was mounted for some player who may — or may not — have been paid for playing a game somewhere. Thomas, as pure as the driven snow and one who was almost more English than the English in his attitude to rugby, was loved by players and journalists for his constant references in speeches to his desire to preserve "this great amateur game of ours for our children and our children's children". It was probably one of Thomas' great regrets that he was never able to get to the bottom of the vexing issue of whether the Cavaliers in South Africa — the rebel All Blacks — in 1986 were paid. He and everyone else was sure they were or, if they weren't, the dividend from the team fund was more than just beer money, but no one could prove a thing. Or at least no one did prove a thing.

Nelson was not the only figure from history with a blind eye. Methods of circumventing the amateur regulations were well known but no one seriously tried to do too much about it. The most common method of ensuring players didn't go short when they were away was for their clubs to have a whip-round and to present them with a plain, brown envelope — along with a travelling clock or something — at an official farewell. The amounts varied according to the wealth of the club's supporters.

Match tickets always used to be another source of income for amateur All Blacks. Host unions gave the visiting team a match allocation of tickets and those that weren't used for close relatives or friends would be sold. Sometimes the selling was at face value, sometimes many times beyond that. It depended on the supply and demand and also on where the All Blacks were. There wasn't much demand for All Black tickets in Argentina, for example, but ticket sales in South Africa or Britain generally swelled the team's coffers. All Blacks who were accountants in civilian life seemed to be especially welcome in touring parties. Since it was assumed they could safely count and hoard money, they were generally the designated keepers of the tickets.

A face value of 11 shillings for this 1937 ticket, but how much could the All Blacks have sold it for?

Ticket selling sometimes landed the All Blacks in trouble though. Some countries don't take too kindly to scalpers outside grounds waving fistfuls of tickets in the air. When the All Blacks did that, they generally tried to appear incognito. In other words, they took off their blazers and ties as if a white-shirted, grey-trousered, fit-looking man outside the ground shouting "Tickets for sale!" fooled anyone. The Japanese police certainly weren't fooled in 1987 when the All Blacks were there. Matthew Cooper was given the job of getting rid of surplus tickets before a match in Kyoto and, being a reasonably tall fair New Zealander in

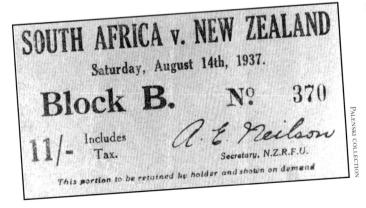

SOUTH AFRICA v. NEW ZEALAND

Saturday, August 14th, 1937.

Block B.   № 370

11/- Includes Tax.   *A. E. Neilson*

Secretary, N.Z.R.F.U.

This portion to be retained by holder and shown on demand

Japan, he was noticed by the vigilant police. They didn't want Japan to be the land of the rising sum and promptly hauled the appalled Cooper off to the nearest guardhouse. After a lot of gesticulating and rapid Japanese, Cooper was released into the care of the All Black manager, Malcolm Dick, and that was the end of ticket selling in Japan.

Ticket tales and other stories of accumulating money on tours didn't mean the All Blacks all came home richer than when they left. Far from it. If there was a dividend for players, it was at best break-even money. More often than not, team funds were used for such purposes as buying gifts for the manager, captain and coach at the end of tours and buying something also for people who helped them while on tour, the local help such as liaison officers, baggagemen and masseurs. Sometimes, there'd be enough for an end-of-tour party in Singapore or some other stopover.

Typically, players in the amateur days had to take leave from work for the duration of the tour (paid leave if they could get it, unpaid if there was no choice), some had to hire someone to work for them while they were away, others had to build up a store of work before they left and others simply didn't have jobs to leave or to go back to.

The South African tour of 1976 may have been typical of long tours of the latter days of amateurism.

Bryan Williams, the wing who had been such a sensation on the tour of South Africa six years before, was then a conveyancing lawyer in Auckland. The 1976 tour was his fourth while with the same law firm and, while he was away, his workload fell on his colleagues. His weeks before departure were spent preparing briefs and notes for those who took over his clients' files. In the lead-up to the tour, he worked a full day in his office, went to rugby practice three nights a week, played on Saturdays, and worked late each night on his cases.

The captain, Andy Leslie, had his own menswear store in Petone, in which he had previously been in partnership with an All Black from an earlier era, Bob Scott. Since Leslie was his own boss, he could decide for himself if he could go and if he could afford drawings while he was away. But for the duration of the tour, he had to employ someone to watch the store. In effect, he like many others paid to be with the All Blacks.

Ian Kirkpatrick was shearing on his farm practically until it was time to go. And while he was away, his three brothers had to hire extra staff to take his place during the busy and demanding lambing season. Kirkpatrick said he found it very demanding to be shearing all day, then have to go to rugby practice at night. But he still found time during the day to go for a run. And was the effort and the expense worthwhile to be an All Black? "Too right," he said.

Alan Sutherland also had to hire someone to replace him on the family's Marlborough farm. At the

The cost of touring . . . Bryan Williams eyes a souvenir stall in South Africa in 1970.

Ross Wiggins

ROSS WIGGINS

time, he was running a shearing gang that was fulfilling contracts at a number of farms, he had sheep in lamb and heifers in calf and he was also in the throes of starting a stud. Sutherland's problems were compounded by his brother, Ivan, being in the New Zealand rowing eight at the Olympics in Montreal. He reckoned the tour would have cost him about $4000, a substantial enough amount in 1976.

Peter Whiting, who was a science teacher at Glendowie College in Auckland, had to take leave on half-pay; if he'd been married, he would have been on full pay. He also had to find a replacement teacher. Lawrie Knight worked at Cook Hospital in Gisborne and three weeks of the time he was away was counted as annual leave, but the rest was leave without pay. Grant Batty was then branch manager of an investment company in Tauranga and while the company was happy to let him go, it cost him about six weeks' wages.

It was from the late 70s and into the 80s that players began complaining publicly, in books or in interviews, that it was illogical for them to be touring for nothing while at the same time the rugby authorities in whatever country were making huge amounts of money. The rugby unions could and did answer that the money was going toward clubs and the development of the game but it was an understandable feeling by the players, who would walk into a stadium such as Twickenham and see it full because of the attraction of the players, not because of the union. It was also around this time that players started earning money from their profiles as rugby players even if a bit of subterfuge had to be employed to keep it legal. During the first World Cup in New Zealand, the cup company chairman, John Kendall-Carpenter, and the British press were incensed that the

PALENSKI COLLECTION

All Black captain, Andy Dalton, was appearing in a television commercial for a farm bike. Thomas, the defender of amateurism, had to point out that nowhere in the commercial did it state that Dalton was a rugby player, much less an All Black.

It wasn't just the players who complained that they were hard done by. Even in 1953, when the All Blacks went to Britain, New Zealand newspapers criticised their weekly allowance of £2 10s, not much better in real terms than the three bob a day paid to the Originals half a century earlier. At the same time, the New Zealand cricketers were in South Africa earning £650 a month, a fortune compared with the All Blacks' paltry offering. The cricketers then were also ostensibly amateurs.

The real amateur days as Bert Cooke and George Nepia join referee Sam Hollander for oranges at halftime in the first test against the Lions in 1930.

A POUND OF FLESH, A FISTFUL OF DOLLARS

"It may be that the allowance for the cricketers is over-generous," the *New Zealand Observer* said, "and inconsistent with the strict principles of amateurism, since some of the players will be better off at the end of the tour than when it starts.

"But the niggardly provision for the footballers goes to the other extreme. £2 10s could be spent in London in the twinkling of an eye in returning hospitality. It is time for a more realistic attitude and New Zealand should endeavour to enlist the support of South Africa and Australia in pressing its viewpoint as forcefully as possible. Under today's conditions, £4 a day would not be an unreasonable allowance and no one could seriously contend that this amount would jeopardise anyone's amateur status."

The *Observer* was long gone by 1995 but its sentiments lived on and it was indeed the three principal southern hemisphere rugby countries who forced a change on the rest of the rugby world. Perhaps not so much forced a change, but reacted in the only way they could to the changes being forced on them.

The daily allowance agreed by the International Rugby Board was increased almost at every board annual meeting but it remained woefully inadequate to meet the daily requirements of players, much less compensate them for loss of earnings (which it was never intended to do).

While the IRB and its British majority continued to hold fast to the amateur principles laid down a century before, the three southern hemisphere countries gradually drifted away in their own time from the hard line (as did Wales in a subtle way by stuffing banknotes into the toes of boots). Money found its way to players in the southern hemisphere in various ways. When a team such as the All Blacks was wanted for a television commercial or for some other form of advertising, payment would be made and divided equally among the players taking part. The All Black Club, an idea hatched between the All Black coach, Laurie Mains, and Kevin Roberts who was then the head of Lion Nathan, also rewarded players in ways that didn't get them into trouble with the national union, which by then was quickly becoming exasperated with the whole amateur business anyway.

The man behind the All Blacks Club and former NZRFU director, Kevin Roberts.

By late 1994, players earmarked as being likely to figure in the World Cup in 1995 were contracted to the New Zealand union and they were paid by a company registered as All Black Promotions in return for various non-taxing duties. When Rupert Murdoch made his assault on league in Australia and split the game in two with his Super League, amateur rugby's days were almost over. New Zealand, Australia and South Africa, fearing that rugby players were ripe for plucking by league's enriched status, worked out their counter-plan. They went to Murdoch's News Corporation and out of a series of meetings came the agreement to sell television rights to Murdoch for the first-class game in the three countries. At almost the same time came the threat from the World Rugby Corporation, the plan devised by a former Wallaby prop and manager, Ross Turnbull, and supposedly backed by Murdoch's Australian rival, Kerry Packer.

Far from facing a loss of players to league, rugby now faced losing a hell of a lot more players to a breakaway rugby group. Amateurism was dead. The corpse may have still twitched in the northern hemisphere, but it was six feet under in the southern.

Players went where the money was. As it turned out, it was with the establishment game, thanks to Murdoch. There was a promise of money from Packer, but not enough up front. The unions' efforts to sign the players became even more desperate when the word came down from on high that all the players had to sign or Murdoch's money would be withdrawn.

It's now history that Jeff Wilson and Josh Kronfeld broke ranks with the All Blacks and signed first with the New Zealand union and that gradually the others fell into line, some gleefully, some grudgingly.

Only the players, their lawyers and Inland Revenue know precisely what was paid to whom, but it's reasonable to assume that those who signed early were looked upon more favourably than those who signed later.

If Billy Wallace could arrive in the Tardis and see what his successors have in the bank, he'd be astonished — and in all likelihood pull out an old pair of boots and try to get back into it.

Money has made an enormous difference to rugby in just over five years, not just to the health of the All Blacks' bank accounts, but across the board in rugby. Some of the impact has had a profound effect on the way the game is administered — even in the way the game is played through the demands for more entertainment to satisfy the television companies which largely bankroll the game. It's had an effect on club rugby because the introduction of the Super 12 and the year-long demands on the elite players mean no All Blacks play club rugby anymore, unless they need a club match to test their recovery from injury. Club rugby is not the focal point of a community that it once was. Players, once they know they're not likely to be in the All Blacks or picked up by one of the Super 12 teams, have the option of heading to Britain or Japan or somewhere where a playing job is guaranteed. In so doing, they take a lot of experience away with them.

Rugby's come a long way since Ian Kirkpatrick returned from South Africa and went straight from the airport to training with his club, Ngatapa.

The money has had a huge effect on the way the game is administered. In 1980, the New Zealand Rugby Union had a staff of three or four. Twenty years later, it had a staff of more than 60 with a branch office in Auckland. The old council was replaced by a board of directors, including independents who aren't necessarily versed in the lore of rugby, and the same applies to provincial unions where the old committees of delegates were replaced by boards.

Rugby has adopted business jargon. Ideas aren't agreed to anymore, there's "buy in". "Protocols" have replaced rules, "culture" has replaced an area's distinctive nature, plans are "signed off on" rather than approved, the All Blacks are a brand, the tests are a product. Players don't go overseas anymore, they go "offshore". Consultants prepare reports that are bulkier than phone books. Those who speak the jargon know where everyone else is coming from, but do they know where rugby is headed?

Life for the All Blacks is vastly different. They earn considerable amounts of money for doing what they do best. A prudent All Black could set himself up for life with his earnings from three or four years at the top level of the game. They're paid sums much, much smaller than what athletes in other sports earn overseas, but they're paid sums much, much bigger than what most people in New Zealand can command.

The life of an All Black revolves around training, either team or individual,

A POUND OF FLESH, A FISTFUL OF DOLLARS

with regular bouts of testing, playing and fulfilling the obligations demanded of the wealth of sponsors that have, to continue the jargon, "come on board". Their year goes from early January to late May (if they're good enough) with their Super 12 team, June to September with the All Blacks, September–October with their NPC team, then October–November if there's a northern hemisphere tour.

What the money does do is enable the All Blacks, or players aspiring to be All Blacks, to train and prepare themselves in a manner to meet the demands placed upon them both as individuals and collectively as a team. No All Black today could work in a "regular" job from 9 until 5 and still adequately fulfil the role of being an All Black. No All Black of today could get away with a couple of training sessions at night after work. The demands of the game dictate this. It is professional sport like any other and should be judged from the viewpoint of professional sport and not, wistfully, from the old days when it was an amateur sport. It's changed and it won't change back again.

But some things have not changed. From my observations and talking with players, the pride in wearing the All Black jersey is as great as it ever was; the desire to be an All Black is as great as it ever was and the desire, once having become an All Black, to be more than a one-match wonder is as great as it ever was. There has been no lessening of desire.

Just to give one example: Anton Oliver was first an All Black in 1996, if his brief stint as a reserve in 1995 is discounted. It took until the first game of the World Cup in 1999 before he would swap his All Black jersey with an opponent. That was against Tonga and the only reason, he says, that he handed his jersey

Black was fine by Anton Oliver, until after this match against Tonga in the 1999 World Cup when he swapped his jersey for the first time.

PHOTOSPORT

PETER BUSH

over was that the Tongan hooker was most insistent and wouldn't take no for an answer. "I just didn't want to give them away," he said. "They were my All Black jerseys. I didn't want any other jersey. Black was fine by me."

Much has been made, especially since adidas became the All Blacks' apparel sponsor in 1999, of the tradition of the All Blacks. It's been featured in television commercials, in posters and in other advertising. It's been using the past to build up the present, to remind followers of the traditions of being an All Black, that the All Blacks are a continuum, not just a team of the moment. Such imagery has also been a help for the players, reminding them that they're responsible for not just their own performances, but for maintaining the standards.

Like most other young men, they know of rugby players of their eras but their knowledge of All Black history is slight. That is not the same thing as saying they don't respect it. They do. They're conscious not of the detail of All Black history, but of the broad thrust and, because of that history, the weight of expectation that is on them. They know the country demands that they win. It helps that they know why. The All Blacks want to win for many reasons. They want to win for their team-mates, they want to win to show that their methods are better, they want to win for the families and friends who support them, they want to win because they're playing for their country, they want to win because they're All Blacks.

The All Blacks were professional in attitude and preparation long before they were professional in financial fact. That hasn't changed either.

The All Blacks wore adidas jerseys for the first time in the South African test in Dunedin in 1999 and to mark the occasion, captain Taine Randell presents a signed and framed jersey to adidas's president and chief executive officer, Robert Louis-Dreyfus.

A POUND OF FLESH, A FISTFUL OF DOLLARS

DANIE'S COSTLY GESTURE

∾ After the controversially bitter tour of New Zealand in 1981 by the Springboks, Danie Craven lavished gifts on members of the New Zealand Rugby Football Union who had insisted on the tour going ahead despite widespread public outrage.

Craven, president of what was then the South African Rugby Board, omitted to declare the gifts to customs when he arrived and thus avoided paying duty.

Somehow this leaked out and All Blacks and other rugby players returning to New Zealand for the next couple of years felt they were singled out by customs officers as retaliation.

Graham Mourie on his Opunake farm, which cost him money while he was playing for the All Blacks.

NEWS MEDIA AUCKLAND

The All Black captain, Graham Mourie, brought a few souvenirs and some wine back with him from the tour of Romania and France later in 1981.

"I was charged $170 duty so thank you Danie," Mourie recorded in his book, *Graham Mourie — Captain.*

Mourie, then running a Taranaki dairy farm, totted up the rest of the cost of being an All Black:

A wages bill of $1200 for a manager he had to employ to run the farm while he was away. The manager proved to be incompetent and Mourie put the cost of the incompetence down as another $1200. A grand total (Craven's dividend included) of $2400.

"A relatively cheap tour," he remarked.

PLAYING THE PRICE IN '76

Many players lost money through touring with the All Blacks because of loss of wages or loss of a job, but the team in Argentina in 1976 suffered a double whammy.

The players also had to sacrifice their daily allowance for the time they were in Uruguay for their first match.

When the team was first chosen, each player received a letter from the New Zealand union saying they'd be paid £2.50 a day — which then equated to $NZ4.40 — but that the payment would begin only when they were in Argentina.

The catch was that their first game was across the River Plate in Montevideo and the New Zealand union decided the Uruguay union was so poor it shouldn't have to pay the daily allowances.

(The usual system was for host unions to pay the allowances to the touring team manager and he then distributed them to the players).

The effect of the New Zealand union's generous gesture toward Uruguay was that the players spent the first week of their tour — three days travelling and three days in Montevideo — living off their own money. It saved the Uruguay union about $660 and the union also benefited from a crowd of about 5000 at the military academy ground where the match was played.

Giving up their "pay", as paltry as it was, wasn't the only money worry the All Blacks had while they were in Uruguay.

The All Blacks in Argentina in 1976. From left, Murray Taylor, Andy Haden, Graham Mourie and John Callesen.

News Media Auckland

A POUND OF FLESH, A FISTFUL OF DOLLARS

Some of the players, their pockets bulging with Uruguayan 1000-peso notes which amounted to not much in real money, decided to reduce their cash flow while waiting at the airport for the flight to Buenos Aires.

They stood on a balcony above the main concourse and watched the money float down to the floor below. A couple of grateful cleaners leapt on to the money from heaven until two militia men, not amused at this display of disrespect for the national currency, raced up the stairs and told the players bluntly to desist or they'd be arrested. They desisted, then helped clean up down below.

No tickets, no game!

ꙮ For 25 years, Stan Dean ruled New Zealand rugby. He was chairman of the New Zealand union from 1922 to 1947 and had managed the

Cliff Porter as he was painted during the Lions' tour in 1930.

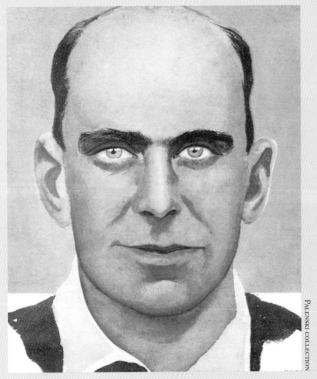

PALENSKI COLLECTION

Invincibles on their spectacularly successful tour of Britain in 1924–25.

When Dean said jump, rugby jumped.

But Cliff Porter, captain of the Invincibles and captain for most of the late 20s, did not jump.

He and Dean had not got on since the Invincibles' tour when Dean stopped Porter from playing in the Welsh and English tests. The pair had a confrontation on the eve of the fourth test against the British Isles in 1930.

The tour had been a financial success and Dean, anxious to wring every last penny out of a grateful public, decided the All Blacks would not be given free tickets to the test as they had been for the previous three.

Dean's decision was conveyed to Porter by Alfred Neilsen, the New Zealand union secretary from 1926 until 1950 and a faithful Dean ally.

Porter told Neilsen he disagreed with the decision and would fight it. The night before the test, Porter called his team together and suggested that if they didn't get free tickets, they should not play the next day. The players agreed.

Porter then told Neilsen of the team's decision, Neilsen relayed it to his boss who quickly if grudgingly reinstated the agreed ration of tickets.

Scotty's bob-a-job

ꙮ Bob Scott, the great All Black of the late 40s and early 50s, thought he would supplement his daily allowance on tour with a bit of exhibition kicking.

In Eastbourne on England's south coast during the All Blacks' 1953–54 tour, Scott was practising his goalkicking when an English journalist asked him if he really could, as reports said, kick bare-footed.

"What will you give me?" Scott asked. "Three attempts for a bob?"

"Certainly," the journalist replied.

OPPOSITE PAGE: Bob Scott demonstrates his barefoot kicking in Britain in 1953-54.

A POUND OF FLESH, A FISTFUL OF DOLLARS

Scott took off his boots and socks and placed the ball on halfway.

The first kick was high and straight, but short.

Scott moved the ball a little to the right for the second attempt. Immediately he'd connected, he shouted, "That's it, that's it."

The ball headed toward the right then veered in and went over the crossbar with plenty to spare.

The journalist rushed over with a half-crown coin (2s 6d).

But Scott had had second thoughts.

"No, no. Professionalism!" he cried.

FARM FIRST FOR CALLESEN

∽ Giving up something for rugby is one thing. Giving up the chance of a lifetime, a tour of South Africa with the All Blacks, is another.

John Callesen, an All Black lock first in 1974, was a surefire choice for the tour of South Africa in 1976. But he agonised for months over whether he could go and finally, painfully, decided he couldn't.

"I would love to have gone, it would have been the fulfilment of an ambition," he recalled recently, "but it just wasn't possible at the time."

Callesen and his father farmed 800 hectares in the Manawatu where they ran 4000 ewes, 800 breeding hoggets and 2000 Angus cattle. They were also heavily involved in cropping and contract harvesting.

"We'd employed someone else to help out but if I'd gone to South Africa we would have had to hire another labourer and the extra wages for four months just wasn't possible," Callesen said.

He and his wife Judy also had two young daughters at the time (the first two of four).

"We were sowing crops at the time of the tour and that in itself pretty much ruled me out," Callesen said. "But going on an All Black tour of South Africa was such a big thing that I thought long and hard about it, even though I knew deep down all along that we couldn't afford to go."

The sowing finished, Callesen was instead able to go on the tour of Argentina later in the year. "That was some consolation," he said, "it was a ripper of a tour."

Unable to go to South Africa, John Callesen went to Argentina instead in 1976. Here he prepares for a lineout against the San Isidro club.

AN ALL BLACK MISCELLANY

CIDER IN THE CELLAR

Every so often, there have been stories about All Blacks and drinking, how sessions foster camaraderie within the group and how drinking can help players wind down after an arduous match.

There've been tales of some epic bouts such as the time Alex Wyllie led his troops to a session at a league club in Sydney in 1988 after a drawn test the day before and how Laurie Mains followed suit with his players in a long night in Liverpool in 1993. There have been other sessions, other tours. Some may not have been recorded for the simple fact that while participants can remember there was a session, the details were a little hazy.

None of this is new.

One night in Devon during the Originals' tour, a group of All Blacks including captain Dave Gallaher were taken away from their hotel for a night of entertainment by a local farmer. The night began, Billy Wallace recalled, with the farmer showing the players what a crack shot he was with a revolver. He had the All Blacks toss pennies in the air and no sooner were the pennies up than the farmer brought them down. The All Blacks had a go but few hits were recorded.

The entrée over, the All Blacks and their host adjourned to the cellar for the main course.

"Here we found about 30 barrels of cider and he would have us taste a sample from each," Wallace wrote. The last of the barrels sampled was also the oldest and, Wallace recalled, it had plenty of kick in it and made the room go round. The exit from the cellar was by means of a rickety ladder.

"It was great fun trying to get up that ladder into fresh air again but we managed it at last after a fair bit of assistance. When we got out into the open air again we could scarcely see our way as the cider seemed to have affected our eyes.

"Somehow or other we stumbled up the steps into the house and took our seats at the table, but we had to guess where the plate of soup was and then try to steer a direct course from the plate to the mouth."

The meal safely negotiated, the players were driven back to their hotel after midnight, no doubt in a pain-free condition.

A presumably sober Billy Wallace in Britain in 1905.

NEW ZEALAND RUGBY MUSEUM

WORLD CUP WAR GAMES HAD NOTHING ON THE REAL THING

∽ The All Blacks, as part of their physical and mental conditioning for the World Cup campaign in 1999, were put through a series of exercises by the elite unit of the New Zealand army, the Special Air Service (motto: Who Dares Wins).

Part of the players' brief stint as soldiers comprised being grouped into fours, deposited out in the middle of nowhere and told to find their way back within a specified time. It was designed to be a test of individual strength of character and leadership qualities as well as the ability to operate as a team, each looking after the other.

Though the players were sworn to secrecy, enough details have emerged for it to be apparent that they were tested far more than they would ever be in the most rugged of test matches.

Though the exercise had a serious purpose and told All Blacks things about themselves they may not have wanted to know, they were in the end just playing at soldiers for a few days. Neither their lives nor livelihood were at risk and they knew they'd be back in their familiar, comfortable environment in a few days. And, after all, no one was shooting at them.

All Blacks of an earlier era indulged in similar activity but with far deadlier purpose and

All Black hooker Norm Hewitt directs his blindfolded team-mates during their SAS exercise in 1999.

without the mental comfort of knowing it would soon be over.

Many All Blacks served in the two world wars. Thirteen were killed in action in the first and seven in the second while many others were injured, some so seriously they could not return to rugby when peace came.

The exercise the All Blacks had in 1999 with the SAS was a remarkably similar echo of a real live action during the Second World War in which the All Black halfback of the early 30s, Merv Corner, played a distinguished part.

Corner in 1944 was a captain with the 1st Battalion of the Fiji Military Forces and their task, in conjunction with American troops, was to rid the island of Bougainville of the Japanese. The enemy were concentrated in the north and south of the island and the Allies occupied a coastal strip and the hilly, jungle country in the middle. The Japanese launched a concentrated attack on the New Zealanders and Fijians and their commander, Lieutenant-Colonel Geoff Upton, decided on a withdrawal to the coast. Corner and the men under his command tried to fight their way through the Japanese but were beaten back and rejoined the main group, which was cut off from all escape routes.

A Fijian sergeant, Usaia Sotutu, who had been a missionary on Bougainville years earlier, remembered an old disused track down a steep ravine and Upton took his men (plus about 200 locals) to safety. Corner was once more in the thick of it.

He returned up the track to show the way to a rearguard patrol commanded by a Captain Gosling.

The operation was conducted in pitch-black darkness and in pouring rain.

The official war history, *The Pacific*, noted: "Gosling and his party were guided in that night by Corner, in such darkness that each man was instructed to hold the equipment of the man in front of him."

The overall commander of the troops on Bougainville, American Major-General Oliver Griswold, later reported to his headquarters: "The success of the battalion . . . was one of the finest examples of troop leading that has ever come to my attention."

Corner, who finished the war as a lieutenant-colonel with the Military Cross, played 25 matches for the All Blacks, including six tests. He was later a North Island and New Zealand selector.

SVENSON'S FLUSH A NEAR THING FOR INVINCIBLES

Kenneth Svenson (above), known forever in rugby as "Snowy", had the unique distinction on the 1924–25 tour by the Invincibles of scoring a try in each of the four tests.

That wasn't the only way he left his mark on British soil.

One of the last survivors of the Invincibles, Canterbury wing Alan Robilliard, once recalled a night in England when some of the players →

celebrated the latest of their wins with a few beers in one of their hotel rooms.

"I can't remember where it was," he said, "but it was a big, high rambling hotel and there were four or five of us in one of the bedrooms having a few beers. The corridors meandered away down the back of the hotel and that was where the toilet was."

The players dutifully trooped down to the toilet each time they felt the need but soon tired of the trek.

Someone found a chamber pot under a bed and it was pressed into service. Inevitably, its capacity was soon tested.

Robilliard continued his story: "Snowy said, 'I'll fix it' and he pulled up a window. He put the pot out and tipped it and he stopped there for quite a while.

"He got a funny expression on his face and then he slowly brought his hand in.

"He just had the handle of the pot and the rest of it had gone down on to the footpath. Five minutes later, in came the hotel manager with a policeman wanting to know what was going on."

The All Blacks affected airs of innocence and denied all knowledge.

The policeman explained in injured tones: "I was proceeding on me beat when this po fell down in front of me."

Assured that these fine examples of colonial manhood were innocent, the policeman continued his beat convinced that the policeman's lot was not a 'appy one.

When All Blacks played — and refereed

It wouldn't have happened in Sean Fitzpatrick's day — not officially anyway — but one of his predecessors as the All Black hooker, Jim Burrows, once took the field for an All Black match as the referee.

Burrows became the first New Zealander to hook in the middle of a three-man front row. It happened in South Africa in 1928 when the All Blacks found their two-man front rows couldn't win the ball against the three-man South African front rows. So the All Blacks switched to a three-man front row for the first time against Griqualand West in Kimberley and Burrows was the man in the middle.

He became a different type of man in the middle later in the tour.

In the week of the fourth test, won by the All Blacks to square the series, the players learnt that the ship scheduled to take them to Australia was delayed for a couple of days. Rather than fill in the extra two days after the test with sightseeing or otherwise relaxing, All Black manager Bill Hornig agreed to play a scratch match against the combined universities of Cape Town and Stellenbosch.

It was a match with a difference because the South Africans agreed to play under different laws then applying in New Zealand. The two main differences were that kicking into touch on the full could be only from within a defender's 25-yard line and that knock-ons wouldn't be ruled if a player knocked the ball on but regained it (both laws later became universal).

The other reason it was a match with a difference was that Burrows was delegated to referee it.

The first Burrows knew of it was when his captain, Maurice Brownlie, went to him and asked him if he had a white jersey.

Burrows recalled in a television interview that he told Brownlie he didn't but that Andy Mercer, their masseur, would probably get him one.

"Oh it's not for me, it's for you," Brownlie told Burrows, adding that he would be refereeing the match against the universities.

"This of course scared the daylights out of me," Burrows said. "A few of the team were listening. It produced all sorts of stories about referees who had been stoned to death and what could happen to him

NEWS MEDIA AUCKLAND

if he made a lot of decisions against the locals etc.

"I came back and said, 'Well, you're the first bloke I'm going to order off with that sort of talk'."

As it turned out, Burrows recalled, any child could have refereed it.

Though it didn't count as an official match because of the law variations, it still was a genuinely competitive match — the All Blacks had 11 players who had been in the fourth test and the universities had two of the test Springboks. The crowd of about 15,000 at Newlands indicated that the Cape Town public took it seriously as well.

When Burrows blew the whistle for the last time in his unique role, the All Blacks had won the match 14–9.

CAREERS DON'T COME MUCH SHORTER THAN COBDEN'S

Many All Blacks had fleeting careers in the black jersey but Don Cobden didn't just have a brief All Black career, his entire rugby career was amazingly brief.

Cobden was a Canterbury wing who played just 20 minutes for the All Blacks — the first 20 minutes of the first test against South Africa in 1937. He was picked up and dumped in a tackle by South African wing Dai Williams, injured a leg and had to leave the field. He never played first-class rugby again.

He had played only eight first-class matches in his entire career, three for Canterbury (two in 1936 and one in 1937), one for the South Island, three trials in 1937 and the test.

Later in 1937, Cobden worked his passage to Britain and joined the Royal Air Force and while training as a fighter pilot, he played club rugby.

He flew Spitfires in the Battle of Britain and on 11 August 1940 — his birthday — Cobden was shot down over the English Channel when attacking a superior force of 40 German fighters.

He was the first of seven All Blacks to be killed in the Second World War.

BERT MARSHALS THE INVINCIBLES IN TOULOUSE

Toulouse was obviously the place to be on Sunday, 18 January 1925. So many people crowded into the Stade des Ponts Jumeaux for the last match of the Invincible All Blacks' tour that the start had to be delayed while spectators were pushed back from the touchline.

There wasn't room, evidently, to swing *un chat*.

After the match, in which the All Blacks vindicated their Invincibles tag with a 30–6 win, the festivities wound up a notch and Bert Cooke, that prince of centres, found more to swing than a mere cat.

Among the guests at the post-match dinner in the plush Hotel de l'Europe was Marshal Henri Pétain, who became the hero of France when his troops held the Germans at Verdun in 1916 (though fell from grace a little when his grand scheme for the Maginot line didn't prove very effective against the Germans in 1940).

Maginot and Germans were far from minds as the dinner continued into the Toulouse night. The wine and the beer flowed and the All Blacks weren't afraid to imbibe because they had only two matches left in Canada and they were a month away.

There had to be some circumspection though because the team was due to catch a train at 11 that night and head off back to Paris.

Cooke and a few of his mates decided to go to the station and they retrieved their straw boater hats from the hat check at the hotel entrance. Cooke couldn't resist what he saw.

There, alongside the straw boaters, the homburgs and a top hat or two were the accoutrements of Pétain's high and mighty military position: dress uniform hat and sword.

He somehow charmed them out of the hat check attendant and, as team-mate Alan Robilliard recalled, "Cookey next thing was out in the street strutting up and down in this gear."

The pilfered items were returned before the marshal made his grand exit.

The rest of the walk to the station didn't proceed without incident either.

Along the way, first five-eighth Neil McGregor began limping and, Robilliard recalled, tottered along for a while before collapsing on the footpath, apparently unconscious. "We couldn't bring him round," Robilliard said, "so Ian Harvey [a powerful Wellington lock] said, 'Well, I'll carry him' and he stuck him on his shoulders and carried him. When we got to the station, he put him down very carefully on the platform.

"Mac got up, looked around, and said, 'Thanks Ian'. There was nothing wrong with him at all."

YOU WOULDN'T READ ABOUT IT

It's a tale to touch the heart, the tale of All Black lock Read Masters and the sweetheart he married 43 years after first meeting her. Then he died a week later.

Masters was one of the 1924–25 Invincibles — and wrote a book about the tour — and had been on the tour of New South Wales that preceded the British tour. While in Sydney, he met Sybil Argyll Smith, one of the stars of early Australian cinema.

They corresponded after the tour but went their separate ways. Masters married and settled down in Christchurch and Smith married an Englishman and the pair lived in Hollywood where her husband was a lawyer. Masters never forgot Smith. He always carried in his wallet a small newspaper clipping about her from 1924.

Masters' wife died early in 1966 and Smith's husband died later the same year.

In 1967, the pair renewed their correspondence and Smith, who had returned to Sydney to live, came to New Zealand to see Masters.

The reunion took place in June and they were married on 21 August 1967. Eight days later, on 29 August 1967, Masters died.

OPPOSITE PAGE: The programme for the Invincibles' test in Toulouse.

Firsts from the Fifties

∾ The 1953–54 All Blacks in Britain, though they lost four matches including the tests against Wales and France, set some All Black firsts:

They were the first team to go to Britain by air;

They were the first All Black team to play in seven countries (England, Scotland, Ireland, Wales, France, Canada, United States);

They were the first to complete a circumnavigation of the globe.

Two All Black captains have also led teams to defeat the All Blacks. The first was Bob Duff (All Black captain 1956) who led Canterbury to beat the All Blacks 11–9 in Christchurch in 1957. The second was Colin Meads (All Black captain 1971) who led a President's XV that beat the All Blacks 35–28 in Wellington in 1973. That match and another the following week in Auckland had been hurriedly arranged to replace the South African tour of New Zealand, which Prime Minister Norman Kirk had ordered should not go ahead. The two matches were widely regarded as farewell matches for Meads.

Bob Duff leads out the All Blacks in the 1956 series against South Africa.

Poet Pearce wowed 'em

∾ All Black managers have not often been noted for their powers of oratory. Speeches by managers, while not descending to the thanking the ladies for the plate variety, have generally been politely listened to and politely applauded, another rugby ritual out of the way.

But one manager was noted for his speaking. He was Tom Pearce, who managed the All Blacks to South Africa in 1960.

Pearce, good enough as a prop to play for Auckland for 10 years and to be an All Black reserve, stunned his audience at the All Blacks' farewell at the old Midland Hotel in Wellington.

He quoted, without a falter, the last 15 lines of Tennyson's poem, *Ulysses*:

'Tis not too late to seek a newer world,
Push off, and sitting well in order smite
The surrounding furrows, for my purpose holds
To sail beyond the sunset, and the baths
Of all the western stars until I die.
It may be that the gulfs will wash us down:
It may be that we shall touch the happy isles
And see the great Achilles, whom we knew,
Though much is taken, much abides;
*   and though*
We are not now that strength which in old days
Moved heaven and earth;
*   that which we are, we are:*

One equal temper of heroic hearts
Made weak by time and fate but strong in will
To strive, to seek, to find, and not to yield.

By all accounts, it wasn't just the classical scholars in the audience (if there were any) who understood Pearce's message.

The All Black coach, Jack Sullivan, and captain Wilson Whineray both said in their speeches they were delighted to have Pearce as manager because his presence would mean he could be assigned all the public speaking duties.

Pearce in South Africa was also reputed to have fallen back on the old joke of making a speech in Maori that delighted his audience: "Tokoroa, Waikato, Te Kuiti, Taumarunui, Taranaki . . ."

NOW HERE'S A PLAYER FOR ALL POSITIONS

Here's one for all the quiz buffs: name the player who played in every backline position except halfback for Manawatu in more than 60 games, but played his one test as a flanker.

Brian Edward Louis Finlay, that's who.

Finlay first played for Manawatu in 1950 and after a career in the backs and at an age when many players would be considering retirement, switched to the forwards midway through 1958.

The Manawatu selectors apparently had little faith in their pack and moved Finlay to flanker for a Ranfurly Shield challenge against Taranaki to add a bit of backbone.

The audacious, it appears, paid off. Finlay was an instant hit and within a year was selected as a flanker for the first test against the Lions in 1959.

"My only regret is that I did not play all my rugby as a forward," he said after his shock All Black selection.

His was a brief career though. He was injured early in the test in Dunedin — the infamous 18–17 victory when Don Clarke kicked six penalties — after tackling halfback Dicky Jeeps. Replacements

News Media Auckland

The versatile Brian Finlay.

couldn't be made and Finlay's effectiveness was reported to have been diminished for the rest of the match.

Finlay's injury kept him out of contention for the second test in which he was replaced by none other than Colin Meads, who had been in the first test reserves. Meads played the second and third tests on the side of the scrum and moved to lock for the fourth.

Finlay wasn't picked for New Zealand again.

Fotopress/Peter Bush

About that lineout . . .

 Sometimes, referees are remembered as much in All Black history as the players themselves . . . there was John Dallas of 1905 fame who didn't award a try to Bob Deans, Albert Freethy who sent Cyril Brownlie from the field in 1925 and Kevin Kelleher who sent Colin Meads packing at Murrayfield in 1967.

And there was Roger Quittenton.

He was the referee in the test against Wales in 1978, the test the All Blacks won 13–12 after replacement Brian McKechnie kicked a penalty goal with a couple of minutes to go. Quittenton had penalised Welsh lock Geoff Wheel for climbing on the shoulder of Frank Oliver.

But incensed Welshmen believed Quittenton had been conned by Andy Haden's theatrical dive out of the lineout in search of a penalty. They had been robbed, they said, of victory over the All Blacks, a victory which had become a national obsession.

Quittenton's name in Wales became mud and a Welsh union official told him that he would never again referee a match in Wales.

The incident was not a five-minute wonder. Two years later, when the All Blacks were back in Wales, the afternoon paper in Cardiff, the *South Wales Echo*, called Quittenton the most hated man in Wales.

Quittenton through it all retained a stoic silence. But not so his wife Ann, who was so sick of her husband being painted as Welsh Public Enemy No 1 that she furiously wrote a letter to the paper.

It was no brief riposte either. It went on for 20 paragraphs and began: "I am Ann, wife of Roger Quittenton, the most hated man in Wales. Before you set fire to this letter, I also am Welsh — unfortunately. I feel like renouncing my Welsh background (sorry, Dad) when I hear of the way Welsh rugby men are behaving."

She then launched into defence of her husband, whom she calls "Rog". It began as a general defence then she moved on to the offending lineout specifically:

"The lineout penalty was proved by video to be correct — even JPR said so at the private dinner after the match. 'You were very brave Rog, but you were right'. [That was true, JPR Williams did say that]. Pity he can't say that in his book.

"Still, a bit silly of Wales in the closing minutes of the game, the ref on their side of the lineout, the ball at their end of the field. Now, if Rog is so bent as to award such a penalty in order for New Zealand to win, don't you think he'd be quick witted enough to realise to do that against Wales is you finished as far as Wales is concerned?"

In what had to be one of the most unusual defences of a referee, Ann Quittenton continued: "I shall probably be told I'm interfering in a man's world (please forgive me for writing this letter, Rog) but when the man I love, respect and know is being character assassinated by my own countrymen, I feel I have to speak up."

Coincidentally, or perhaps not so coincidentally, the same paper on the same day quoted the *Daily Telegraph* rugby writer at the time, John Reason, as writing that thanks to television and slow-motion replays, the 1978 lineout had superseded the disallowed Deans try in 1905 as the high point of controversy in matches between Wales and New Zealand.

"Within the space of two years," Reason wrote, that is, from 1978 to 1980, "the Welsh have erected around that lineout the biggest Celtic myth of all time. This myth asserts that when Haden dived out of the lineout to try to persuade the referee to award New Zealand a penalty . . . the referee should somehow have had eyes in his posterior and should have reversed the penalty award and, for all I know, should have awarded Wales the games they lost to the All Blacks in 1924, 1964, 1969 (two), 1972 and 1974."

Opposite Page: The All Blacks in a more orthodox lineout against Wales in 1978. From the front, Brad Johnstone, Frank Oliver, Andy Haden and Gary Seear.

An All Black miscellany

REDS UNDER RUGBY BEDS

All Blacks are OK, but Reds? Never.

The All Blacks went to Britain in 1953–54 at the height of the era of McCarthyism in the United States and each player was interviewed at the American Embassy in Wellington for about three-quarters of an hour before a visa to enter the United States was issued.

Each player had finger and palm prints taken, had to answer a lengthy questionnaire and had to swear he was not, nor ever had been, "a Communist, Fascist, Nazi or Falangist".

The process was so lengthy it took the embassy two days to get through the 30 players plus management.

In the language of the time, *The Dominion* headed its report of the interviews: "All Blacks must not be Reds".

McCarthyism was named after Republican Senator Joseph McCarthy who conducted a witch-hunt into the number of supposed communists in influential positions in American life, including the State Department and the military. His allegations led to a series of hearings which ultimately told the American people more about his paranoid hysteria than it did about any other type of extremists.

The All Blacks spent a few hours in New York and played in San Francisco without posing a threat to America's national security.

All Blacks Ian Clarke, Arthur Woods and Peter Jones swear their political purity to an American official in Wellington.

News Media Auckland

Long and the Short of it

The Invincibles of 1924–25 were rightly reckoned to be one of the strongest and best of All Black teams. Their biggest forward was Cyril Brownlie, listed then as 15 stone and now would be listed as 95kg.

Of current or recent All Blacks, utility back Leon MacDonald, whose listed weight is 96kg, is heavier than any of the Invincibles.

Wallaby Fred Wood and All Black Bolla Francis show the long and the short of it in this 1907 photo.

PALENSKI COLLECTION

An All Black miscellany

It's funny what you find in the mail

~ All Blacks today would squirm with embarrassment if someone wrote a poem about them, especially if it was published for all the world to see.

But poems about sports stars were quite common in the early days of organised sport.

Among several published about the Original All Blacks of 1905 was this one about Billy Wallace in the *Daily Mail*.

Gliding away at a deuce of a pace,
Swerving and dodging all over the place,
Doubling and twisting,
Stout tacklers resisting,
To snap up the leather he's ever persisting;
All hot sand and ginger,
He's trouble a harbinger,
And scarcely the chief you would care to embrace.

Note how he's working with verve, vim and flip,
He gives nought away — unless it's the slip,
Jumping and bumping,
And o'er the line dumping,
The leather (his comrades the while
*   are "galumphing"),*
With goal never tiring,
While foemen, perspiring,
Are marvelling how he escaped from their grip.

Watch him when steering the ball with his toe,
Sure as a Vardon when putting, you know,
'Tween the sticks sailing,
With skill never failing,
While in the home ranks there is weeping
*   and wailing,*
A djina* with the ball is
This wonderful Wallace,
And — abracadabra! — his goal crop will grow.

* A mythological being with supernatural powers.

No news was often Badeley news

~ All Blacks in the old amateur days weren't supposed to write for newspapers, but some of them did anyway.

Among them on the Invincibles' tour in 1924 was inside back Cec Badeley, one of the senior players and captain on the preceding tour of Australia.

Badeley, who was then 27, adopted the convenient method of sending his unofficial dispatches to his father, who then passed them on to the Auckland morning paper, the *New Zealand Herald*.

But Badeley revealed in a letter to his mother from on board the ship taking the team to Britain that he may have had opposition.

"I'll give Dad all the news though there isn't much to say as our programme has been much the same as before we reached the [Panama] Canal," Badeley told his mother.

Chronicler Cec Badeley.

He then added a PS, showing all the secretive instincts of a trained journalist: "Tell Dad to take his letters to the *Herald* as soon as he gets them as I believe another fellow with the party is writing to them. Also tell him not to say I know about it."

Badeley didn't say who his rival was but he may have been talking about Arthur Carman, who took leave without pay from his job with the Audit Department in Wellington to write about the tour for a variety of news outlets.

Carman was later a co-founder of the *New Zealand Rugby Almanack*.

But he may also have been talking about his team-mate Read Masters, who wrote a book about the tour.

THE FORGOTTEN ALL BLACK

  Every so often mention is made of a forgotten All Black. Usually, such a reference is to a player who perhaps had a brief All Black career and who had enjoyed public anonymity since.

But there was one real forgotten All Black.

He was an Otago loose forward, John Turnbull, whose one appearance for New Zealand was as a replacement against New South Wales in 1921. That All Black team comprised players who were not involved in the main event of the year, the first series against South Africa.

A couple of years later a publication called the *New Zealand Rugby Annual* was produced and its list of New Zealand representatives since 1884 didn't include Turnbull.

And when that indefatigable and normally punctilious recorder of early New Zealand rugby minutiae, Arthur Swan, compiled his first volume of *History of New Zealand Rugby Football,* published in 1945, Turnbull still didn't get a mention.

When the second volume of Swan's work was published in 1957, Turnbull was still among the missing.

Subsequently, other lists of All Blacks which put their reliance in Swan — a reliance normally justified — also left Turnbull out.

Turnbull's name was missing from *The Reed Book of All Black Records* and even from the first edition of the *New Zealand Rugby Encyclopedia,* published in 1981. He also missed being listed as one of Otago's All Blacks in the Otago centenary book, *Pride of Southern Rebels.*

One of the *Encyclopedia*'s editors, Rod Chester, was researching records for *Centenary,* published in 1984, when he found a newspaper account that mentioned Turnbull took the field against New South Wales. He checked and checked again and yep, Turnbull was an All Black.

For his one appearance, he replaced another Otago All Black, Sid Cabot and, ironically enough, that was also his only match for New Zealand.

When Turnbull made it into the later editions of the *Encyclopedia,* it noted that ill health forced him to give up rugby later in 1921.

The first edition of *The Encyclopedia of New Zealand Rugby*.

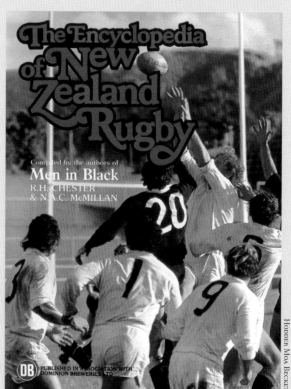

AN ALL BLACK MISCELLANY

TALLEST

2.04 metres	Chris Tregaskis
2.03	Hud Rickit
	Jock Ross
	Mark Cooksley
	Richard Fromont
2.01	Chresten Davis
1.99	Peter Whiting
	Glenn Taylor
1.98	Andy Haden
	Murray Pierce
	Gary Whetton
	Steve Gordon
	Blair Larsen
	Ian Jones
	Royce Willis
	Norm Maxwell

The tallest back has been Jonah Lomu at 1.96m.

Chris Tregaskis.

SHORTEST

1.60 metres	Kevin Briscoe
	Ponty Reid
	Percy Tetzlaff
1.63	Bill Dalley
	Neil Wolfe
	Tu Wyllie
1.65	Grant Batty
	Merv Corner
	Joey Sadler

The shortest forward was Bill Francis at 1.68m.

Percy Tetzlaff.

OLDEST

40 years 123 days	Ned Hughes
35 years 305 days	Frank Bunce
35 years 287 days	John Ashworth
35 years 226 days	Richard Loe
35 years 136 days	Tane Norton
35 years 72 days	Colin Meads
35 years 54 days	Charlie Sonntag
35 years 37 days	Andy Haden
35 years 11 days	Gary Knight
34 years 327 days	Wiremu Heke
34 years 219 days	Bill Lindsay
34 years 178 days	Sean Fitzpatrick
34 years 109 days	John Spiers
34 years 28 days	Simon Mynott
34 years 17 days	Bill Cunningham

Bunce and Mynott were the oldest backs.

Tane Norton.

OLDEST ON DEBUT

35 years ?? days	Angus Stuart
35 years 26 days	Charlie Sonntag
34 years 299 days	Wiremu Heke
34 years 184 days	Bill Lindsay
33 years 268 days	Edwin Davy
32 years 261 days	Ken Going
32 years 192 days	Nelson Dalzell
32 years 179 days	Jock Ross
32 years 165 days	Lin Davis
32 years 96 days	Alf Kivell
32 years 20 days	Phil Coffin

Ken Going.

Youngest

17 years 36 days	Lui Paewai
18 years 196 days	Craig Wickes
18 years 331 days	Jasin Goldsmith
19 years 2 days	Jamie Hendrie
19 years 45 days	Jonah Lomu
19 years 71 days	George Nepia
19 years 79 days	Edgar Wrigley
19 years 106 days	Pat Walsh
19 years 140 days	George Dickinson
19 years 183 days	John Kirwan
19 years 200 days	Billie Mitchell
19 years 221 days	Bill Francis
19 years 224 days	Neil Wolfe
19 years 233 days	Geoff Hines
19 years 246 days	Ron Stewart
19 years 264 days	Bryan Williams
19 years 270 days	Jim Baird
19 years 277 days	Bruce Hunter
19 years 291 days	Ken Stewart
19 years 311 days	Handley Brown
19 years 344 days	Chris Laidlaw
19 years 357 days	Walter Little
19 years 364 days	Jeff Wilson

Only Francis, Hines, Ken Stewart and Ron Stewart were forwards.

Lui Paewai.

Jonah Lomu.

HEAVIEST

125kg	Mark Cooksley
123	Kees Meeuws
122	Isitolo Maka
121	Craig Dowd
121	Jonah Lomu
120	Phil Coffin
119	Royce Willis
117	Greg Feek
116	Richard Loe
115	Mark Allen
115	Con Barrell

The "big rig", Mark Cooksley.

LIGHTEST

58.93kg	Ginger Nicholls
58.93	Merv Corner
58.93	Ponty Reid
59.40	Arthur Humphries
60.71	Ray Williams
61.16	Roger Urbahn
61.60	Bert Cooke
62.06	Joey Sadler

"Ginger" Nicholls.

Many of the earlier players did not have accurate weights recorded. John Dumbell was said to have weighed 7 stone 6lb (46.45kg) at the time of the 1884 tour. Although a utility back, he played two tour matches in the forwards. Even in later years, player heights and weights have been notoriously unreliable.

ALL BLACK LISTS

ALL BLACK BROTHERS (38)

Bachop, Graeme and Stephen

Badeley, Ces and Vic

Bayly, Alf and Walter

Brooke, Robin and Zinzan

Brown, Handley and Henry

Brownlie, Cyril, Laurence and Maurice

Clarke, Adrian and Phil

Clarke, Don and Ian

Cooke, Alfred and Reuben

Cooper, Greg and Matthew

Deans, Robbie and Bruce

Donald, Jim and Quentin

Dunn, Eddie and Ian

Fanning, Alfred and Bernie

Goddard, Jack and Maurice

Going, Sid and Ken

Good, Alan and Hugh

Gordon, Rob and Steve

Hadley, Bill and Swin

Haig, Jim and Laurie

Jaffray, Lyn and Merv

Knight, Arthur and Laurie

Meads, Colin and Stan

Meates, Bill and Kevin

Millton, Edward and William

McMinn, Archie and Paddy

New Zealand Rugby Museum

The three Brownlies, Laurence, Maurice and Cyril.

Nicholls, Doc, Ginger and Mark

Purdue, Charles and Pat

Ryan, Eddie and Jim

Shearer, Jack and Syd

Smith, Johnny and Peter

Solomon, Dave and Frank

Spencer, George and Jack

Stuart, Bob and Kevin

Taylor, Murray and Warwick

Tilyard, Fred and Jim

Whetton, Alan and Gary

Woodman, Fred and Kawhena

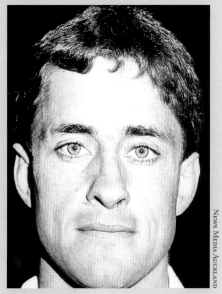
Warwick Taylor.

Murray Taylor.

Father and son All Blacks (15)

Barry, Ned and Kevin

Barry, Kevin and Liam

Brown, Handley and Ross

Dalton, Ray and Andy

Dick, John and Malcom

Fitzpatrick, Brian and Sean

Irvine, "Bull" and Ian

Knight, Laurie and Lawrie

Lynch, Tom and Tommy

McCormick, Archie and Fergie

Mexted, Graham and Murray

Oliver, Frank and Anton

Purdue, Pat and Jack

Roberts, Harry and Teddy

Stanley, Joe and Jeremy

Archie McCormick.

Fergie McCormick.

ALL BLACK CENTURIES

145–17	v	Japan	Bloemfontein	1995
117–6	v	South Australia	Adelaide	1974
106–4	v	Japan	Tokyo	1987
103–9	v	Northern New South Wales	Quirindi	1962
102–0	v	Tonga	Albany	2000
101–3	v	Italy	Huddersfield	1999

MOST POINTS IN A MATCH

45	**Simon Culhane v Japan**	**1995**	**(1t, 20c)**
43	Robbie Deans v South Australia	1984	(3t, 14c, 1p)
41	Joe Karam v South Australia	1974	(2t, 15c, 1p)
38	Ron Jarden v Central West (Aus)	1951	(6t, 10c)
36	John Gallagher v Victoria Inv XV	1988	(4t, 10c)
36	**Tony Brown v Italy**	**1999**	**(1t, 11c, 3p)**
34	Gerald Kember v North East Cape	1970	(14c, 2p)
34	Shane Howarth v South of Scotland	1993	(2t, 9c, 2p)
33	**Carlos Spencer v Argentina**	**1997**	**(2t, 10c, 1p)**
33	**Andrew Mehrtens v Ireland**	**1997**	**(1t, 5c, 6p)**
32	Don Clarke v South West Zone (Aus)	1957	(13c, 2p)
32	Alan Hewson v Queensland Country	1984	(13c, 1p, 1dg)
32	**Tony Brown v Tonga**	**1999**	**(1t, 12c, 1p)**
30	John Gallagher v Japan	1987	(1t, 10c, 2p)
30	Grant Fox v Japan	1987	(15c)
30	**Marc Ellis v Japan**	**1995**	**(6t)**

bold = test match

MOST TRIES BY A PLAYER IN A MATCH

8	Rod Heeps	v	Northern New South Wales	1962
7	Charles Rushbrook	v	Victoria	1928
7	Russell Watt	v	South West Zone (Aus)	1957
6	Mona Thomson	v	British Columbia	1906
6	Ron Jarden	v	Central West (Aus)	1951
6	**Marc Ellis**	**v**	**Japan**	**1995**
5	George Smith	v	New England (Aus)	1897
5	Jimmy Hunter	v	Northumberland	1905
5	Hunter	v	Oxford University	1905
5	Frank Fryer	v	Queensland	1907
5	Harry Taylor	v	Central West Districts (Aus)	1914
5	Jim Parker	v	North Midlands	1924
5	Bill Elvy	v	Victoria	1926
5	Wally Argus	v	Australian Capital Territory	1947
5	Ron Jarden	v	Australia XV	1951
5	Don McKay	v	Northern New South Wales	1962
5	Graham Williams	v	Tasmania	1968
5	Terry Wright	v	Rosario	1991
5	**Jeff Wilson**	**v**	**Fiji**	**1997**

bold = test match

News Media Auckland

Rod Heeps.

Photosport

Marc Ellis.

Most games for the All Blacks

133	Colin Meads
128	Sean Fitzpatrick
117	Andy Haden
113	Ian Kirkpatrick, Bryan Williams
105	Ian Jones
102	Bruce Robertson
101	Gary Whetton
100	Zinzan Brooke

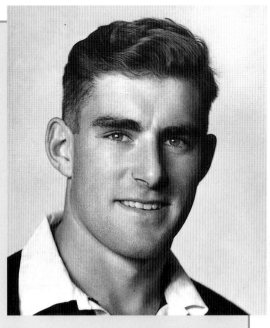

Colin Meads.

Most tests for the All Blacks

92	Sean Fitzpatrick
79	Ian Jones
63	John Kirwan
62	Robin Brooke
60	Craig Dowd
58	Gary Whetton, Zinzan Brooke
56	Olo Brown
55	Frank Bunce, Michael Jones, Colin Meads
54	Josh Kronfeld, Jeff Wilson
51	Christian Cullen
50	Walter Little

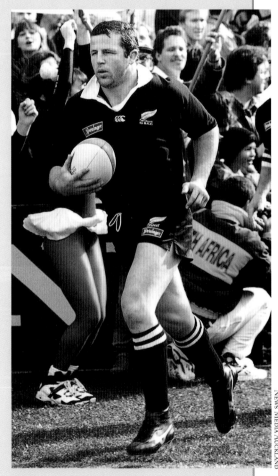

Sean Fitzpatrick.

MOST MATCHES FOR THE ALL BLACKS WITHOUT PLAYING A TEST

31	Bevan Holmes
23	Kevin Barry
21	Lin Colling
20	Keith Bagley
20	Handley Brown
20	Frederick Murray*
20	William McKenzie*
19	Alf Bayly*

whole career before 1903, when the All Blacks played their first test

News Media Auckland

Bevan Holmes.

MOST POINTS IN ALL MATCHES FOR THE ALL BLACKS

1067	Grant Fox
781	Don Clarke
747	Andrew Mehrtens
453	Fergie McCormick
401	Bryan Williams
379	Billy Wallace
357	Alan Hewson
345	Joe Karam
316	Kieran Crowley

MOST TRIES IN ALL MATCHES FOR THE ALL BLACKS

67	John Kirwan
66	Bryan Williams
50	Ian Kirkpatrick, Stu Wilson
49	Jimmy Hunter, Terry Wright
48	Christian Cullen
46	Bernie Fraser
45	Grant Batty, Jeff Wilson

ALL BLACKS BORN OVERSEAS (54)

Barney Armit	Inverkeithing, Scotland
Walter Batty	Tonga
Reg Bell	Birnie, Tasmania
Henry Braddon	Calcutta
Olo Brown	Apia
Eroni Clarke	Apia
Des Connor	Ashgrove, Queensland
John Cuthill	Inverleithen, Scotland
John Dumbell	Liverpool
Alf Eckhold	Adelaide
Bernie Fraser	Lautoka
John Gallagher	London
Mike Gilbert	Rothesay, Scotland
Colin Gilray	Broughty Ferry, Scotland
Maurice Graham	Blayney, NSW
Jimmy Haig	Prestonpans, Scotland
Laurie Haig	Prestonpans, Scotland
Jamie Hendrie	Singapore
Maurice Herrold	Calcutta
George Humphreys	Wolverhampton
Alama Ieremia	Apia
Frederick Ivimey	London
Arthur Jennings	Lautoka
Evan Jessep	Sydney
Alex Kirkpatrick	Northern Ireland
Arty Lambourn	Maryborough, Queensland
Scott McLeod	Brisbane
Tabai Matson	Nausori
Andrew Mehrtens	Durban
William Mitchell	Melbourne
Timothy O'Connor	Kilenenan, Ireland
Bernard O'Dowda	India
Robert Oliphant	County Tyrone, Ireland

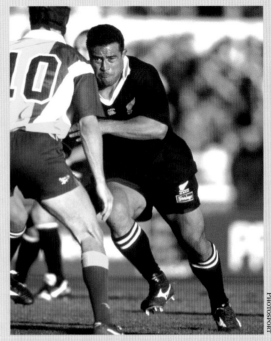

Olo Brown.

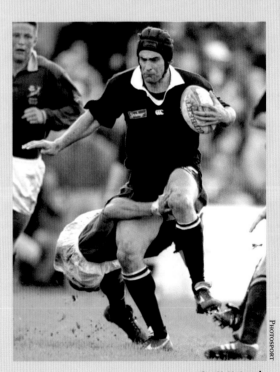

Scott McLeod.

Sydney Orchard	Elmore, Australia
Cliff Porter	Edinburgh
Charles Reichelmann	Nuku'alofa
Jamie Salmon	Hong Kong
John Schuster	Apia
David Solomon	Levuka
Frank Solomon	Pago Pago
Robert Souter	Cambusnethan, Scotland
Eddie Stapleton	Sydney
David Stewart	Fasque, Scotland
Angus Stuart	Scotland
Snowy Svenson	Toowoomba
John Swain	Sydney
Frederick Tilyard	Waratah, Tasmania
James Tilyard	Waratah, Tasmania
Va'aiga Tuigamala	Faleasiu, Samoa
Hubert Turtill	London
James Watson	Rochdale, England
Ron Williams	Suva
Len Wilson	Dunfermline, Scotland
Francis Young	Tasmania

Andrew Mehrtens.

Va'aiga Tuigamala.

ALL BLACK CAPTAINS (122)

1884	William Millton, George Robertson
1893	Tom Ellison, Alf Bayly
1894	Bayly
1896	Davy Gage
1897	Alf Bayly, Arthur Humphries
1901	Jimmy Duncan
1903	Duncan (first test captain), Mickey Kiernan, Morris Wood
1904	Billy Stead
1905–06	Dave Gallaher, Jimmy Hunter, Fred Roberts, Stead, John Spencer
1907	Hunter, Roberts
1908	Stead, Hunter
1910	Roberts, Simon Mynott
1913	Alex McDonald, Frank Mitchinson, Joe O'Leary
1914	Dick Roberts, James Ryan
1920	Jim Tilyard, Beethoven Algar

A trio of All Black captains from the early 1900s. From left, Frank Mitchinson, Simon Mynott and Fred Roberts.

Rival captains Frank Kilby and Tom Lawton before the first test against Australia in 1932.

1921	George Aitken, Teddy Roberts
1922	Moke Belliss, Jack Steel
1923	Jock Richardson, "Ginger" Nicholls
1924–25	Ces Badeley, Cliff Porter, Richardson, Mark Nicholls, "Son" White
1925	Porter, Jim Donald
1926	Porter, Mark Nicholls, Maurice Brownlie
1928	Brownlie, Mark Nicholls, Ron Stewart, Porter
1929	Porter, Bill Dalley, Harry Lilburne, Lew Hook
1930	Porter
1931	Archie Strang
1932	Frank Kilby, Dick Steere, Harry Lilburne
1934	Kilby, Lilburne, "Rusty" Page
1935–36	Jack Manchester, Charlie Oliver, Merv Corner
1936	Jack Griffiths
1937	Ron King
1938	Norm Mitchell, Rod McKenzie
1946	Fred Allen
1947	Allen, Fred Hobbs, Roy White

ALL BLACK CAPTAINS CONTINUED

1949	Allen, Ray Dalton, Jim Kearney, Ron Elvidge, Johnny Smith
1950	Elvidge, Peter Johnstone
1951	Johnstone, John Tanner, Lachie Grant
1952	Kevin Skinner
1953–54	Bob Stuart, Laurie Haig, Skinner, Bill McCaw
1955	Ian Clarke
1956	Pat Vincent, Bob Duff
1957	Ponty Reid, Stan Hill, Robin Archer, Clarke
1958	Wilson Whineray
1959	Whineray
1960	Whineray, Mick Bremner, John Graham, Nev MacEwan, Colin Meads
1961	Whineray
1962	Whineray, Des Connor, Graham, MacEwan, Clarke
1963–64	Whineray, Clarke, Kevin Briscoe, Kel Tremain, Pat Walsh, Meads, Graham
1964	Graham
1965	Whineray
1966	Brian Lochore
1967	Lochore, Ian MacRae, Meads
1968	Lochore, Chris Laidlaw, Tremain, Meads
1969	Lochore
1970	Lochore, Meads, Laidlaw, MacRae, Ian Kirkpatrick
1971	Meads
1972–73	Kirkpatrick, Sid Going, Alex Wyllie
1973	Kirkpatrick
1974	Andy Leslie, Graeme Crossman, Kirkpatrick
1975	Leslie
1976	Leslie, Tane Norton, Alan Sutherland, Crossman, Graham Mourie, Ian Stevens
1977	Norton, Mourie, Bruce Robertson, Robbie Stuart
1978	Frank Oliver, Mourie, Robertson
1979	Mourie, Andy Haden, Dave Loveridge
1980	Loveridge, Brad Johnstone, Haden, Mourie, Mark Donaldson
1981	Mourie, Andy Dalton, Haden
1982	Mourie

1983	Dalton, Stu Wilson
1984	Dalton, Murray Mexted, Jock Hobbs
1985	Dalton, Hobbs, Mexted
1986	David Kirk, Hobbs, Mark Shaw
1987	Kirk, Wayne Shelford
1988	Shelford, Albert Anderson, Gary Whetton
1989	Shelford, Whetton
1990	Shelford, Whetton, Mike Brewer, Joe Stanley
1991	Whetton, Brewer, Grant Fox, Stanley
1992	Sean Fitzpatrick, Brewer, Zinzan Brooke, Richard Loe, Steve McDowell, Ian Jones
1993	Fitzpatrick, Brooke, John Mitchell
1994	Fitzpatrick
1995	Fitzpatrick, Paul Henderson, Frank Bunce, Brooke, Loe
1996	Fitzpatrick, Taine Randell
1997	Fitzpatrick, Justin Marshall, Todd Blackadder
1998	Randell
1999	Randell
2000	Blackadder

Sean Fitzpatrick.

Todd Blackadder.

ALL BLACK LISTS

MOST POINTS ON TEST DEBUT

45	Simon Culhane	v	Japan	1995	(1t, 20c)
33	Carlos Spencer	v	Argentina	1997	(2t, 10c, 1p)
28	Andrew Mehrtens	v	Canada	1995	(1t, 7c, 3p)
26	Tony Brown	v	Samoa	1999	(7c, 4p)
23	Matthew Cooper	v	Ireland	1992	(2t, 6c, 1p)
18	Kieran Crowley	v	England	1985	(6p)
17	Jeff Wilson	v	Scotland	1993	(3t, 1c)

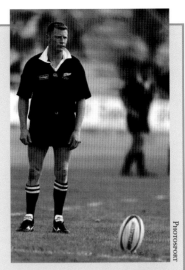

Simon Culhane.

PHOTOSPORT

MOST TRIES ON ALL BLACK DEBUT

4	James Mackay	v	West Coast Buller	1928
	George Hart	v	North Otago	1930
	Jack McLean	v	Australian Capital Territory	1947
	Jon McLachlan	v	South Australia	1974
	Steve Scott	v	Queensland Country	1980
	Paul Simonsson	v	Japan B	1987
3	William Fuller	v	Wellington	1910
	Tom Lynch	v	Australia	1913
	Bill Currey	v	Tasmania	1928
	Scott Cartwright	v	Uruguay	1976
	Christian Cullen	v	Western Samoa	1996

Most tries on test debut

3	Frank Mitchinson	v	Australia	1907
	Tom Lynch	v	Australia	1913
	Jeff Wilson	v	Scotland	1993
	Christian Cullen	v	Samoa	1996
	Troy Flavell	v	Tonga	2000
2	George Smith	v	Scotland	1905
	Bunny Abbot	v	France	1906
	Jock McKenzie	v	Australia	1913
	Hugh McLean	v	Great Britain	1930
	Charlie Saxton	v	Australia	1938
	Wally Argus	v	Australia	1946
	Ralph Caulton	v	British Isles	1959
	Bruce Watt	v	Australia	1962
	Earle Kirton	v	England	1967
	Craig Innes	v	Wales	1989
	Eroni Clarke	v	World XV	1992
	Matthew Cooper	v	Ireland	1992
	Marc Ellis	v	Scotland	1993
	Glen Osborne	v	Canada	1995
	Carlos Spencer	v	Argentina	1997
	Doug Howlett	v	Tonga	2000

Christian Cullen.

CHOSEN FOR THE ALL BLACKS BUT DID NOT PLAY*

Charles Anderson	1931
Allan Andrews	1934
Don Beard	1950
Ivan Bramwell	1929
Paddy Byrne	1922
George Campbell	1884
Buff Caradus	1893
Don Carlson	1949
Jim Carroll	1978, 79
Michael Carroll	1914
Frank Clayton	1884
Frank Colthurst	1965
Daniel Cooper	1884
Alan Couling	1950
Cliff Crossman	1937
Edward d'Auvergne	1884
Alan Dawson	1981
Greg Denholm	1976, 77
William Dickson	1950
Ernest Dive	1907
"Mother" Elliott	1893
Ross Fraser	1979
Peter Gerrard	1904
Clem Green	1914
Francis Green	1913
Max Grierson	1921
David Halligan	1981
Hugh Harkness	1950
Brian Hegarty	1977
F Herring	1910
Peter Hurley	1981
James King	1905

Greg Denholm.

David Halligan.

Joe Leota	1986
Bruce Mackenzie	1955
Jack McKenzie	1949
Harold Marett	1955
Bruce Middleton	1980
Percy Minns	1928
Alfred Mitchell	1910
Henry Mullins	1921
Bill O'Leary	1920
"Doc" Paewai	1946
Dave Pescini	1973
Alan Rowlands	1958
Brian Russell	1950
David Scott	1913
Paul Scott	1966
Brian Stack	1966
Alex Sutherland	1937
Barry Sweet	1950
Tony Thorpe	1986
John Webster	1884
David Weston	1950
"Tiddly" White	1896
Robert Whiteside	1884

includes reserves who didn't take the field

Bruce Middleton.

Joe Leota.

Dave Pescini.

Tony Thorpe.

All Blacks —
THE COMPLETE REGISTER

NAME	DOB	DOD	PROVINCE(S)	POSITION(S)	YEARS	TESTS	GAMES	POINTS
ABBOTT, Harold Louis	17.6.1882	17.1.1972	Taranaki	Wing	1905-06	1	11	47: 15 tries
ADKINS, George Thomas Augustus	21.8.1910	24.5.1976	South Canterbury	Prop	1935-36	0	11	6: 2 tries
AITKEN, George Gothard	2.7.1898	8.7.1952	Wellington	Centre	1921	2	2	0
ALATINI, Pita Paiva Fimoana	11.3.1976		Otago	Midfield back	1999-2000	10	11	10: 2 tries
ALGAR, Beethoven	28.5.1894	28.11.1989	Wellington	Centre/five-eighth	1920-21	0	6	9: 3 tries
ALLAN, James	11.9.1860	2.9.1934	Otago	Forward	1884	0	8	6: 3 tries
ALLEN, Frederick Richard	9.2.1920		Auckland	Five-eighth	1946-47, 49	6	21	21: 7 tries
ALLEN, Lewis	30.1.1870	?	Taranaki	Centre/five-eighth	1896, 97, 1901	0	11	32: 10 tries, 1 con
ALLEN, Mark Richard	27.7.1967		Taranaki, Central Vikings	Prop	1993, 95-97	8	20	5: 1 try
ALLEN, Nicholas Houghton	30.8.1958	7.10.1984	Auckland, Counties	First five-eighth	1980	2	9	28: 4 tries, 4 dg
ALLEY, Geoffrey Thomas	4.2.1903	25.9.1986	Southland, Canterbury	Lock	1926, 28	3	19	3: 1 try
ANDERSON, Albert	5.2.1961		Canterbury	Lock	1983-85, 87-88	6	25	4: 1 try
ANDERSON, Brent Leslie	10.3.1960		Wairarapa-Bush	Lock	1986-87	1	3	4: 1 try
ANDERSON. Eric James	4.4.1931		Bay of Plenty	Prop	1960	0	10	6: 2 tries
ARCHER, James Albert	31.5.1900	15.7.1979	Southland	Wing forward	1925	0	2	0
ARCHER, William Roberts	19.9.1930		Otago, Southland	Five-eighth	1955-57	4	12	15: 5 tries
ARGUS, Walter Garland	29.5.1921		Canterbury	Wing	1946-47	4	10	42: 14 tries
ARMIT, Alexander McNaughton	1874	12.11.1899	Otago	Wing	1897	0	9	18: 6 tries
ARMSTRONG, Adam Loftus	13.4.1878	30.1.1959	Wairarapa	Wing forward	1903	0	5	3: 1 try
ARNOLD, Derek Austin	10.1.1951		Canterbury	Second five-eighth	1963-64	4	15	24: 7 tries, 1 dg
ARNOLD, Keith Dawson	1.3.1920		Waikato	Flanker	1947	2	8	6: 2 tries
ASHBY, David Lloyd	15.2.1931		Southland	Fullback	1958	1	1	0
ASHER, Albert Arapeha	3.12.1879	8.1.1965	Auckland	Wing	1903	1	11	51: 17 tries
ASHWORTH, Barry Graeme	23.9.1949		Auckland	Flanker	1978	2	8	8: 2 tries
ASHWORTH, John Colin	15.9.1949		Canterbury, Hawke's Bay	Prop	1977-85	24	52	4: 1 try
ATKINSON, Henry James	17.7.1888	21.7.1949	West Coast	Lock	1913	1	10	3: 1 try
AVERY, Henry Esau	3.10.1885	22.3.1961	Wellington	Wing forward	1910	3	6	0
BACHOP, Graeme Thomas Miro	11.6.1967		Canterbury	Halfback	1987-92, 94-95	31	54	79: 19 tries
BACHOP, Stephen John	2.4.1966		Otago	First five-eighth	1992-94	5	18	15: 3 tries
BADELEY, Cecil Edward Oliver	7.11.1896	10.11.1986	Auckland	Five-eighth	1920-21, 24	2	15	27: 9 tries
BADELEY, Victor Ivan Roskill	22.11.1898	19.2.1971	Auckland	Threequarter	1922	0	5	13: 3 tries, 2 cons
BAGLEY, Keith Parker	10.2.1931	5.7.1999	Manawatu	Lock	1953-54	0	20	3: 1 try
BAIRD, David Lindsay	26.7.1894	11.12.1947	Southland	Loose forward	1920	0	9	17: 4 tries, 1 con, 1 pen
BAIRD, James Alexander Steenson	17.12.1893	7.6.1917	Otago	Centre	1913	1	1	0
BALCH, William	17.10.1871	4.4.1949	Canterbury	Wing	1894	0	1	0
BALL, Nelson	11.10.1908	9.5.1986	Wellington	Wing	1931-32, 35-36	5	22	37: 11 tries, 1 dg
BARBER, Robert John	14.1.1945		Southland	No 8	1974	0	5	16: 4 tries

Name	Born	Died	Province	Position	Years	Tests	Matches	Points
BARRELL, Connan Keith	15.4.1967		Canterbury	Prop	1996-97	0	4	0
BARRETT, James	8.10.1888	31.8.1971	Auckland	Loose forward	1913-14	2	3	0
BARRY, Edward Fitzgerald	3.9.1905	12.12.1993	Wellington	Loose forward	1932, 34	1	10	6: 2 tries
BARRY, Kevin Edward	22.4.1936		Thames Valley	Utility forward	1962-64	0	23	26: 8 tries, 1 con
BARRY, Liam John	15.3.1971		North Harbour	Flanker	1993, 95	1	10	5: 1 try
BATTY, Grant Bernard	31.8.1951		Wellington	Wing	1972-77	15	55	180: 45 tries
BATTY, Walter	1.1.1905	10.5.1979	Auckland	Loose forward	1928, 30-31	4	6	3: 1 try
BAYLY, Alfred	20.5.1866	14.12.1907	Taranaki	Centre	1893-94, 97	0	19	22: 6 tries, 1 gm
BAYLY, Walter	18.11.1869	20.8.1950	Taranaki	Wing forward	1894	0	1	0
BEATTY, George Edward	29.3.1925		Taranaki	First five-eighth	1950	1	1	0
BELL, James Raymond	1900	7.5.1963	Southland	Five-eighth	1923	1	1	0
BELL, Raymond Henry	31.12.1925		Otago	Wing/fullback	1951-52	3	9	29: 4 tries, 7 cons, 1 pen
BELL, Reginald Clive	11.12.1894	19.11.1960	Otago	Fullback	1922	0	8	5: 1 try, 1 con
BELLISS, Ernest Arthur	1.4.1894	22.4.1974	Wanganui	Wing forward	1920-23	3	20	27: 9 tries
BENNET, Robert	23.7.1879	9.4.1962	Otago	Centre	1905	1	1	0
BERGHAN, Trevor	13.7.1914	23.9.1998	Otago	First five-eighth	1938	3	6	0
BERRY, Martin Joseph	13.7.1966		Wairarapa-Bush, Wellington	Utility back	1986, 93	1	10	9: 2 tries
BERRYMAN, Norman Rangi	15.4.1973		Northland	Centre	1998	1	1	0
BEST, John Jeffries	19.3.1914		Marlborough	Loose forward	1935-36	0	6	0
BEVAN, Vincent David	24.12.1921	25.5.1994	Wellington	Halfback	1947,49-50,53-54	6	25	3: 1 try
BIRTWISTLE, William Murray	4.7.1939	26.5.1996	Canterbury, Waikato	Wing	1965, 67	7	12	33: 11 tries
BLACK, John Edwin	25.7.1951		Canterbury	Hooker	1976-80	3	26	12: 3 tries
BLACK, Neville Wyatt	25.4.1925		Auckland	First five/halfback	1949	1	11	3: 1 try
BLACK, Robert Stanley	25.4.1893	21.9.1916	Buller	First five-eighth	1914	1	6	9: 3 tries
BLACKADDER, Todd Julian	20.9.1971		Canterbury	Loose forward/lock	1995-98, 2000	12	25	15: 3 tries
BLAIR, John Alexander	1872	12.4.1911	Wanganui	Hooker	1897	0	9	5: 1 try, 1 con
BLAKE, Alan Walter	3.11.1922		Wairarapa	Flanker	1949	1	1	0
BLAKE, John Muldoon	21.6.1902	11.5.1988	Hawke's Bay	Threequarter	1925-26	0	13	15: 5 tries
BLIGH, Samuel	8.1.1887	25.3.1955	Buller	Hooker	1910	0	5	0
BLOWERS, Andrew Francis	23.3.1975		Auckland	Flanker	1996-97, 99	11	18	5: 1 try
BLOXHAM, Kenneth Charles	4.1.1954	10.10.2000	Otago	Hooker	1980	0	2	0
BOE, John William	23.11.1955		Waikato	First five-eighth	1981	0	2	0
BOGGS, Eric George	28.3.1922	29.7.1999	Auckland	Wing	1946, 49	2	9	3: 1 try
BOND, Jack Garth Parker	24.5.1920		Canterbury	Prop	1949	1	1	0
BOON, Roger John	23.2.1935		Taranaki	Hooker	1960	0	6	0
BOOTH, Ernest Edward	24.2.1876	18.10.1935	Otago	Fullback/¾	1905-07	3	24	19: 5 tries, 2 cons
BOROEVICH, Kevin Grant	4.10.1960		King Country, Wellington	Prop	1983-84, 86	3	20	0
BOTICA, Frano Michael	3.8.1963		North Harbour	First five-eighth	1986-89	7	27	123: 13 tries, 19 cons, 9 pens, 2 dgs
BOTTING, Ian James	18.5.1922	9.7.1980	Otago	Wing	1949	0	9	6: 2 tries
BOWDEN, Noel James Gordon	19.3.1926	11.6.2000	Taranaki	Fullback	1952	1	1	3: 1 pen
BOWERS, Richard (Guy)	5.11.1932		Wellington	First five-eighth	1953-54	2	15	6: 2 tries

NAME	DOB	DOD	PROVINCE(S)	POSITION(S)	YEARS	TESTS	GAMES	POINTS
BOWMAN, Albert William	5.5.1915	20.1.1992	Hawke's Bay	Flanker	1938	3	6	6: 2 tries
BRADANOVICH, Nicholas Martin	13.9.1907	14.4.1961	Otago	Five-eighth	1928	0	2	19: 2 cons, 5 pens
BRADDON, Henry Yule	27.4.1863	7.9.1955	Otago	Fullback	1884	0	7	0
BRAID, Gary John	25.7.1960		Bay of Plenty	Lock	1983-84	2	13	0
BRAKE, Leonard John	3.7.1952		Bay of Plenty	First five-eighth	1976	0	5	8: 2 tries
BREMNER, Selwyn George	2.8.1930		Auckland, Canterbury	Five-eighth	1952, 56, 60	2	18	0
BREWER, Michael Robert	6.11.1964		Otago, Canterbury	Loose forward	1986-95	32	61	49: 12 tries
BRISCOE, Kevin Charles	20.8.1936		Taranaki	Halfback	1959-60, 62-64	9	43	55: 10 tries, 8 cons, 3 pens
BROOKE, Robin Matthew	10.12.1966		Auckland	Lock	1992-99	62	69	20: 4 tries
BROOKE, Zinzan Valentine	14.2.1965		Auckland	Loose forward	1987-97	58	100	190: 41 tries, 3 dgs
BROOKE-COWDEN, Mark	12.6.1963		Auckland	Flanker	1987	4	7	16: 4 tries
BROOOKER, Frank Jenner	11.10.1876	25.7.1939	Canterbury	Flanker	1897	0	4	0
BROWN, Charles	19.12.1887	2.4.1966	Taranaki	Halfback	1913, 20	2	11	5: 1 try, 1 con
BROWN, Handley Welbourne	29.8.1904	5.12.1973	Taranaki	Centre	1924-26	0	20	35: 8 tries, 4 cons, 1 pen
BROWN, Henry Mackay	14.6.1910	1.6.1965	Auckland	Wing	1935-36	0	8	15: 5 tries
BROWN, Olo Max	24.10.1967		Auckland	Prop	1990, 92-98	56	69	20: 4 tries
BROWN, Ross Handley	8.9.1934		Taranaki	Five-eighth/centre	1955-59, 61-62	16	25	27: 7 tries, 2 dgs
BROWN, Tony Eion	17.1.1975		Otago	First five-eighth	1999-2000	13	14	108: 2 tries, 34 cons, 10 pens
BROWNLIE, Cyril James	6.8.1895	7.5.1954	Hawke's Bay	Loose forward	1924-26, 28	3	31	33: 11 tries
BROWNLIE, Jack Laurence	25.11.1899	8.10.1972	Hawke's Bay	Loose forward	1921	0	1	0
BROWNLIE, Maurice John	10.8.1897	21.1.1957	Hawke's Bay	Loose forward	1922-26, 28	8	61	63: 21 tries
BRUCE, John Alexander	11.11.1887	20.10.1970	Auckland	Loose forward	1913-14	2	10	6: 2 tries
BRUCE, Oliver Douglas	23.5.1947		Canterbury	First five-eighth	1974, 76-78	15	41	51: 6 tries, 2 pens, 7 dgs
BRYERS, Ronald Frederick	14.11.1919	20.8.1987	King Country	Lock	1949	1	1	0
BUCHAN, John Alexander Shepherd	17.6.1961		Canterbury	Hooker	1987	0	2	0
BUDD, Alfred	22.1.1880	7.11.1962	South Canterbury	Loose forward	1910	0	3	0
BUDD, Thomas Alfred	1.8.1922	8.3.1989	Southland	Lock	1946, 49	2	2	0
BULLOCK-DOUGLAS, George Arthur Hardy	4.6.1911	24.8.1958	Wanganui	Wing	1932, 34	5	15	45: 15 tries
BUNCE, Frank Eneri	4.2.1962		North Harbour	Second five/centre	1992-97	55	69	131: 27 tries
BURGESS, George Francis	1.11.1876	2.7.1961	Southland	Halfback	1905	1	1	0
BURGESS, Gregory Alexander John	6.7.1953		Auckland	Prop	1980-81	1	2	0
BURGESS, Robert Edward	26.3.1949		Manawatu	First five-eighth	1971-73	7	30	50: 13 tries
BURGOYNE, Michael Martin	27.3.1949		North Auckland	Flanker	1979	0	6	4: 1 try
BURKE, Peter Standish	22.9.1927		Taranaki	Lock	1951, 55, 57	3	12	6: 2 tries
BURNS, John Francis	17.2.1941		Canterbury	Lock	1970	0	9	0
BURNS, Patrick James	10.3.1881	24.2.1943	Canterbury	Halfback/¾	1908, 10, 13	5	9	15: 5 tries
BURROWS, James Thomas	14.7.1904	10.6.1991	Canterbury	Hooker	1928	0	9	6: 2 tries
BURRY, Hugh Cameron	29.10.1930		Canterbury	No 8	1960	0	11	24: 8 tries

BURT, John Robert	27.8.1874	16.1.1933	Otago	Loose forward	1901	0	1	0
BUSH, Ronald George	3.5.1909	10.5.1996	Otago	Fullback	1931	1	1	14: 1 con, 4 pens
BUSH, William Kingita Te Pohe	24.1.1949		Canterbury	Prop	1974-79	11	37	4: 1 try
BUTLAND, Henry	11.2.1872	2.12.1956	West Coast	Halfback	1893-94	0	9	6: 2 tries
BUTLER, Victor Claude	11.7.1907	1.2.1971	Auckland	Fullback	1928	0	1	0
BUXTON, John Burns	31.10.1933		Canterbury	Flanker	1955-56	2	2	0
CABOT, Phillippe Sidney de Quetteville	18.7.1900	12.12.1998	Otago	Wing forward	1921	0	1	0
CAIN, Michael Joseph	7.7.1885	27.8.1951	Taranaki	Hooker	1913-14	4	24	14: 4 tries, 1 con
CALCINAI, Umberto Primo	2.2.1892	26.7.1963	Wellington	Hooker	1922	0	5	0
CALLESEN, John Arthur	24.5.1950		Manawatu	Lock	1974-76	4	16	4: 1 try
CALNAN, Joseph John	24.6.1876	31.12.1947	Wellington	Loose forward	1897	0	9	8: 2 tries, 1 con
CAMERON, Dennis Hugh	17.11.1938		Mid-Canterbury	Wing	1960	0	8	6: 2 tries
CAMERON, Donald	15.7.1887	25.8.1947	Taranaki	Wing	1908	3	3	3: 1 try
CAMERON, Lachlan Murray	12.4.1959	23.10.1973	Waikato	Midfield back	1979-81	5	17	16: 4 tries
CARLETON, Sydney Russell	22.2.1904		Canterbury	Utility back	1928-29	6	21	6: 2 tries
CARRINGTON, Kenneth Roy	3.9.1950		Auckland	Wing	1971-72	3	9	20: 5 tries
CARROLL, Alphonsus John	20.4.1895	1.12.1974	Manawatu	Hooker	1920-21	0	8	13: 3 tries, 2 cons
CARSON, William Nicol	16.7.1916	8.10.1944	Auckland	Flanker	1938	0	3	3: 1 try
CARTER, George	9.4.1854	1.4.1922	Auckland	Forward	1884	0	7	0
CARTER, Mark Peter	7.11.1968		Auckland	Flanker	1991, 97-98	7	10	5: 1 try
CARTWRIGHT, Scott Calvert	7.1.1954		Canterbury	Wing	1976	0	7	28: 7 tries
CASEY, Stephen Timothy	24.12.1882	10.8.1960	Otago	Hooker	1905-08	8	38	0
CASHMORE, Adrian Richard	25.7.1973		Auckland	Fullback/wing	1996-97	2	2	0
CATLEY, Evelyn Haswell	23.9.1915	23.3.1975	Waikato	Hooker	1946-47, 49	7	21	3: 1 try
CAUGHEY, Thomas Harcourt Clarke	4.7.1911	4.8.1993	Auckland	Wing/midfield back	1932, 34-37	9	39	106: 34 tries, 1 dg
CAULTON, Ralph Walter	10.1.1937		Wellington	Wing	1959-61, 63-64	16	50	93: 31 tries
CHERRINGTON, Nau Paora	5.3.1924	26.6.1979	North Auckland	Wing	1950-51	1	7	27: 9 tries
CHRISTIAN, Desmond Lawrence	9.9.1923	30.8.1977	Auckland	No 8/prop	1949	1	11	0
CLAMP, Michael	26.12.1961		Wellington	Wing	1984-85	2	15	72: 18 tries
CLARK, Donald William	22.2.1940		Otago	Flanker	1964	2	2	0
CLARK, Francis Leslie	25.9.1902	12.11.1972	Canterbury	Hooker	1928	0	4	0
CLARK, Lindsay Allan	1.5.1944		Otago	Prop	1972-73	0	7	0
CLARK, William Henry	16.11.1929		Wellington	Flanker	1953-56	9	24	21: 7 tries
CLARKE, Adrian Hipkins	23.2.1938		Auckland	Five-eighth	1958-60	3	14	9: 3 tries
CLARKE, Donald Barry	10.11.1933		Waikato	Fullback	1956-64	31	89	781: 8 tries, 173 cons, 120 pens, 15 dgs, 2 gm
CLARKE, Eroni	31.7.1968		Auckland	Wing/midfield	1992-93, 98	10	24	50: 11 tries
CLARKE, Ian James	5.3.1931	29.6.1997	Waikato	Prop/No 8	1953-64	24	83	16: 4 tries, 2 cons
CLARKE, Philip Hipkins	23.1.1942		Marlborough	Wing	1967	0	4	0
CLARKE, Ray Lancelot	7.7.1908	3.6.1972	Taranaki	Lock	1932	2	9	0

ALL BLACKS — THE COMPLETE REGISTER

NAME	DOB	DOD	PROVINCE(S)	POSITION(S)	YEARS	TESTS	GAMES	POINTS
COBDEN, Donald Gordon	11.8.1914	11.8.1940	Canterbury	Wing	1937	1	1	0
COCKERILL, Maurice Stanley	8.12.1928		Taranaki	Fullback	1951	3	11	50: 1 try, 16 cons, 5 pens
COCKROFT, Eric Arthur Percy	10.9.1890	2.4.1973	South Canterbury	Wing/fullback	1913-14	3	7	7: 1 pen, 1 dg
COCKROFT, Samuel George	13.5.1864	1.1.1955	Manawatu, Hawke's Bay	Hooker	1893-94	0	12	3: 1 try
CODLIN, Brett William	29.11.1956		Counties	Fullback	1980	3	13	127: 1 try, 30 cons, 21 pens
COFFIN, Phillip Hone	24.7.1964		King Country	Prop	1996	0	3	0
COLLING, George Lindsay	27.8.1946		Otago	Halfback	1972-73	21	21	24: 6 tries
COLLINS, Arthur Harold	19.7.1906	11.1.1988	Taranaki	Fullback	1932, 34	3	15	110: 1 try, 35 cons, 11 pens, 1 dg
COLLINS, John Law	1.2.1939		Poverty Bay	Second five-eighth	1964-65	3	3	0
COLLINS, William Reuben	18.10.1910	9.9.1993	Hawke's Bay	Lock	1935	0	7	0
COLMAN, John Thomas Henry	14.1.1887	28.9.1965	Taranaki	Utility/wing fwd	1907-08	4	6	8: 2 tries, 1 con
CONN, Stuart Bruce	11.3.1953		Auckland	Flanker	1976, 80	0	6	0
CONNOLLY, Leo Stephen	2.12.1921		Southland	Prop	1947	0	5	0
CONNOR, Desmond Michael	9.9.1935		Auckland	Halfback	1961-64	12	15	3: 1 try
CONRAD, William John McKeown	10.5.1925	14.8.1972	Waikato	Halfback	1949	0	10	3: 1 try
CONWAY, Richard James	22.4.1935		Otago, Bay of Plenty	Flanker	1959-60, 65	10	25	12: 4 tries
COOKE, Albert Edward	5.10.1901	29.9.1977	Auckland, Hawke's Bay, Wairarapa, Wellington	Midfield back	1924-26, 28, 30	8	44	120: 38 tries, 3 cons
COOKE, Alfred Ernest	1870	3.6.1900	Canterbury	Halfback	1894	0	1	0
COOKE, Reuben James	1880	10.5.1940	Canterbury	Loose forward	1903	1	10	3: 1 try
COOKSLEY, Mark Stephen Bill	11.4.1971		Counties, Waikato	Lock	1992-95, 97	9	21	5: 1 try
COOPER, Gregory John Luke	10.6.1965		Auckland, Otago	Fullback	1986, 92	7	7	63: 2 tries, 14 cons, 7 pens, 2 dgs
COOPER, Matthew James Andrew	10.10.1966		Hawke's Bay, Waikato	Midfield/fullback	1987, 92-94, 96	8	26	224: 12 tries, 35 cons, 33 pens
CORBETT, John	1880	11.4.1945	West Coast	Forward	1905	0	15	0
CORKILL, Thomas George	9.7.1901	9.5.1966	Hawke's Bay	Halfback/five-eighth	1925	0	4	0
CORNER, Mervyn Miles Nelson	5.7.1908	2.2.1992	Auckland	Halfback	1930-32, 34-36	6	25	25: 1 try, 11 cons
COSSEY, Raymond Reginald	21.1.1935	24.5.1986	Counties	Wing	1958	1	1	0
COTTRELL, Anthony Ian	10.2.1907	10.12.1988	Canterbury	Hooker/prop	1929-32	11	22	12: 4 tries
COTTRELL, Wayne David	30.9.1943		Canterbury	Five-eighth	1967-68, 1970-71	7	37	33: 9 tries, 2 dgs
COUCH, Manuera Ben Riwai	27.6.1925	3.6.1996	Wairarapa	First five-eighth	1947-49	3	7	3: 1 try
COUGHLAN, Thomas Desmond	9.4.1934		South Canterbury	Flanker	1958	1	1	0
CREIGHTON, John Neville	10.3.1937		Canterbury	Hooker	1962	1	6	12: 4 tries
CRIBB, Ronald Te Huia	7.7.1976		North Harbour	No 8	2000	9	9	20: 4 tries
CRICHTON, Scott	18.2.1954		Wellington	Prop	1983-85	2	7	0
CRON, Stewart Edward George	7.7.1946		Canterbury	Flanker	1976	0	6	8: 2 tries
CROSS, Thomas	21.1.1876	?	Canterbury, Wellington	Loose forward	1901, 04-05	2	3	3: 1 try
CROSSMAN, Graeme Murray	30.11.1945		Bay of Plenty	Hooker	1974, 76	0	19	12: 3 tries
CROWLEY, Kieran James	21.8.1961		Taranaki	Fullback	1983-87, 90, 91	20	36	320: 14 tries, 36 cons,

61 pens, 3 dgs

Name	Born	Died	Union	Position	Tests			Points
CROWLEY, Patrick Joseph Bourke	20.10.1923	9.6.1981	Auckland	Flanker	1949-50	6	21	6: 2 tries
CULHANE, Simon David	10.3.1968		Southland	First five-eighth	1995-96	6	9	150: 1 try, 38 cons, 22 pens, 1 dg
CULLEN, Christian Mathias	12.2.1976		Manawatu, Central Vikings, Wellington	Fullback/wing	1996-2000	51	52	246: 48 tries, 3 cons
CUMMINGS, William	13.3.1889	28.5.1955	Canterbury	Loose forward	1913, 21	2	3	3: 1 try
CUNDY, Rawi Tama	15.8.1901	9.2.1955	Wairarapa	Utility back	1929	1	6	31: 2 tries, 11 cons, 1 pen
CUNNINGHAM, Gary Richard	12.5.1955		Auckland	Wing/midfield	1979-80	5	17	12: 3 tries
CUNNINGHAM, William	8.7.1874	3.9.1927	Auckland	Lock	1901, 05-08	9	39	22: 2 tries, 8 cons
CUPPLES, Leslie Frank	8.2.1898	10.8.1972	Bay of Plenty	Loose forward	1922-25	2	29	18: 6 tries
CURREY, William Douglas Roy	2.6.1944		Taranaki	Wing	1968	0	7	24: 8 tries
CURRIE, Clive James	25.12.1955		Canterbury	Fullback	1978	2	4	18: 6 cons, 2 pens
CUTHILL, John Elliot	24.8.1892	22.4.1970	Otago	Fullback/wing	1913	2	16	31: 7 tries, 5 cons
DALLEY, William Charles	18.11.1901	9.2.1989	Canterbury	Halfback	1924-26, 28-29	5	35	15: 5 tries
DALTON, Andrew Grant	16.11.1951		Counties	Hooker	1977-85	35	58	12: 3 tries
DALTON, Douglas	18.1.1913		Hawke's Bay	Prop/hooker	1935-38	9	21	3: 1 try
DALTON, Raymond Alfred	14.7.1919	2.2.1997	Wellington, Otago	Prop	1947, 49	2	20	3: 1 try
DALZELL, George Nelson	26.4.1921	30.4.1989	Canterbury	Lock	1953-54	5	22	15: 5 tries
D'ARCY, Archibald Edgar	18.9.1870	22.6.1919	Wairarapa	Fullback	1893-94	0	7	0
DAVIE, Murray Geoffrey	19.9.1955		Canterbury	Prop	1983	1	5	4: 1 try
DAVIES, William Anthony	16.9.1939		Auckland, Otago	Fullback/five-eighth	1960, 62	3	17	94: 3 tries, 20 cons, 11 pens, 4 dgs
DAVIS, Chresten Scott	16.9.1975		Manawatu	Loose forward	1996	0	2	0
DAVIS, Keith	21.5.1930		Auckland	Halfback	1952-55, 58	10	25	12: 4 tries
DAVIS, Lyndon John	22.12.1943		Canterbury	Halfback	1976-77	3	16	12: 3 tries
DAVIS, William Leslie	15.12.1942		Hawke's Bay	Centre	1963-64, 67-70	11	53	75: 25 tries
DAVY, Edwin	9.9.1850	22.5.1935	Wellington	Halfback	1884	0	3	2: 1 try
DEANS, Ian Bruce	25.11.1960		Canterbury	Halfback	1987-89	10	23	56: 14 tries
DEANS, Robert George	19.2.1884	30.9.1908	Canterbury	Centre	1905-06, 08	5	24	63: 21 tries
DEANS, Robert Maxwell	4.9.1959		Canterbury	Fullback	1983, 85	5	19	252: 8 tries, 59 cons, 34 pens
DELAMORE, Graham Wallace	3.4.1920		Wellington	Five-eighth	1949	1	9	0
DEWAR, Henry	13.10.1883	19.8.1915	Taranaki	Loose forward	1913	2	16	3: 1 try
DIACK, Ernest Sinclair	22.7.1930		Otago	Wing	1959	1	1	0
DICK, John	3.10.1912		Auckland	Wing	1937-38	3	5	6: 2 tries
DICK, Malcolm John	3.1.1941		Auckland	Wing	1963-67, 69-70	15	54	120: 40 tries
DICKINSON, George Ritchie	11.3.1903	17.3.1978	Otago	Five-eighth	1922	0	5	6: 2 tries
DICKSON, David McKee	25.9.1900	19.4.1978	Otago	Loose forward	1925	0	7	13: 2 tries, 2 cons, 1 pen
DIXON, Maurice James	6.2.1929		Canterbury	Wing	1953-54, 56-57	10	28	51: 17 tries
DOBSON, Ronald Leslie	26.3.1923	26.10.1994	Auckland	Second five-eighth	1949	1	1	0
DODD, Ernest Henry	21.3.1880	11.9.1918	Wellington	Hooker	1901, 05	1	3	0
DONALD, Andrew John	11.5.1957		Wanganui	Halfback	1981, 83-84	7	20	20: 5 tries

ALL BLACKS — THE COMPLETE REGISTER

NAME	DOB	DOD	PROVINCE(S)	POSITION(S)	YEARS	TESTS	GAMES	POINTS
DONALD, James George	4.6.1898	29.8.1981	Wairarapa	Wing forward	1920-22, 25	2	22	20: 6 tries, 1 con
DONALD, Quentin	13.3.1900	27.12.1965	Wairarapa	Hooker	1923-25	4	23	18: 6 tries
DONALDSON, Mark William	6.11.1955		Manawatu	Halfback	1977-81	13	34	20: 5 tries
DOUGAN, John Patrick	22.12.1946		Wellington	First five-eighth	1972-73	2	12	11: 2 tries, 1 dg
DOUGLAS, James Burt	11.7.1890	21.12.1964	Otago	Loose forward	1913	0	9	24: 8 tries
DOWD, Craig William	26.10.1969		Auckland	Prop	1993-2000	60	67	15: 3 tries
DOWD, Graham William	17.12.1963		North Harbour	Hooker	1992	1	8	0
DOWNING, Albert Joseph	12.7.1886	8.8.1915	Auckland	Flanker, lock	1913-14	5	26	21: 7 tries
DRAKE, John Alan	22.1.1959		Auckland	Prop	1985-87	8	12	4: 1 try
DRAKE, Walter Augustus	21.2.1879	27.1.1941	Canterbury	Loose forward	1901	0	1	0
DUFF, Robert Hamilton	5.8.1925		Canterbury	Lock	1951-52, 55-56	11	18	0
DUGGAN, Rhys John Llewellyn	31.7.72		Waikato	Halfback	1999	1	1	0
DUMBELL, John Thomas	1859	31.12.1936	Wellington	Utility back/forward	1884	0	5	7: 1 con, 1 dg
DUNCAN, James	12.11.1869	19.10.1953	Otago	Five-eighth/forward	1897, 1901, 03	1	10	9: 3 tries
DUNCAN, Michael Gordon	8.8.1947		Hawke's Bay	Midfield back	1971	2	2	0
DUNCAN, William Dow	11.6.1892	14.12.1961	Otago	Hooker	1920-21	3	11	3: 1 try
DUNN, Edward James	19.1.1955		North Auckland	First five-eighth	1978-79, 81	2	20	22: 4 tries, 2 dgs
DUNN, Ian Thomas Wayne	11.6.1960		North Auckland	First five-eighth	1983-84	3	13	8: 2 tries
DUNN, John Markham	17.11.1918		Auckland	Wing	1946	1	1	0
EARL, Andrew Thomas	12.9.1961		Canterbury	Utility forward	1986-89, 91-92	13	45	57: 14 tries
EASTGATE, Barry Peter	10.7.1927		Canterbury	Prop	1952-54	3	17	3: 1 try
ECKHOLD, Alfred George	28.12.1885	24.10.1931	Otago	Five-eighth	1907	0	3	0
ELIASON, Ian Matheson	6.6.1945		Taranaki	Lock	1972-73	0	19	8: 2 tries
ELLIOTT, Kenneth George	3.3.1922		Wellington	Lock/No 8	1946	2	2	0
ELLIS, Marc Christopher Gwynne	8.10.1971		Otago	Utility back	1992-93, 95	8	20	98: 19 tries, 1 dg
ELLISON, Thomas Rangiwahia	11.11.1867	2.10.1904	Wellington	Forward	1893	0	7	20: 2 tries, 5 cons, 1gm
ELSOM, Allan Edwin George	18.7.1925		Canterbury	Centre	1952-55	6	22	42: 13 tries, 1 dg
ELVIDGE, Ronald Rutherford	2.3.1923		Otago	Midfield back	1946, 49-50	9	19	15: 5 tries
ELVY, William Lister	2.12.1901	29.7.1977	Canterbury	Wing	1925-26	0	12	36: 12 tries
ERCEG, Charles Percy	28.11.1928		Auckland	Wing	1951-52	4	9	9: 3 tries
EVANS, Cyril Edward	10.1.1896	13.5.1975	Canterbury	Fullback	1921	0	1	0
EVANS, David Alexander	4.10.1886	12.10.1940	Hawke's Bay	Lock	1910	1	4	3: 1 try
EVELEIGH, Kevin Alfred	8.11.1947		Manawatu	Flanker	1974, 76-77	4	30	4: 1 try
FANNING, Alfred Henry Netherwood	31.3.1890	11.3.1963	Canterbury	Lock	1913	1	1	3: 1 try
FANNING, Bernard John	11.11.1874	9.7.1946	Canterbury	Lock	1903-04	2	9	0
FARRELL, Colin Paul	19.3.1956		Auckland	Fullback	1977	2	2	0
FAWCETT, Christopher Louis	28.10.1954		Auckland	Fullback/wing	1976	2	13	44: 4 tries, 8 cons, 4 pens
FEA, William Rognvald	5.10.1898	22.12.1988	Otago	Five-eighth	1921	1	1	0
FEEK, Gregory Edward	20.7.1975		Canterbury	Prop	1999	8	8	0

FINLAY, Brian Edward Louis	7.11.1927	9.3.1982	Manawatu	Flanker	1959	1	1	0
FINLAY, Jack	31.1.1916		Manawatu	No 8	1946	1	1	3: 1 try
FINLAY, Mark Clayton	10.5.1963		Manawatu	Fullback	1984	0	2	18: 2 tries, 5 cons
FINLAYSON, Innes	4.7.1899	29.1.1980	North Auckland	Flanker	1925-26, 28-30	6	36	35: 11 tries, 1 con
FISHER, Thomas	27.5.1891	20.3.1968	Buller	Loose forward	1914	0	5	3: 1 try
FITZGERALD, Charles James	6.6.1899	8.5.1961	Marlborough	Midfield back	1922	0	5	3: 1 pen
FITZGERALD, James Train	6.8.1928	13.5.1993	Wellington	Midfield back	1952-54	1	17	46: 11 tries, 5 cons, 1 pen
FITZPATRICK, Brian Bernard James	5.3.1931		Poverty Bay, Wellington	Second five-eighth	1951, 53-54	3	22	15: 5 tries
FITZPATRICK, Sean Brian Thomas	4.6.1963		Auckland	Hooker	1986-97	92	128	90: 20 tries
FLAVELL, Troy Vandem	4.11.1976		North Harbour	Lock	2000	8	8	20: 4 tries
FLEMING, John Kingsley	2.5.1953		Wellington, Waikato	Lock	1978-80	5	35	16: 4 tries
FLETCHER, Charles John Compton	9.5.1894	9.9.1973	Auckland, North Auckland	Loose forward	1920-21	1	2	0
FOGARTY, Richard	12.12.1891	9.9.1980	Taranaki	Flanker/hooker	1921	2	2	0
FORD, Brian Robert	10.7.1951		Marlborough	Wing	1977-79	4	20	32: 8 tries
FORD, William August	25.8.1895	7.7.1959	Canterbury	Wing	1921-23	0	9	21: 7 tries
FORSTER, Stuart Thomas	12.2.1969		Otago	Halfback	1993-95	6	12	0
FOX, Grant James	16.6.1962		Auckland	First five-eighth	1984-93	46	78	1067: 2 tries, 225 cons, 192 pens, 11 dgs
FRANCIS, Arthur Reginald Howe	8.6.1882	15.6.1957	Auckland	Loose forward	1905, 07-08, 10	10	18	31: 8 tries, 2 cons, 1 pen
FRANCIS, William Charles	4.2.1894	28.11.1981	Wellington	Hooker	1913-14	5	12	9: 3 tries
FRASER, Bernard Gabriel	21.7.1953		Wellington	Wing	1979-84	23	55	184: 46 tries
FRAZER, Harry Frederick	21.4.1916		Hawke's Bay	Lock/prop	1946-47, 49	5	15	6: 2 tries
FREEBAIRN, William Stuart Scott	12.1.1932		Manawatu	Wing	1953-54	0	14	27: 9 tries
FREITAS, David Frank Errol	23.2.1901	10.4.1968	West Coast	Loose forward	1928	4	4	3: 1 try
FROMONT, Richard Trevor	17.9.1969		Auckland	Lock	1993, 95	0	10	0
FROST, Harry	27.2.1869	6.7.1954	Canterbury	Forward	1896	1	1	0
FRYER, Frank Cunningham	2.11.1886	22.9.1958	Canterbury	Wing	1907-08	4	8	33: 11 tries
FULLER, William Bennett	9.4.1883	25.7.1957	Canterbury	Wing/midfield	1910	2	6	15: 5 tries
FURLONG, Blair Donald Marie	10.3.1945		Hawke's Bay	First five/fullback	1970	1	11	32: 10 cons, 3 pens, 1 dg
GAGE, David Richmond	11.1.1868		Hawke's Bay, Wellington	Utility back	1893, 96	0	8	6: 2 tries
GALLAGHER, John Anthony	29.1.1964		Wellington	Centre/fullback	1986-89	18	41	251: 35 tries, 39 cons, 11 pens
GALLAHER, David	30.10.1873	4.10.1917	Auckland	Hooker/wing forward	1903-06	6	36	14: 4 tries, 1 con
GARD, Philip Charles	20.11.1947	3.6.1990	North Otago	Midfield back	1971-72	1	7	0
GARDINER, Ashley John	10.12.1946		Taranaki	Prop	1974	1	11	8: 2 tries
GARDNER, John Henry	30.1.1870	1909	South Canterbury	Forward	1893	0	4	0
GATLAND, Warren David	17.9.1963		Waikato	Hooker	1988-91	0	17	8: 2 tries
GEDDES, John Herbert	9.1.1907	16.8.1990	Southland	Wing	1929	1	6	23: 7 tries, 1 con
GEDDES, William McKail	13.5.1893	1.7.1950	Auckland	First five-eighth	1913	1	1	0
GEMMELL, Bruce McLeod	12.5.1950		Auckland	Halfback	1974	2	5	4: 1 try
GEMMELL, Samuel William	28.8.1896	28.6.1970	Hawke's Bay	Hooker	1923	0	1	0
GEORGE, Victor Leslie	5.6.1908	10.8.1996	Southland	Prop	1938	3	7	0

ALL BLACKS — THE COMPLETE REGISTER

NAME	DOB	DOD	PROVINCE(S)	POSITION(S)	YEARS	TESTS	GAMES	POINTS
GIBSON, Daryl Peter Earl	2.3.1975		Canterbury	Midfield back	1999-2000	13	13	5: 1 try
GILBERT, Graham Duncan McMillan	11.3.1911	22.1.1964	West Coast	Fullback	1935-36	4	27	125: 31 cons, 17 pens, 3 dgs
GILLESPIE, Charles Theodore	24.6.1883		Wellington	Lock	1913	1	1	0
GILLESPIE, William David	6.8.1934		Otago	Flanker	1957, 58, 60	1	23	3: 1 try
GILLETT, George Arthur	23.4.1877	27.9.1956	Canterbury, Auckland	Wing forward/fullback	1905-08	8	38	41: 4 tries, 13 cons, 1 gm
GILLIES, Colin Cuthbert	8.10.1912	2.7.1996	Otago	First five-eighth	1936	1	2	0
GILRAY, Colin MacDonald	17.3.1885	15.7.1994	Otago	Wing	1905	1	1	0
GIVEN, Frederick James	21.5.1876	12.6.1921	Otago	Flanker	1903	0	9	3: 1 try
GLASGOW, Francis Turnbull	17.8.1880	20.2.1939	Hawke's Bay, Southland	Loose forward	1905-06, 08	6	35	43: 10 tries, 5 cons, 1 pen
GLENN, William Spiers	21.2.1887	5.10.1953	Taranaki	Loose forward	1904-06	2	19	0
GLENNIE, Ernest	1871	?	Canterbury	Utility	1897	0	6	9: 3 tries
GODDARD, John Wood	31.1.1920	22.10.1996	South Canterbury	Fullback	1949	0	8	32: 10 cons, 4 pens
GODDARD, Maurice Patrick	28.9.1921	19.6.1974	South Canterbury	Centre	1946-47, 49	5	20	27: 9 tries
GOING, Kenneth Tautohe	18.2.1942		North Auckland	Fullback	1974	0	3	11: 1 con, 3 pens
GOING, Sidney Milton	19.8.1943		North Auckland	Halfback	1966-77	29	86	164: 33 tries, 18 cons, 5 pens, 1 dg
GOLDSMITH, Jasin Alex	24.7.1969		Waikato	Utility back	1988	0	8	20: 5 tries
GOOD, Alan	12.7.1867	30.4.1938	Taranaki	Wing	1893	0	4	0
GOOD, Hugh Maurice	29.9.1871	3.7.1941	Taranaki	Wing	1894	0	1	0
GORDON, Steven Bryan	16.5.1967		Waikato	Lock	1989-91, 93	2	19	0
GORDON, William Robert	7.8.1965		Waikato	Loose forward	1990	0	3	0
GRAHAM, David John	1.1.1935		Canterbury	Loose forward	1958, 60-64	22	53	33: 11 tries
GRAHAM, James Buchan	23.4.1884	15.5.1941	Otago	Loose forward	1913-14	3	19	74: 4 tries, 28 cons, 2 pens
GRAHAM, Maurice Gordon	20.12.1931		New South Wales	Fullback	1960	0	1	0
GRAHAM, Wayne Geoffrey	13.4.1957		Otago	Loose forward	1978-79	1	8	0
GRANGER, Kenneth William	20.3.1951		Manawatu	Wing	1976	0	6	20: 5 tries
GRANT, Lachlan Ashwell	4.10.1923		South Canterbury	Flanker/lock	1947, 49, 51	4	23	12: 4 tries
GRAY, George Donaldson	1880	16.4.1961	Canterbury	Five-eighth	1908, 13	3	14	12: 4 tries
GRAY, Kenneth Francis	24.6.1938	18.11.1992	Wellington	Prop	1963-69	24	50	27: 9 tries
GRAY, Roderick	22.10.1870	27.5.1951	Wairarapa	Forward	1893	0	2	6: 2 tries
GRAY, William Ngataiawhio	23.12.1932	10.1.1993	Bay of Plenty	Second five-eighth	1955-57	6	11	6: 2 tries
GREEN, Craig Ivan	23.3.1961		Canterbury	Wing	1983-87	20	39	108: 27 tries
GREENE, Kevin Michael	31.12.1949		Waikato	Halfback	1976-77	0	8	0
GRENSIDE, Bertram Arthur	9.4.1899	2.10.1989	Hawke's Bay	Wing	1928-29	6	21	42: 14 tries
GRIFFITHS, Jack Lester	9.9.1912		Wellington	Midfield back	1934-36, 38	7	30	50: 3 tries, 14 cons, 3 pens, 1 dg
GUDSELL, Keith Eric	19.10.1924		Wanganui	Midfield back	1949	0	6	0
GUY, Richard Alan	6.4.1941		North Auckland	Prop	1971-72	4	9	8: 2 tries
HADEN, Andrew Maxwell	26.9.1950		Auckland	Lock	1972-73, 76-85	41	117	32: 8 tries

Name	Born	Died	Province	Position	Years	Tests	Games	Points
HADLEY, Swinbourne	19.9.1904	30.4.1970	Auckland	Hooker	1928	4	11	0
HADLEY, William Edward	11.3.1910	30.9.1992	Auckland	Hooker	1934-36	8	25	6: 2 tries
HAIG, James Scott	7.12.1924	28.10.1996	Otago	Halfback	1946	2	2	3: 1 try
HAIG, Laurence Stokes	18.10.1922	10.7.1992	Otago	First five-eighth	1950-51, 53-54	9	29	15: 2 tries, 3 cons, 1dg
HALES, Duncan Alister	22.11.1947		Canterbury	Centre/wing	1972-73	4	27	48: 12 tries
HAMILTON, Donald Cameron	19.1.1883	14.4.1925	Southland	Wing forward	1908	1	1	0
HAMMETT, Mark Garry	13.7.1972		Canterbury	Hooker	1999-2000	14	15	10: 2 tries
HAMMOND, Ian Arthur	25.10.1925	20.5.1998	Marlborough	Hooker	1951-52	1	8	3: 1 try
HANDCOCK, Robert Alexander	6.4.1874	27.1.1956	Auckland	Forward	1897	0	8	9: 3 tries
HARDCASTLE, William Robert	30.8.1874	11.7.1944	Wellington	Forward	1897	0	7	3: 1 try
HARPER, Eric Tristram	1.12.1877	30.4.1918	Canterbury	Threequarter	1904-06	2	11	24: 6 tries, 3 cons
HARPER, George	19.8.1867	7.6.1937	Nelson	Threequarter	1893	0	3	7: 1 pen, 1gm
HARRIS, Jack Hardy	26.7.1903	19.5.1944	Canterbury	Fullback	1925	0	8	4: 1 dg
HARRIS, Perry Colin	11.1.1946		Manawatu	Prop	1976	1	4	0
HARRIS, William Albert	30.6.1876	15.6.1950	Otago	Hooker	1897	0	9	0
HART, Augustine Henry	28.3.1897	1.2.1965	Taranaki	Wing	1924-25	1	17	69: 23 tries
HART, George Fletcher	10.2.1909	3.6.1944	Canterbury	Wing	1930-32, 34-36	11	35	84: 28 tries
HARVEY, Brett Andrew	6.10.1959		Wairarapa-Bush	Flanker	1986	1	1	0
HARVEY, Ian Hamilton	1.1.1903	22.10.1966	Wairarapa	Lock	1924-26, 28	1	18	0
HARVEY, Lester Robert	14.4.1919	3.6.1993	Otago	Lock	1949-50	8	22	0
HARVEY, Patrick	3.4.1880	29.10.1949	Canterbury	Halfback	1904	1	1	0
HASELL, Edward William	26.4.1889	7.4.1966	Canterbury	Hooker	1913, 20	2	7	21: 3 tries, 6 cons
HAY-MacKENZIE, William Edward	2.7.1874	1.12.1942	Auckland	Fullback	1901	0	2	0
HAYWARD, Harold Owen	23.5.1883	25.7.1970	Auckland	Loose forward	1908	1	1	3: 1 try
HAZLETT, Edward John	21.7.1938		Southland	Prop	1966-67	6	12	3: 1 try
HAZLETT, William Edgar	8.11.1905	13.4.1978	Southland	Loose forward	1926, 28, 30	8	26	18: 6 tries
HEEPS, Thomas Roderick	7.3.1938		Wellington	Wing	1962	5	10	47: 15 tries, 1 con
HEKE, Wiremu Rika	3.9.1894	30.11.1989	North Auckland	Loose forward	1929	3	6	0
HELMORE, George Henry Noble	15.6.1862	28.5.1922	Canterbury	Utility back	1884	0	7	16: 4 tries, 2 dgs
HEMARA, Bruce Stephen	19.10.1957		Manawatu	Hooker	1985	0	3	0
HEMI, Ronald Courtney	15.5.1933	13.9.2000	Waikato	Hooker	1953-57, 59-60	16	46	18: 6 tries
HENDERSON, Paul William	21.9.1964		Otago, Southland	Flanker	1989-91, 93, 95	7	25	21: 5 tries
HENDERSON, Peter	18.4.1926		Wanganui	Wing	1949-50	7	19	24: 8 tries
HENDRIE, James Malcolm	12.6.1951		Western Australia	Halfback	1970	0	1	0
HEREWINI, MacFarlane Alexander	17.10.1940		Auckland	First five/fullback	1962-67	10	32	92: 2 tries, 13 cons, 10 pens, 10 dgs
HERROLD, Maurice	1869		Auckland	Halfback	1893	0	2	0
HEWETT, Jason Alexander	17.10.1968		Auckland	Halfback	1991	1	1	4: 1 try
HEWITT, Norman Jason	11.11.1968		Hawke's Bay, Southland	Hooker	1993, 96-98	9	23	35: 7 tries
HEWSON, Allan Roy	6.6.1954		Wellington	Fullback	1979, 81-84	19	34	357: 6 tries, 66 cons, 61 pens, 6 dgs
HICKEY, Percy Hubert	28.4.1899	1942	Taranaki	Wing	1922	0	2	0

ALL BLACKS — THE COMPLETE REGISTER

NAME	DOB	DOD	PROVINCE(S)	POSITION(S)	YEARS	TESTS	GAMES	POINTS
HIGGINSON, Graeme	14.12.1954		Canterbury	Lock	1980-83	6	20	12: 3 tries
HILL, Stanley Frank	9.4.1927		Canterbury	Lock/flanker	1955-59	11	19	2: 1 con
HINES, Geoffrey Robert	10.10.1960		Waikato	Flanker	1980	1	12	16: 4 tries
HOBBS, Frederick George	18.3.1920	15.10.1985	Canterbury	Flanker	1947	0	6	9: 3 tries
HOBBS, Michael James Bowie	15.2.1960		Canterbury	Flanker	1983-86	21	39	52: 13 tries
HOEFT, Carl Henry	13.11.1974		Otago	Prop	1998-2000	20	21	0
HOGAN, John	3.9.1881	15.11.1945	Wanganui	Forward	1907	0	2	0
HOLDEN, Arthur William	8.4.1907	27.7.1970	Otago	Halfback	1928	0	3	0
HOLDER, Edward Catchpole	26.7.1908	2.7.1974	Buller	Wing	1932, 34	1	10	29: 9 tries, 1 con
HOLMES, Bevan	7.4.1946		North Auckland	Loose forward	1970, 72-73	0	31	31: 9 tries
HOOK, Llewellyn Simpkin	4.5.1905	4.8.1979	Auckland	Threequarter	1928-29	3	12	5: 1 try, 1 con
HOOPER, John Alan	10.9.1913	21.4.1976	Canterbury	Second five-eighth	1937-38	3	7	9: 3 tries
HOPA, Aaron Remana	13.11.1971	8.12.1998	Waikato	Loose forward	1997	0	4	5: 1 try
HOPKINSON, Alister Ernest	30.5.1941	17.1.1999	Canterbury	Prop	1967-70	9	35	12: 4 tries
HORE, John	9.8.1907		Otago	Hooker/prop	1928, 30, 32, 34-36	10	45	33: 11 tries
HORSLEY, Ronald Hugh	4.7.1932		Wellington	Lock	1960, 63-64	3	31	3: 1 try
HOTOP, John	7.12.1929		Canterbury	First five-eighth	1952, 55	3	3	6: 1 try, 1 dg
HOWARTH, Shane Paul	8.7.1968		Auckland	Fullback	1993-94	4	10	151: 5 tries, 18 cons, 30 pens
HOWDEN, James	1905	12.3.1978	Southland	Hooker	1928	0	1	0
HOWLETT, Douglas Charles	21.9.1978		Auckland	Wing	2000	4	4	25: 5 tries
HUGHES, Arthur Maitland	11.10.1924		Auckland	Hooker	1947, 49-50	6	7	0
HUGHES, Daniel John	19.9.1869	11.2.1951	Taranaki	Hooker	1894	0	1	0
HUGHES, Edward	26.4.1881	1.5.1928	Southland	Hooker	1907-08, 21	6	9	3: 1 try
HULLENA, Laurence Clifford	24.8.1965		Wellington	Prop	1990-91	0	9	0
HUMPHREYS, George William	15.3.1870	11.5.1933	Canterbury	Loose forward	1894	0	1	3: 1 try
HUMPHRIES, Arthur Larwill	15.2.1874	13.4.1953	Taranaki	Halfback	1897, 1901, 03	0	15	47: 3 tries, 18 cons, 1 pen
HUNTER, Bruce Anthony	16.9.1950		Otago	Wing	1970-71	3	10	24: 8 tries
HUNTER, James	6.3.1879	14.12.1962	Taranaki	Second five-eighth	1905-08	11	36	147: 49 tries
HURST, Ian Archibald	27.8.1951		Canterbury	Midfield back	1972-74	5	32	44: 11 tries
IEREMIA, Alama	27.10.1970		Wellington	Midfield back	1994-97, 99-2000	30	40	45: 9 tries
IFWERSEN, Karl Donald	6.1.1893	19.5.1967	Auckland	Second five-eighth	1921	1	1	0
INNES, Craig Ross	20.9.1969		Auckland	Centre/wing	1989-91	17	30	60: 15 tries
INNES, Gordon Donald	8.9.1910	6.11.1992	Canterbury	Second five-eighth	1932	1	7	6: 2 tries
IRVINE, Ian Bruce	6.3.1929		North Auckland	Hooker	1952	1	1	0
IRVINE, John Gilbert	1.7.1888	10.6.1939	Otago	Lock	1914	3	10	0
IRVINE, William Richard	2.12.1898	26.4.1952	Hawke's Bay, Wairarapa	Hooker	1923-26, 30	5	41	24: 8 tries
IRWIN, Mark William	10.2.1935		Otago	Prop	1955, 56, 58-60	7	25	0
IVIMEY, Frederick Elder Birbeck	28.3.1880	6.12.1961	Otago	Loose forward	1910	0	1	0
JACKSON, Everard Stanley	12.1.1914	20.9.1975	Hawke's Bay	Prop	1936-38	6	11	3: 1 try

Name	Born	Died	Province	Position	Years			Points
JACOB, Hohepa	16.11.1894	30.5.1955	Horowhenua	Wing forward/loose forward	1920	0	8	25: 7 tries, 2 cons
JACOB, John Phillip le Grande	19.5.1877	3.11.1909	Wellington	Wing	1901	0	2	6: 2 tries
JAFFRAY, John Lyndon	17.4.1950		Otago, South Canterbury	Five-eighth	1972, 75-79	7	23	28: 7 tries
JAFFRAY, Mervyn William Rutherford	18.1.1949		Otago	Loose forward	1976	0	4	12: 3 tries
JARDEN, Ronald Alexander	14.12.1929	18.2.1977	Wellington	Wing	1951-56	16	37	213: 35 tries, 36 cons, 12 pens
JEFFERD, Andrew Charles Reeves	13.6.1953		East Coast	Second five-eighth	1980-81	3	5	0
JENNINGS, Arthur Grahn	1939		Bay of Plenty	Lock	1967	0	6	0
JERVIS, Francis Mahon	1870	20.12.1952	Auckland	Wing	1893	0	10	38: 5 tries, 6 cons, 1 dg, 2 gm
JESSEP, Evan Morgan	11.10.1904	10.1.1983	Wellington	Hooker/prop	1931-32	2	8	0
JOHNS, Peter Arthur	16.3.1944		Wanganui	Five-eighth/fullback	1968	0	6	6: 1 try, 1 dg
JOHNSON, Lancelot Matthew	9.8.1897	11.1.1983	Wellington	Five-eighth	1925, 28, 30	4	25	19: 3 tries, 5 cons
JOHNSTON, David	24.3.1903	5.7.1938	Taranaki	Five-eighth	1925	0	2	4: 2 cons
JOHNSTON, William	13.9.1881	9.1.1951	Otago	Loose forward	1905, 07	3	27	12: 4 tries
JOHNSTONE, Bradley Ronald	30.7.1950		Auckland	Prop	1976-80	13	45	28: 7 tries
JOHNSTONE, Peter	9.8.1922	18.10.1997	Otago	Flanker/No 8	1949-51	9	26	12: 4 tries
JONES, Ian Donald	17.4.1969		North Auckland, North Harbour	Lock	1989-99	79	105	65: 14 tries
JONES, Michael Niko	8.4.1965		Auckland	Loose forward	1987-98	55	74	69: 16 tries
JONES, Murray Gordon	26.10.1942	12.2.1975	North Auckland	Prop	1973	1	5	0
JONES, Peter Frederick	24.3.1932	7.6.1994	North Auckland	Loose forward	1953-56, 58-60	11	37	60: 20 tries
JOSEPH, Howard Thornton	25.8.1949		Canterbury	Centre	1971	2	2	0
JOSEPH, James Whitinui	21.11.1969		Otago	Loose forward/lock	1992-95	20	30	15: 3 tries
KANE, Gregory Norman	12.10.1952		Waikato	Midfield back	1974	0	7	16: 4 tries
KARAM, Joseph Francis	21.11.1951		Wellington, Horowhenua	Fullback	1972-75	10	41	343: 6 tries, 80 cons, 51 pens, 2 dgs
KATENE, Thomas	14.8.1929		Wellington	Wing	1955	1	1	0
KEANE, Kieran James	9.2.1953		Canterbury	Second five-eighth	1979	0	6	0
KEARNEY, James Charles	4.4.1920	6.6.1992	Otago	First five-eighth	1947, 49	4	22	30: 6 tries, 4 dgs
KELLEHER, Byron Terrance	3.12.1976		Otago	Halfback	1999-2000	11	12	10: 2 tries
KELLY, John Wallace	7.12.1926	1.10.1998	Auckland	Fullback/wing	1949, 53-54	2	16	86: 5 tries, 22 cons, 7 pens, 2 dgs
KEMBER, Gerald Francis	15.11.1945		Wellington	Fullback/second five-eighth	1967, 70	1	19	158: 43 cons, 24 pens
KENNY, Dean Julian	22.5.1961		Otago	Halfback	1986	0	3	0
KERR, Alexander	3.5.1871	18.6.1936	Canterbury	Loose forward	1896	0	1	3: 1 try
KETELS, Rodney Clive	11.11.1954		Counties	Prop	1979-81	5	16	0
KIERNAN, Henry Arthur Douglas	24.7.1876	15.1.1947	Auckland	Halfback	1903	1	8	9: 3 tries
KILBY, Francis David	24.4.1906	3.9.1985	Wellington	Halfback	1928, 32, 34	4	18	10: 2 tries, 1 dg
KILLEEN, Brian Alexander	13.4.1911	9.3.1993	Auckland	Second five/wing	1936	1	2	3: 1 try

ALL BLACKS — THE COMPLETE REGISTER

NAME	DOB	DOD	PROVINCE(S)	POSITION(S)	YEARS	TESTS	GAMES	POINTS
KING, Ronald Russell	19.8.1909	10.1.1988	West Coast	Lock	1934-38	13	42	21: 7 tries
KINGSTONE, Charles Napoleon	2.7.1895	6.5.1960	Taranaki	Fullback	1921	3	3	0
KIRK, David Edward	5.10.1960		Otago, Auckland	Halfback	1983-87	17	34	68: 17 tries
KIRKPATRICK, Alexander	4.10.1898	25.8.1971	Hawke's Bay	Hooker	1925-26	0	12	6: 2 tries
KIRKPATRICK, Ian Andrew	24.5.1946		Canterbury, Poverty Bay	Loose forward	1967-77	39	113	180: 50 tries
KIRTON, Earle Weston	29.12.1940		Otago	First five-eighth	1963-64, 67-70	13	48	42: 13 tries, 1 dg
KIRWAN, John James	16.12.1964		Auckland	Wing	1984-94	63	96	275: 67 tries
KIVELL, Alfred Louis	12.4.1897	13.2.1987	Taranaki	Loose forward	1929	2	5	0
KNIGHT, Arthur	26.1.1906	26.4.1990	Auckland	Loose forward/lock	1926, 28, 34	1	14	12: 4 tries
KNIGHT, Gary Albert	26.8.1951		Manawatu	Prop	1977-86	36	66	12: 3 tries
KNIGHT, Lawrence Alfred George	16.7.1901		Auckland	Loose forward	1925	0	5	6: 2 tries
KNIGHT, Lawrence Gibb	24.9.1949		Auckland, Poverty Bay	Loose forward/lock	1974, 76-77	6	35	52: 13 tries
KNIGHT, Michael Orton	20.5.1945		Counties	Wing	1968	0	8	18: 6 tries
KOTEKA, Tohoa Tauroa	30.9.1956		Waikato	Prop	1981-82	2	6	4: 1 try
KREFT, Anthony John	27.3.1945		Otago	Prop	1968	1	4	6: 2 tries
KRONFELD, Joshua Adrian	20.6.1971		Otago	Flanker	1995-2000	54	56	80: 16 tries
KURURANGI, Robert	4.7.1957		Counties	Wing	1978	0	8	16: 4 tries
LAIDLAW, Christopher Robert	16.11.1943		Otago, Canterbury	Halfback	1963-68, 70	20	57	48: 11 tries, 5 dgs
LAIDLAW, Kevin Francis	9.8.1934		Southland	Centre	1960	3	17	21: 7 tries
LAM, Patrick Richard	29.9.1968		Auckland	Loose forward	1992	0	1	0
LAMBERT, Kent King	23.3.1952		Manawatu	Prop	1972-74, 76-77	11	40	6: 1 try, 1 con
LAMBIE, James Taylor	9.4.1870	15.4.1905	Taranaki	Forward	1893-94	0	12	12: 4 tries
LAMBOURN, Arthur	11.1.1910	24.9.1999	Wellington	Hooker, prop	1934-38	10	40	9: 3 tries
LARSEN, Blair Peter	20.1.1969		North Harbour	Lock/flanker	1992-96	17	40	14: 3 tries
LAW, Arthur Douglas	8.5.1904	4.9.1961	Manawhenua	Wing	1925	0	4	3: 1 try
LAWSON, Gordon Pirie	15.9.1899	13.9.1985	South Canterbury	First five-eighth	1925	0	2	0
LECKY, John Gage	4.11.1863	6.4.1917	Auckland	Forward	1884	0	7	8: 4 tries
LEESON, John	15.11.1909	11.3.1960	Waikato	Prop	1934	0	5	0
LE LIEVRE, Jules Mathew	17.8.1933		Canterbury	Prop	1962-64	1	25	8: 2 tries, 1 con
LENDRUM, Robert Noel	22.3.1948		Counties	Fullback	1973	1	3	32: 1 try, 5 cons, 5 pens, 1 dg
LESLIE, Andrew Roy	10.11.1944		Wellington	No 8	1974-76	10	34	28: 7 tries
LEVIEN, Howard Joseph	6.9.1935		Otago	Midfield back	1957	0	7	30: 9 tries, 1 dg
LEYS, Eric Tiki	25.5.1907	21.1.1989	Wellington	Halfback	1929	1	5	0
LILBURNE, Herbert Theodore	16.3.1908	12.7.1976	Canterbury, Wellington	Five-eighth/ fullback	1928-32, 34	10	40	65: 6 tries, 12 cons, 5 pens, 2 dgs
LINDSAY, David Frederick	9.12.1906	7.3.1978	Otago	Fullback/wing	1928	3	14	63: 22 cons, 5 pens, 1 dg
LINDSAY, William George	29.12.1879	15.5.1965	Southland	Hooker	1914	0	4	3: 1 try
LINEEN, Terence Raymond	5.1.1936		Auckland	Midfield back	1957-60	12	35	48: 16 tries
LISTER, Thomas Norman	27.10.1943		South Canterbury	Flanker	1968-71	8	26	33: 11 tries

Player	Born	Died	Province	Position	Span	Tests	Matches	Points
LITTLE, Paul Francis	14.9.1934	7.8.1993	Auckland	Centre	1961-64	10	29	27: 9 tries
LITTLE, Walter Kenneth	14.10.1969		North Harbour	Five-eighth/centre	1989-98	50	75	71: 15 tries
LOADER, Colin James	10.3.1931		Wellington	Midfield	1953-54	4	16	12: 4 tries
LOCHORE, Brian James	3.9.1940		Wairarapa, Wairarapa-Bush	Lock/No 8	1963-71	24	68	21: 7 tries
LOCKINGTON, Terence McClatchey	26.3.1913		Auckland	Flanker	1936	0	1	3: 1 try
LOE, Richard Wyllie	6.4.1960		Waikato, Canterbury	Prop	1986-92, 94-95	49	78	44: 10 tries
LOMAS, Arthur Robert	15.11.1894	24.3.1975	Auckland	Hooker	1925-26	0	15	9: 3 tries
LOMU, Jonah Tali	12.5.1975		Counties-Manukau, Wellington	Wing	1994-2000	45	55	175: 35 tries
LONG, A J	?	?	Auckland	Forward	1903	1	10	12: 4 tries
LOVEDAY, John Kelman	1.5.1949		Manawatu	Lock	1978	0	7	0
LOVERIDGE, David Steven	1.5.1949		Taranaki	Halfback	1978-83, 85	24	54	36: 9 tries
LOVERIDGE, George	15.10.1890	28.11.1970	Taranaki	Wing	1913-14	0	11	20: 6 tries, 1 con
LUCAS, Frederick William	30.1.1902	17.9.1957	Auckland	Threequarter	1923-25, 28, 30	7	41	75: 25 tries
LUNN, William Albert	17.9.1926	22.12.1996	Otago	Flanker	1949	2	2	0
LYNCH, Thomas William	6.3.1892	6.5.1950	South Canterbury	Wing	1913-14	4	23	113: 37 tries, 1 con
LYNCH, Thomas William	20.7.1927		Canterbury	Second five-eighth	1951	3	10	27: 8 tries, 1dg
MABER, George	2.11.1869	?	Wellington	Forward	1894	0	1	0
McATAMNEY, Francis Stevens	15.5.1934		Otago	Prop	1956-57	1	9	6: 2 tries
McCAHILL, Bernard Joseph	28.6.1964		Auckland	Midfield back	1987-91	10	32	16: 4 tries
McCARTHY, Patrick	28.6.1893	1.7.1976	Canterbury	Halfback	1923	0	1	0
McCASHIN, Terence Michael	18.1.1944		Horowhenua	Hooker	1968	0	7	3: 1 try
McCAW, William Alexander	26.8.1927		Southland	Loose forward	1951, 53-54	5	32	18: 6 tries
McCLEARY, Brian Verdon	17.1.1897	2.7.1978	Canterbury	Hooker	1924-25	0	12	0
McCLYMONT, William Graham	22.6.1905	21.5.1970	Otago	Wing	1928	0	3	3: 1 try
McCOOL, Michael John	15.9.1951		Wairarapa-Bush	Lock	1979	1	2	0
McCORMICK, Archibald George	23.2.1899	8.2.1969	Canterbury	Hooker	1925	0	1	0
McCORMICK, James	15.10.1923		Hawke's Bay	Hooker	1947	0	3	0
McCORMICK, William Fergus	24.4.1939		Canterbury	Fullback	1965, 67-71	16	43	453: 10 tries, 112 cons, 62 pens, 1 dg
McCULLOUGH, John Francis	8.1.1936		Taranaki	First five-eighth	1959	3	3	0
McDONALD, Alexander	23.4.1883	4.5.1967	Otago	Loose forward	1905, 08, 13	6	41	50: 16 tries, 1 con
MACDONALD, Hamish Hugh	11.1.1947		Canterbury, North Auckland	Lock	1972-76	12	48	8: 2 tries
MACDONALD, Leon Raymond	21.12.1977		Canterbury	Fullback	2000	4	4	0
McDONNELL, Peter	1874	24.5.1950	Wanganui	Wing	1896	1	1	0
McDOWELL, Steven Clark	27.8.1961		Auckland	Prop	1985-92	46	81	28: 7 tries
McELDOWNEY, John Thompson	26.10.1947		Taranaki	Prop	1976-77	2	10	0
MacEWAN, Ian Neven	1.5.1934		Wellington	Lock/No 8	1956-62	20	52	27: 9 tries
McGAHAN, Paul William	12.10.1964		North Harbour	Halfback	1990-91	0	6	4: 1 try
McGRATTAN, Brian	31.12.1959		Wellington	Prop	1983-86	6	23	16: 4 tries
McGREGOR, Alwin John	16.12.1889	15.4.1963	Auckland	Wing	1913	2	11	45: 15 tries
McGREGOR, Ashley Alton	3.9.1953		Southland	Loose forward	1978	0	3	0

ALL BLACKS — THE COMPLETE REGISTER

NAME	DOB	DOD	PROVINCE(S)	POSITION(S)	YEARS	TESTS	GAMES	POINTS
McGREGOR, Duncan	16.7.1881	11.3.1947	Canterbury, Wellington	Wing	1903-06	4	31	106: 34 tries, 2 cons
McGREGOR, Neil Perriam	29.12.1901	12.7.1973	Canterbury	Five-eighth	1924-25, 28	2	27	21: 7 tries
McGREGOR, Robert Wylie	31.12.1874	22.11.1925	Auckland	Centre/fullback	1901, 03-04	2	10	12: 4 tries
McHUGH, Maurice James	19.2.1917		Auckland	Loose forward/lock	1946, 49	3	14	3: 1 try
MACINTOSH, Charles Nicholson	6.4.1869	?.12.1918	South Canterbury	Forward	1893	0	4	3: 1 try
McINTOSH, Donald Neil	1.4.1931		Wellington	Flanker	1956-57	4	13	9: 3 tries
McKAY, Donald William	7.8.1937		Auckland	Wing	1961-63	5	12	54: 18 tries
MACKAY, James Douglas	21.9.1905	?.?.1985	Wellington	Wing	1928	0	2	12: 4 tries
McKECHNIE, Brian John	6.11.1953		Southland	Fullback/first five	1977-79, 81	9	26	148: 2 tries, 22 cons, 28 pens, 4 dgs
McKELLAR, Gerald Forbes	9.1.1884	16.1.1960	Wellington	Wing/ loose forward	1910	3	5	3: 1 try
McKENZIE, Richard John	15.3.1892	25.9.1968	Wellington, Auckland	Five-eighth	1913-14	4	20	57: 17 tries, 1 con, 1 dg
MACKENZIE, Robert Henry Craig	17.2.1904	19.7.1993	Wellington	First five-eighth	1928	0	2	0
McKENZIE, Robert Hugh	1.6.1869	24.6.1940	Auckland	Forward	1893	0	2	0
McKENZIE, Roderick McCulloch	16.9.1909	24.3.2000	Manawatu	Flanker/lock	1934-38	9	35	36: 11 tries, 1 gm
McKENZIE, William	12.6.1871	1.7.1943	Wairarapa	Wing forward	1893-94, 96-97	0	20	24: 8 tries
MACKRELL, William Henry Clifton	20.7.1881	15.7.1917	Auckland	Hooker	1905-06	1	7	3: 1 try
MACKY, John Victor	3.3.1887	15.9.1951	Auckland	Wing	1913	1	1	0
McLACHLAN, Jon Stanley	23.6.1949		Auckland	Wing	1974	1	8	32: 8 tries
McLAREN, Hugh Campbell	8.6.1926	9.5.1992	Waikato	No 8	1952	1	1	0
McLEAN, Andrew Leslie	31.10.1898	18.1.1964	Bay of Plenty	Flanker/fullback	1921, 23	2	3	17: 1 try, 4 cons, 2 pens
McLEAN, Charles	20.9.1892	7.3.1965	Buller	Loose forward	1920	0	5	21: 7 tries
McLEAN, Hugh Foster	18.7.1907	24.4.1997	Wellington, Auckland	Loose forward	1930, 32, 34-36	9	29	50: 16 tries, 1 con
McLEAN, John Kenneth	3.10.1923		King Country, Auckland	Wing	1947, 49	2	5	21: 7 tries
McLEAN, Robert John	23.5.1960		Wairarapa-Bush	Prop	1987	0	2	0
McLEOD, Bruce Edward	30.1.1940	18.5.1996	Counties	Hooker	1964-70	24	46	21: 7 tries
McLEOD, Scott James	28.2.1973		Waikato	Midfield back	1996-98	10	17	30: 6 tries
McMEEKING, David Thomas McLagan	30.1.1896	30.8.1976	Otago	Hooker	1923	0	2	3: 1 try
McMINN, Archibald Forbes	14.8.1880	23.4.1919	Wairarapa, Manawatu	Loose forward	1903, 05	2	10	9: 3 tries
McMINN, Francis Alexander	10.11.1874	8.8.1947	Manawatu	Hooker	1904	1	1	0
McMULLEN, Raymond Frank	18.1.1933		Auckland	Wing	1957-60	11	29	45: 15 tries
McNAB, John Alexander	14.12.1895	23.7.1979	Hawke's Bay	Loose forward	1925	0	1	0
McNAB, John Ronald	26.3.1924		Otago	Flanker	1949-50	6	18	3: 1 try
McNAUGHTON, Alan Murray	20.9.1947		Bay of Plenty	Flanker	1971-72	3	9	12: 3 tries
McNEECE, James	24.12.1885	21.6.1917	Southland	Forward	1913-14	5	11	6: 2 tries
McNICOL, Alasdair Lindsay Robert	15.6.1944		Wanganui	Prop	1973	0	5	0
McPHAIL, Bruce Eric	26.1.1937		Canterbury	Wing	1959	2	2	0
MACPHERSON, Donald Gregory	23.7.1882	26.11.1956	Otago	Wing	1905	1	1	0

Name	Born	Died	Position	Province	Seasons	Tests	Games	Points
MACPHERSON, Gordon	9.10.1962		Lock	Otago	1986	1	1	0
MacRAE, Ian Robert	6.4.1943		Midfield back	Hawke's Bay	1963-64, 66-70	17	45	42: 14 tries
McRAE, John Alexander	29.4.1914	24.2.1977	Hooker/prop	Southland	1946	2	2	0
McROBIE, Nisbet	1873	27.9.1929	Hooker	Southland	1896	0	1	0
McWILLIAMS, Ruben George	12.6.1901	27.1.1984	Loose forward	Auckland	1928-30	10	27	25: 7 tries, 2 cons
MAGUIRE, James Richard	6.2.1886	1.12.1966	Hooker	Auckland	1910	3	6	0
MAHONEY, Atholstan	15.7.1908	13.7.1979	Loose forward	Bush	1929, 34-36	4	26	6: 2 tries
MAINS, Laurence William	16.2.1946		Fullback	Otago	1971, 76	4	15	153: 2 tries, 31 cons, 28 pens
MAJOR, John	8.8.1940		Hooker	Taranaki	1963-64, 67	1	24	0
MAKA, Isitolo	25.5.1975		Loose forward	Otago	1998	4	4	5: 1 try
MANCHESTER, John Eaton	29.1.1908	6.9.1983	Flanker	Canterbury	1932, 34-36	9	36	23: 7 tries, 1 con
MANNIX, Simon James	10.8.1971		First five-eighth	Wellington	1990-91, 94	1	9	70: 2 tries, 19 cons, 8 pens
MARKHAM, Paul Francis	27.11.1891		Second five-eighth	Wellington	1921	0	1	0
MARSHALL, Justin Warren	5.8.1973		Halfback	Canterbury	1995-2000	28	55	125: 25 tries
MASON, David Frank	21.11.1923	3.7.1981	Wing	Wellington	1947	1	6	9: 3 tries
MASTERS, Frederick Harold	20.12.1893	27.5.1980	Lock	Taranaki	1922	0	4	0
MASTERS, Robin Read	19.10.1900	29.8.1967	Lock	Canterbury	1923-25	4	31	18: 6 tries
MATAIRA, Hawea Karepa	3.12.1910	15.11.1979	Loose forward	Hawke's Bay	1934	1	5	3: 1 try
MATHESON, Jeffrey David	30.3.1948		Prop	Otago	1972	5	13	0
MATHIESON, Robert George	11.1.1899	16.4.1966	First five-eighth/halfback	Otago	1922	0	4	0
MATSON, John Tabaiwalu Fakavale	14.5.1973		Midfield back	Canterbury	1995-96	0	5	5: 1 try
MATTSON, Herman Alfred	4.11.1900	6.7.1980	Midfield back	Auckland	1925	0	5	3: 1 try
MAX, Donald Stanfield	7.3.1906	4.3.1972	Loose forward/lock	Nelson	1931-32, 34	3	8	3: 1 try
MAXWELL, Norman Maxwell	5.3.1976		Lock	Canterbury	1999-2000	20	20	10: 2 tries
MAYERHOFLER, Mark Andrew	8.10.1972		Midfield back	Canterbury	1998	6	6	10: 2 tries
MEADS, Colin Earl	3.6.1936		Lock/loose forward	King Country	1957-71	55	133	86: 28 tries, 1 con
MEADS, Stanley Thomas	12.7.1938		Lock/loose forward	King Country	1961-66	15	30	17: 5 tries, 1 con
MEATES, Kevin Francis	20.2.1930		Flanker	Canterbury	1952	2	2	0
MEATES, William Anthony	26.5.1923		Wing	Otago	1949-50	7	20	9: 3 tries
MEEUWS, Kees Junior	26.7.74		Prop	Otago	1998-2000	18	19	0
MEHRTENS, Andrew Philip	28.4.1973		First five-eighth	Canterbury	1995-2000	48	50	747: 7 tries, 125 cons, 145 pens, 9 dgs
MEHRTENS, George Martin	5.2.1907	30.8.1954	Fullback	Canterbury	1928	0	3	0
METCALFE, Thomas Charles	13.5.1909	26.5.1969	Loose forward/lock	Southland	1931-32	2	7	6: 2 tries
MEXTED, Graham George	3.2.1927		No 8	Wellington	1950-51	1	6	15: 5 tries
MEXTED, Murray Graham	5.9.1953		No 8	Wellington	1979-85	34	72	76: 19 tries
MIKA, Dylan Gabriel	17.4.1972		Loose forward	Auckland	1999	7	8	5: 1 try
MILL, James Joseph	19.11.1899	29.3.1950	Halfback	Hawke's Bay, Wairarapa	1923-26, 30	4	33	53: 15 tries, 4 cons
MILLER, Todd James	2.12.1974		Fullback	Waikato	1997	0	4	20: 4 tries
MILLIKEN, Harold Maurice	27.2.1914	10.1.1993	Lock	Canterbury	1938	3	7	6: 2 tries

ALL BLACKS — THE COMPLETE REGISTER

NAME	DOB	DOD	PROVINCE(S)	POSITION(S)	YEARS	TESTS	GAMES	POINTS
MILLS, Hugh Parsons	6.6.1873	26.3.1905	Taranaki	Forward	1897	0	8	12: 4 tries
MILLS, John Gordon	23.2.1960		Auckland	Hooker	1984	0	2	4: 1 try
MILLTON, Edward Bowler	7.3.1861	11.3.1942	Canterbury	Forward	1884	0	7	2: 1 try
MILLTON, William Varnham	10.2.1858	22.6.1887	Canterbury	Forward	1884	0	8	35: 4 tries, 9 cons
MILNER, Henare Pawhara	12.2.1946	2.3.1996	Wanganui	Utility back	1970	1	16	27: 9 tries
MITCHELL, John Eric Paul	23.3.1964		Waikato	No 8	1993	0	6	10: 2 tries
MITCHELL, Neville Alfred	22.11.1913	21.5.1981	Southland, Otago	Threequarter	1935-38	8	32	60: 20 tries
MITCHELL, Terry William	11.9.1950		Canterbury	Wing	1974, 76	1	17	36: 9 tries
MITCHELL, William James	28.11.1890	2.6.1959	Canterbury	Wing	1910	2	5	6: 2 tries
MITCHINSON, Frank Edwin	3.9.1884	27.3.1978	Wellington	Wing/midfield	1907-08, 10, 13	11	31	80: 22 tries, 2 cons, 2 pens, 1 dg
MOFFITT, James Edward	3.6.1889	16.3.1964	Wellington	Lock	1920-21	3	12	14: 4 tries, 1 con
MOLLOY, Brian Peter John	12.8.1931		Canterbury	Halfback	1957	0	5	3: 1 try
MOORE, Graham John Tarr	18.3.1923	27.1.1991	Otago	Wing	1949	1	1	3: 1 try
MORETON, Raymond Claude	30.1.1942		Canterbury	Midfield back	1962, 64-65	7	12	24: 7 tries, 1 dg
MORGAN, Herman David	13.6.1902	19.1.1969	Otago	Wing	1923	0	1	3: 1 try
MORGAN, Joseph Edward	7.8.1945		North Auckland	Second five-eighth	1974, 76	5	22	20: 5 tries
MORRIS, Trevor James	3.1.1942		Nelson Bays	Fullback	1972-73	3	23	175: 1 try, 39 cons, 25 pens, 6 dgs
MORRISON, Terry Geoffrey	16.6.1951		Otago	Wing	1973	1	5	4: 1 try
MORRISON, Thomas Clarence	28.7.1913	31.8.1985	South Canterbury	Wing	1938	3	5	14: 2 tries, 2 dgs
MORRISSEY, Brian Lewis	14.9.1952		Waikato	Loose forward	1981	0	3	4: 1 try
MORRISSEY, Peter John	18.7.1939		Canterbury	Wing	1962	3	3	6: 2 tries
MOURIE, Graham Neil Kenneth	8.9.1952		Taranaki	Flanker	1976-82	21	61	64: 16 tries
MOWLEM, John	9.8.1870	12.10.1951	Manawatu	Forward	1893	0	4	0
MULLER, Brian Leo	11.6.1942		Taranaki	Prop	1967-71	14	34	9: 3 tries
MUMM, William John	26.3.1922	11.12.1993	Buller	Prop	1949	1	1	0
MUNRO, Henry Gordon	8.12.1896	26.11.1974	Otago	Hooker	1924-25	0	9	9: 3 tries
MURDOCH, Keith	9.9.1943		Otago	Prop	1970, 72	3	27	20: 6 tries
MURDOCH, Peter Henry	17.6.1941	16.10.1995	Auckland	First five-eighth	1964-65	5	5	6: 2 tries
MURRAY, Frederick Steele Miller	20.8.1871	5.8.1952	Auckland	Forward	1893, 97	0	20	16: 4 tries, 1 gm
MURRAY, Harold Vivian	9.2.1888	4.7.1971	Canterbury	Wing forward	1913-14	4	22	36: 12 tries
MURRAY, Peter Chapman	23.1.1884	6.2.1968	Wanganui	Hooker	1908	1	1	0
MYERS, Richard George	6.7.1950		Waikato	Loose forward	1977-78	1	5	4: 1 try
MYNOTT, Harry Jonas	4.6.1876	2.1.1924	Taranaki	First five-eighth	1905-07, 10	8	39	55: 17 tries, 2 cons
NATHAN, Waka Joseph	8.7.1940		Auckland	Flanker	1962-64, 66-67	14	37	69: 23 tries
NELSON, Keith Alister	26.11.1938		Otago, Auckland	Loose forward	1962-64	2	18	6: 2 tries
NEPIA, George	25.4.1905	27.8.1986	Hawke's Bay, East Coast	Fullback	1924-25, 1929-30	9	46	99: 1 try, 39 cons, 6 pens
NESBIT, Steven Roberto	13.2.1936		Auckland	First five-eighth	1960	2	13	6: 2 tries
NEVILLE, Wayne Ronald	10.12.1954		North Auckland	Prop	1981	0	4	0
NEWTON, Frederick	7.5.1881	10.12.1955	Canterbury	Lock/loose forward	1905-06	3	19	3: 1 try

Name	Birth	Death	Province	Position	Years			Points
NICHOLLS, Harold Garwood	19.11.1897	10.8.1977	Wellington	Second five-eighth	1923	0	1	3: 1 try
NICHOLLS, Harry Edgar	21.1.1900	1.4.1978	Wellington	Halfback	1921-23	1	7	3: 1 try
NICHOLLS, Marcus Frederick	13.7.1901	10.6.1972	Wellington	Five-eighth	1921-22, 24-26, 28, 30	10	51	284: 5 tries, 93 cons, 20 pens, 5 dgs, 1 gm
NICHOLSON, George William	3.8.1878	13.9.1968	Auckland	Loose forward	1903-07	4	39	24: 8 tries
NORTON, Rangitane Will	30.3.1942		Canterbury	Hooker	1971-77	27	61	4: 1 try
O'BRIEN, Andrew James	22.9.1897	9.5.1969	Auckland	Loose forward	1922	0	3	3: 1 try
O'BRIEN, John	28.10.1871	26.4.1946	Wellington	Forward	1901	0	1	0
O'BRIEN, John Gerald	9.12.1889	9.1.1958	Auckland	Fullback	1914, 20	1	12	5: 1 try, 1 con
O'CALLAGHAN, Michael William	27.4.1946		Manawatu	Wing	1968	3	3	0
O'CALLAGHAN, Thomas Raymond	19.1.1925		Wellington	Second five-eighth	1949	1	1	3: 1 pen
O'CONNOR, Timothy Beehane	1860	5.2.1936	Auckland	Forward	1884	0	7	4: 2 tries
O'DEA, Robert John	27.1.1930	16.7.1986	Thames Valley	Flanker	1953-54	0	5	0
O'DONNELL, Desmond Hillary	7.10.1921	18.1.1992	Wellington	Prop	1949	1	1	0
O'DONNELL, James	?	?	Otago	Forward	1884	0	7	8: 4 tries
O'DOWDA, Bernard Clement	23.3.1874	26.7.1954	Taranaki	Forward	1901	0	2	0
O'HALLORAN, Jason David	28.2.1972		Wellington	Midfield back	2000	1	1	0
OLD, Geoffrey Haldane	22.1.1956		Manawatu	Loose forward	1980-83	3	17	4: 1 try
O'LEARY, Michael Joseph	29.9.1883	12.12.1963	Auckland	Utility back	1910, 13	4	8	33: 13 cons, 1 pen, 1 dg
OLIPHANT, Robert	?.1.1870	18.1.1956	Wellington, Auckland	Wing forward	1893, 96	0	3	3: 1 try
OLIVER, Anton David	9.9.1975		Otago	Hooker	1996-2000	29	36	20: 4 tries
OLIVER, Charles Joshua	1.11.1905	25.9.1977	Canterbury	Midfield back	1928-29, 34-36	7	33	69: 16 tries, 9 cons, 1 pen
OLIVER, Desmond Oswald	26.10.1930	25.10.1997	Otago	Flanker	1953-54	2	20	12: 4 tries
OLIVER, Donald Joseph	29.4.1909	25.6.1990	Wellington	Wing	1930	2	3	6: 2 tries
OLIVER, Francis James	24.12.1948		Southland, Otago, Manawatu	Lock	1976-81	17	43	8: 2 tries
ORCHARD, Sydney Arthur	1875	19.4.1947	Canterbury	Fullback	1896-97	0	9	0
ORMOND, Jack	1.12.1891	24.6.1970	Hawke's Bay	Loose forward	1923	0	1	0
ORR, Rex William	19.6.1924		Otago	Fullback	1949	1	1	0
OSBORNE, Glen Matthew	27.8.1971		North Harbour	Fullback/wing	1995-97, 99	19	29	85: 17 tries
OSBORNE, William Michael	24.4.1955		Wanganui	Midfield back	1975-78, 80, 82	16	48	40: 10 tries
O'SULLIVAN, James Michael	5.2.1883	21.12.1960	Taranaki	Loose forward	1905, 07	5	29	6: 2 tries
O'SULLIVAN, Terence Patrick Anthony	27.11.1936	25.4.1997	Taranaki	Midfield back	1960-62	4	16	21: 7 tries
PAEWAI, Lui	10.8.1906	2.1.1970	Hawke's Bay	Five-eighth	1923-24	0	8	6: 2 tries
PAGE, James Russell	10.5.1908	22.5.1985	Wellington	First five-eighth/centre	1931-32, 34-35	6	18	9: 3 tries
PAGE, Milford Laurenson	8.5.1902	13.2.1987	Canterbury	Halfback	1928	0	1	0
PALMER, Bertram Pitt	14.11.1901	4.9.1932	Auckland	Hooker/prop	1928-29, 32	3	18	14: 4 tries, 1 con
PARKER, James Hislop	1.2.1897	11.9.1980	Canterbury	Wing forward	1924-25	3	21	56: 18 tries, 1 con
PARKHILL, Allan Archibald	22.4.1912	26.8.1986	Otago	No 8	1937-38	6	10	9: 3 tries
PARKINSON, Ross Michael	30.5.1948		Poverty Bay	Midfield back	1972-73	7	20	20: 5 tries
PATERSON, Alexander Marshall	31.10.1885	29.7.1933	Otago	Loose forward	1908, 10	5	9	6: 2 tries

ALL BLACKS — THE COMPLETE REGISTER

NAME	DOB	DOD	PROVINCE(S)	POSITION(S)	YEARS	TESTS	GAMES	POINTS
PATON, Henry	12.2.1881	21.1.1964	Otago	Lock	1907, 10	2	8	18: 6 tries
PAULING, Thomas Gibson	17.6.1873	27.8.1927	Wellington	Forward	1896-97	0	9	16: 4 tries, 2 cons
PENE, Arran Rewi Brett	26.10.1967		Otago	No 8	1992-94	15	26	16: 4 tries
PEPPER, Cyril Stennart	18.11.1911	31.5.1943	Auckland	Prop	1935-36	0	17	12: 4 tries
PERRY, Arnold	18.4.1899	2.10.1977	Otago	First five-eighth	1923	0	1	0
PERRY, Richard Grant	26.5.1953		Mid Canterbury	Hooker	1980	0	1	0
PETERSEN, Louis Charles	19.4.1897	25.6.1961	Canterbury	Loose forward	1921-23	0	8	3: 1 try
PHILLIPS, William John	30.1.1914	10.11.1982	King Country	Wing	1937-38	3	7	6: 2 tries
PHILPOTT, Shayne	21.9.1965		Canterbury	Utility back	1988, 90-91	2	14	33: 5 tries, 2 cons, 3 pens
PICKERING, Ernest Arthur Rex	23.11.1936		Waikato	Loose forward/lock	1957-60	3	21	21: 7 tries
PIERCE, Murray James	1.11.1957		Wellington	Lock	1984-90	26	54	16: 4 tries
POKERE, Steven Tahurata	11.8.1958		Southland, Auckland	Centre/first five-eighth	1981-85	18	39	36: 9 tries
POLLOCK, Harold Raymond	7.9.1909	10.1.1984	Wellington	Utility back	1932, 36	5	8	41: 13 cons, 1 pen, 3 dgs
PORTEOUS, Harry Graeme	20.1.1875	19.12.1951	Otago	Wing forward	1903	0	3	0
PORTER, Clifford Glen	5.5.1899	12.11.1976	Wellington	Wing forward	1923-26, 28-30	7	41	48: 16 tries
POTAKA, Waate Pene	1903	3.11.1967	Wanganui	Threequarter	1923	0	2	3: 1 try
PRESTON, Jon Paul	15.11.1967		Canterbury, Wellington	Halfback/first five-eighth	1991-93, 96-97	10	27	83: 4 tries, 12 cons, 13 pens
PRINGLE, Alexander	9.11.1899	21.2.1973	Wellington	Loose forward	1923	0	1	3: 1 try
PRINGLE, Walter Peter	17.7.1869	24.2.1945	Wellington	Forward	1893	0	5	0
PROCTER, Albert Charles	22.5.1906	11.10.1989	Otago	Wing	1932	1	4	18: 6 tries
PURDUE, Charles Alfred	10.6.1874	10.10.1941	Southland	Loose forward	1901, 05	3	3	0
PURDUE, Edward	1878	16.7.1939	Southland	Lock	1905	1	1	0
PURDUE, George Bambery	4.5.1909		Southland	Lock/flanker	1931-32	4	7	3: 1 try
PURVIS, Graham Herbert	14.10.1960		Waikato	Prop	1989-93	2	28	4: 1 try
PURVIS, Neil Alexander	31.1.1953		Otago	Wing	1976	1	12	36: 9 tries
QUAID, Charles Edward	17.8.1908	18.2.1984	Otago	Hooker	1938	2	4	0
RALPH, Caleb Stanley	10.9.1977		Auckland	Centre	1998	1	1	0
RANDELL, Taine Cheyenne	5.11.1974		Otago	Loose forward	1995-2000	40	50	55: 11 tries
RANGI, Ronald Edward	4.2.1941	13.9.1988	Auckland	Centre	1964-66	10	10	9: 3 tries
RANKIN, John George	14.2.1914	8.12.1989	Canterbury	Flanker	1936-37	3	4	9: 3 tries
REEDY, William Joseph	1880	1.4.1939	Wellington	Hooker	1908	2	2	0
REID, Alan Robin	12.4.1929	16.11.1994	Waikato	Halfback	1951-52, 56-57	5	17	6: 2 tries
REID, Hikatarewa Rockcliffe	8.4.1958		Bay of Plenty	Hooker	1980-81, 83, 85-86	7	38	32: 8 tries
REID, Keith Howard	25.5.1904	24.5.1972	Wairarapa	Hooker	1929	2	5	3: 1 try
REID, Sana Torium	22.9.1912		Hawke's Bay	Lock/flanker	1935-37	9	27	20: 6 tries, 1 con
REIHANA, Bruce Trevor	6.4.1976		Waikato	Wing	2000	2	2	10: 2 tries
RESIDE, Walter Brown	6.10.1905	3.5.1985	Wairarapa	Loose forward	1929	1	6	0
RHIND, Patrick Keith	20.6.1915	10.9.1996	Canterbury	Prop	1946	2	2	0

Name	Born	Died	Province	Position	Seasons	Tests	Matches	Points
RICHARDSON, Johnstone	2.4.1899	28.10.1994	Otago, Southland	Loose forward	1921-25	7	42	58: 18 tries, 2 cons
RICKIT, Haydn	19.2.1951		Waikato	Lock	1981	2	2	0
RIDGE, Matthew John	27.8.1969		Auckland	Fullback	1989	0	6	4: 1 try
RIDLAND, Alexander James	3.3.1882	5.11.1918	Southland	Forward	1910	3	6	0
RIECHELMANN, Charles Calvin	26.4.1972		Auckland	Lock/flanker	1997	6	10	15: 3 tries
RIGHTON, Leonard Stephen	12.10.1898	14.2.1972	Auckland	Lock/loose forward	1923, 25	0	9	9: 3 tries
ROBERTS, Edward James	10.5.1891	27.2.1972	Wellington	Halfback	1913-14, 20-21	5	26	112: 14 tries, 35 cons
ROBERTS, Frederick	7.4.1881	21.7.1956	Wellington	Halfback	1905-08, 10	12	52	72: 19 tries, 4 cons, 1 pen, 1 dg
ROBERTS, Henry	1862	1.1.1949	Wellington	Halfback	1884	0	7	8: 4 tries
ROBERTS, Richard William	23.1.1889	8.3.1973	Taranaki	Centre	1913-14	5	23	102: 22 tries, 15 cons, 2 pens
ROBERTS, William	28.10.1871	25.8.1937	Wellington	Midfield back	1896-97	0	8	18: 6 tries
ROBERTSON, Bruce John	9.4.1952		Counties	Centre	1972-74, 76-81	34	102	142: 34 tries, 2 dgs
ROBERTSON, Duncan John	6.2.1947		Otago	First five-eighth/fullback	1974-77	10	30	50: 11 tries, 2 dgs
ROBERTSON, George Scott	1859	26.4.1920	Otago	Forward	1884	0	8	8: 4 tries
ROBERTSON, Scott Maurice	21.8.1974		Canterbury	Flanker	1998-2000	13	13	5: 1 try
ROBILLIARD, Alan Charles	20.12.1903	23.4.1990	Canterbury	Wing	1924-26, 28	4	27	75: 25 tries
ROBINS, Bryce Graeme	12.12.1958		Taranaki	Wing	1985	0	4	16: 4 tries
ROBINSON, Alastair Garth	5.11.1956		North Auckland	Lock	1983	0	4	0
ROBINSON, Charles Edward	5.4.1927	4.3.1983	Southland	Flanker	1951-52	5	11	3: 1 try
ROBINSON, John Topi	1906	29.3.1968	Canterbury	Loose forward	1928	0	3	9: 3 tries
ROBINSON, Mark Darren	21.8.1975		North Harbour	Halfback	1997-98	1	4	5: 1 try
ROBINSON, Mark Powell	17.1.1974		Canterbury	Centre	2000	2	2	5: 1 try
ROLLERSON, Douglas Leslie	14.5.1953		Manawatu	Five-eighth/fullback	1976, 80	8	24	110: 7 tries, 14 cons, 13 pens, 5 dgs
ROPER, Roy Alfred	11.8.1923		Taranaki	Threequarter	1949-50	5	5	9: 3 tries
ROSS, John Charles	24.4.1949		Mid-Canterbury	Lock	1981	0	5	0
ROWLANDS, Gregory David	10.12.1947		Bay of Plenty	Fullback	1976	4	4	44: 10 cons, 8 pens
ROWLEY, Harrison Cotton Banks	15.6.1924	16.12.1956	Wanganui	No 8	1949	1	1	0
RUSH, Eric James	11.2.1965		North Harbour	Wing	1992-93, 95-96	9	29	90: 18 tries
RUSH, Xavier Joseph	13.7.1977		Auckland	No 8	1998	1	1	0
RUSHBROOK, Charles Archibald	6.1.1907	31.7.1987	Wellington	Wing	1928	0	10	53: 17 tries, 1 con
RUTLEDGE, Leicester Malcolm	12.4.1952		Southland	Flanker	1978-80	13	31	28: 7 tries
RYAN, Edmond	17.2.1891	29.8.1965	Wellington	Centre	1921	0	1	0
RYAN, James	8.2.1887	17.7.1957	Wellington	Utility back	1910, 14	4	15	20: 6 tries, 1 con
RYAN, Patrick John	20.4.1950	5.3.1985	Hawke's Bay	Loose forward	1976	0	5	4: 1 try
RYAN, Thomas	2.12.1863	22.2.1927	Auckland	Threequarter	1884	0	9	35: 1 try, 7 cons, 3 dgs
SADLER, Bernard Sydney	28.7.1914		Wellington	Halfback	1935-36	5	19	12: 4 tries
SALMON, James Lionel Broome	16.10.1959		Wellington	Centre	1980-81	3	7	8: 2 tries
SAPSFORD, Herbert Paul	8.9.1949		Otago	Prop	1976	0	7	8: 2 tries
SAVAGE, Laurence Theodore	17.2.1928		Canterbury	Halfback	1949	3	12	3: 1 try

ALL BLACKS — THE COMPLETE REGISTER

NAME	DOB	DOD	PROVINCE(S)	POSITION(S)	YEARS	TESTS	GAMES	POINTS
SAXTON, Charles Kesteven	23.5.1913		South Canterbury	Halfback	1938	3	7	12: 4 tries
SAYERS, Mark	1.5.1947		Wellington	Second five-eighth	1972-73	0	15	16: 4 tries
SCHULER, Kevin James	11.3.1967		Manawatu, North Harbour	Loose forward	1989-90, 92, 95	4	13	8: 2 tries
SCHUSTER, Nesetorio Johnny	17.1.1964		Wellington	Second five-eighth	1987-89	10	26	32: 8 tries
SCOTT, Robert William Henry	6.2.1921		Auckland	Fullback	1946-47, 49-50, 53-54	17	52	242: 1 try, 58 cons, 33 pens, 8 dgs
SCOTT, Stephen John	11.9.1955		Canterbury	Halfback	1980	0	4	20: 5 tries
SCOWN, Alistair Ian	21.10.1948		Taranaki	Loose forward	1972-73	5	17	8: 2 tries
SCRIMSHAW, George	1.12.1902	13.7.1971	Canterbury	Wing forward	1928	1	11	15: 5 tries
SEEAR, Gary Alan	19.2.1952		Otago	No 8	1976-79	12	34	42: 8 tries, 2 cons, 2 pens
SEELING, Charles Edward	14.5.1883	29.5.1956	Auckland	Loose forward	1904-08	11	39	33: 11 tries
SELLARS, George Maurice Victor	16.4.1886	7.6.1917	Auckland	Hooker	1913	2	15	6: 2 tries
SEYMOUR, Dallas James	19.8.1967		Canterbury	Loose forward	1992	0	3	5: 1 try
SHANNON, Graham	13.6.1869	25.10.1911	Manawatu	Halfback/forward	1893	0	6	9: 3 tries
SHAW, Mark William	23.5.1956		Manawatu, Hawke's Bay	Flanker	1980-86	30	69	104: 26 tries
SHEARER, Jack Douglas	19.8.1896	18.9.1963	Wellington	Loose forward	1920	3	5	3: 1 try
SHEARER, Sydney David	23.10.1890	26.2.1973	Wellington	Hooker	1921-22	0	8	3: 1 try
SHEEN, Thomas Reginald	29.3.1905	?.3.1979	Auckland	Midfield back	1926, 28	0	8	3: 1 try
SHELFORD, Frank Nuki Ken	16.5.1955		Bay of Plenty	Flanker	1981, 83-85	4	22	36: 9 tries
SHELFORD, Wayne Thomas	13.12.1957		North Harbour	No 8	1985-90	22	48	88: 22 tries
SHERLOCK, Kurt	31.12.1961		Auckland	Second five-eighth	1985	0	3	0
SIDDELLS, Stanley Keith	16.7.1897	3.3.1979	Wellington	Wing	1921	1	1	0
SIMON, Harold James	7.3.1911	1.10.1979	Otago	Halfback	1937	3	3	0
SIMONSSON, Paul Lennard James	16.2.1967		Waikato	Wing	1987	0	2	28: 7 tries
SIMPSON, John George	18.3.1922		Auckland	Prop	1947, 49-50	9	30	6: 2 tries
SIMPSON, Victor Lenard James	26.2.1960		Canterbury	Centre	1985	2	4	0
SIMS, Graham Scott	25.6.1951		Otago	Centre	1972	1	1	0
SINCLAIR, Robert Gemmell Burnett	31.8.1896	27.6.1932	Otago	Fullback	1923	0	2	23: 7 cons, 3 pens
SKEEN, Jack Robert	23.12.1928		Auckland	Flanker	1952	1	1	0
SKINNER, Kevin Lawrence	24.11.1927		Otago, Counties	Prop	1949-54, 56	20	63	9: 3 tries
SKUDDER, George Rupuha	10.2.1948		Waikato	Wing	1969, 72-73	1	14	15: 4 tries
SLATER, Gordon Leonard	21.11.1971		Taranaki	Prop	1997, 2000	3	6	5: 1 try
SLOANE, Peter Henry	10.9.1948		North Auckland	Hooker	1973, 76, 79	1	16	12: 3 tries
SMITH, Alan Edward	10.12.1942		Taranaki	Lock	1967, 69-70	3	18	3: 1 try
SMITH, Bruce Warwick	4.1.1959		Waikato	Wing	1983-84	3	13	28: 7 tries
SMITH, Charles Herbert	13.2.1909	10.4.1976	Otago	Centre	1934	0	2	3: 1 try
SMITH, George William	20.9.1874	8.12.1954	Auckland	Threequarter	1897, 1901-06	2	39	102: 34 tries
SMITH, Ian Stanley Talbot	20.8.1941		Otago, North Otago	Wing	1963-66	9	24	30: 10 tries
SMITH, John Burns	25.9.1922	3.12.1974	North Auckland	Midfield back	1946-47, 49	4	9	9: 2 tries, 1 dg
SMITH, Peter	1.8.1924	26.1.1954	North Auckland	Second five-eighth	1947	0	3	12: 4 tries
SMITH, Ross Mervyn	21.4.1929		Canterbury	Wing	1955	1	1	0

Name	Born	Died	Province	Position	Years	Tests	Games	Points
SMITH, Wayne Ross	19.4.1957		Canterbury	First five-eighth	1980, 82-85	17	35	36: 6 tries, 4 dgs
SMITH, William Ernest	9.3.1881	25.5.1945	Nelson	First five-eighth	1905	1	1	0
SMYTH, Bernard Francis	11.2.1891	1.7.1972	Canterbury	Hooker	1922	0	3	0
SNODGRASS, Wallace Frankham	24.4.1898	16.7.1976	Nelson	Wing	1923, 28	0	3	13: 1 try, 5 cons
SNOW, Eric McDonald	19.4.1898	24.7.1974	Nelson	Loose forward	1928-29	3	16	3: 1 try
SOLOMON, David	31.5.1913	15.8.1997	Auckland	Five-eighth/fullback	1935-36	0	8	3: 1 try
SOLOMON, Frank	30.5.1906	12.12.1991	Auckland	Wing forward/No 8	1931-32	3	9	9: 3 tries
SOMERVILLE, Greg Mardon	28.11.1977		Canterbury	Prop	2000	6	6	0
SONNTAG, William Theodore Charles	3.6.1894	30.6.1988	Otago	Lock	1929	3	8	0
SOPER, Alistair John	7.9.1936		Southland	No 8	1957	0	8	3: 1 try
SOUTER, Robert	5.1.1905		Otago	Hooker	1929	0	4	0
SPEIGHT, Charles Richard Barton	13.7.1870	23.12.1935	Auckland	Forward	1893	0	7	3: 1 try
SPEIGHT, Michael Wayne	24.2.1962		North Auckland	Lock	1986	1	5	0
SPENCER, Carlos James	14.10.1975		Auckland	First five-eighth	1995-98, 2000	14	23	266: 8 tries, 62 cons, 34 pens
SPENCER, George	3.11.1878		Wellington	Fullback	1907	0	5	6: 3 cons
SPENCER, John Clarence	27.11.1880	21.5.1936	Wellington	Loose forward	1903, 05, 07	2	6	6: 2 tries
SPIERS, John Edmunde	4.8.1947		Counties	Prop	1976, 79-81	5	27	4: 1 try
SPILLANE, Augustine Patrick	10.5.1888	16.9.1974	South Canterbury	Second five-eighth	1913	2	2	0
STALKER, John	11.2.1881	28.11.1931	Otago	Midfield back	1903	0	6	6: 2 tries
STANLEY, Jeremy Crispian	26.3.1975		Auckland	Threequarter	1997	0	3	0
STANLEY, Joseph Tito	13.4.1957		Auckland	Centre	1986-91	27	49	28: 7 tries
STAPLETON, Edgar Thomas	21.11.1930		New South Wales	Wing	1960	0	1	3: 1 try
STEAD, John William	18.9.1877	21.7.1958	Southland	Five-eighth	1903-06, 08	7	42	36: 12 tries
STEEL, Anthony Gordon	31.7.1941		Canterbury	Wing	1966-68	9	23	60: 20 tries
STEEL, John	10.11.1898	4.8.1941	West Coast	Wing	1920-25	6	38	114: 35 tries, 3 cons, 1 pen
STEELE, Leo Brian	19.1.1929		Wellington	Halfback	1951	3	9	5: 1 con, 1 dg
STEERE, Edward Richard George	10.7.1908	1.6.1967	Hawke's Bay	Lock	1928-31	6	21	3: 1 try
STENSNESS, Lee	24.12.1970		Auckland	Five-eighth	1993, 97	8	14	15: 3 tries
STEPHENS, Owen George	9.1.1947		Wellington	Wing	1968	1	1	0
STEVENS, Ian Neal	13.4.1948		Wellington	Halfback/first five-eighth	1972-74, 76	3	33	32: 8 tries
STEVENSON, Donald Robert Louis	3.2.1903	11.4.1962	Otago	Fullback	1926	0	4	0
STEWART, Allan James	11.10.1940		Canterbury	Lock	1963-64	8	26	6: 2 tries
STEWART, David	24.1.1871	?	South Canterbury	Loose forward	1894	0	1	0
STEWART, Edward Barrie	29.10.1901	13.12.1979	Otago	Wing	1923	0	1	6: 2 tries
STEWART, James Douglas	3.10.1890	5.5.1973	Auckland	Threequarter	1913	2	2	0
STEWART, Kenneth William	3.1.1953		Southland	Flanker	1972-76, 79, 81	13	55	24: 6 tries
STEWART, Ronald Terowie	12.1.1904	15.12.1982	South Canterbury, Canterbury	Loose forward	1923-26, 28, 30	5	39	32: 10 tries, 1 con
STEWART, Vance Edmond	28.10.1948		Canterbury	Lock	1976, 79	0	12	8: 2 tries

ALL BLACKS — THE COMPLETE REGISTER

NAME	DOB	DOD	PROVINCE(S)	POSITION(S)	YEARS	TESTS	GAMES	POINTS
STOHR, Leonard	13.11.1889	25.7.1973	Taranaki	Threequarter	1910, 13	3	15	73: 10 tries, 14 cons, 5 pens
STOKES, Edward James Taite	26.6.1950		Bay of Plenty	Centre	1976	0	5	4: 1 try
STONE, Arthur Massey	19.12.1960		Waikato, Bay of Plenty	Midfield back	1981, 83-84, 86	9	23	23: 5 tries, 1 dg
STOREY, Percival Wright	11.2.1897	4.10.1975	South Canterbury	Wing	1920-21	2	12	50: 16 tries, 1 con
STRACHAN, Anthony Duncan	7.6.1966		Auckland, North Harbour	Halfback	1992-93, 95	11	17	18: 4 tries
STRAHAN, Samuel Cunningham	25.12.1944		Manawatu	Lock	1967-68, 70, 72-73	17	45	6: 2 tries
STRANG, William Archibald	18.10.1906	11.2.1989	South Canterbury	Five-eighth/halfback	1928, 30-31	5	17	44: 5 tries, 11 cons, 1 pen, 1 dg
STRINGFELLOW, John Clinton	26.2.1905	3.1.1959	Wairarapa	Centre/fullback	1929	2	7	16: 4 tries, 1 dg
STUART, Angus John	1858	8.10.1923	Wellington	Forward	1893	0	7	0
STUART, Kevin Charles	19.9.1928		Canterbury	Fullback	1955	1	1	0
STUART, Robert Charles	28.10.1920		Canterbury	Loose forward	1949, 53-54	7	27	3: 1 try
STUART, Robert Locksdale	9.1.1949		Hawke's Bay	Lock/prop	1977	1	6	4: 1 try
SULLIVAN, John Lorraine	30.3.1915	9.7.1990	Taranaki	Midfield back	1936-38	6	9	18: 6 tries
SURMAN, Frank	?	?	Auckland	Midfield	1896	0	1	0
SURRIDGE, Stephen Dennis	17.7.1970		Canterbury	No 8	1997	0	3	5: 1 try
SUTHERLAND, Alan Richard	4.1.1944		Marlborough	Lock/No 8	1969, 70-73, 76	10	64	157: 32 tries, 17 cons, 3 pens
SVENSON, Kenneth Sydney	6.12.1898	7.12.1955	Buller, Wellington	Midfield back	1922-26	4	34	97: 26 tries, 8 cons, 1 pen
SWAIN, John Patterson	1902	29.8.1960	Hawke's Bay	Hooker	1928	4	16	9: 3 tries
SWINDLEY, James	?	?.10.1918	Wellington	Forward	1894	0	1	0
TAIAROA, John Grey	16.9.1862	31.12.1907	Otago	Halfback	1884	0	9	21: 9 tries, 1 con
TAITUHA, Peina	30.4.1901	25.2.1958	Wanganui	Second five-eighth/wing	1923	0	2	0
TANNER, John Maurice	11.1.1927		Auckland	Midfield back	1950-51, 53-54	5	24	33: 11 tries
TANNER, Kerry John	25.4.1945		Canterbury	Prop	1974-76	7	27	0
TAYLOR, Glenn Lyndon	23.9.1970		North Auckland	Flanker/lock	1992, 96	1	6	0
TAYLOR, Henry Morgan	5.2.1889	20.6.1955	Canterbury	Halfback/threequarter	1913-14	4	23	60: 20 tries
TAYLOR, John McLeod	12.1.1913	5.5.1979	Otago	Fullback	1937-38	6	9	45: 15 cons, 5 pens
TAYLOR, Kenneth John	30.11.1957		Hawke's Bay	Wing	1980	0	1	8: 2 tries
TAYLOR, Murray Barton	25.8.1956		Waikato	Five-eighth	1976, 79-80	7	30	28: 4 tries, 4 dgs
TAYLOR, Norman Mark	11.1.1951		Bay of Plenty, Hawke's Bay	Midfield/wing	1976-78, 82	9	27	51: 11 tries, 2 cons, 1 dg
TAYLOR, Reginald	23.3.1889	20.6.1917	Taranaki	Wing forward	1913	2	2	3: 1 try
TAYLOR, Warwick Thomas	11.3.1960		Canterbury	Second five-eighth	1983-88	24	40	32: 8 tries
TETZLAFF, Percy Laurence	14.7.1920		Auckland	Halfback	1947	2	7	0
THIMBLEBY, Neil William	19.6.1939		Hawke's Bay	Prop	1970	1	13	0
THOMAS, Barry Trevor	21.7.1937		Auckland, Wellington	Prop	1962, 64	4	4	0
THOMAS, Leslie Arthur	13.8.1897	3.6.1971	Wellington	Loose forward	1925	0	3	0
THOMPSON, Barry Alan	28.12.1947		Canterbury	Prop	1979	0	8	0

Name	Born	Died	Province	Position	Years	Tests	Matches	Points
THOMSON, Hector Douglas	20.2.1881	9.8.1939	Wellington	Wing	1905-06, 08	1	15	50: 16 tries, 1 con
THORNE, Grahame Stuart	25.2.1946		Auckland	Threequarter/midfield back	1967-70	10	39	119: 35 tries, 4 cons, 1 pen, 1 dg
THORNE, Reuben David	2.1.1975		Canterbury	Lock/flanker	1999-2000	11	11	0
THORNTON, Neville Henry	12.12.1918	12.9.1998	Auckland	No 8	1947, 49	3	19	21: 6 tries, 1 pen
TIATIA, Filogia Ian	4.6.1971		Wellington	No 8	2000	2	2	10: 2 tries
TILYARD, Frederick Joseph	5.7.1896	8.2.1954	Wellington	First five-eighth	1923	0	1	3: 1 try
TILYARD, James Thomas	27.8.1889	1.11.1966	Wellington	Five-eighth	1913, 20	1	10	20: 4 tries, 2 cons, 1 dg
TIMU, John Kahukura Raymond	8.5.1969		Otago	Wing/fullback	1989-94	26	50	117: 27 tries
TINDILL, Eric William Thomas	18.12.1910		Wellington	Halfback/first five-eighth	1935-36, 38	1	17	24: 6 dgs
TIOPIRA, Hoeroa	10.1.1871	?	Hawke's Bay	Forward	1893	0	8	0
TONU'U, Ofisa Francis Junior	3.2.1970		Auckland	Halfback	1996-98	5	8	10: 2 tries
TOWNSEND, Lindsay James	3.3.1934		Otago	Halfback	1955	2	2	0
TREGASKIS, Christopher David	5.1.1965		Wellington	Lock	1991	0	4	0
TREMAIN, Kelvin Robin	21.2.1938	2.5.1992	Canterbury, Auckland, Hawke's Bay	Flanker	1959-68	38	86	108: 36 tries
TREVATHAN, David	6.5.1912	11.4.1986	Otago	First five-eighth	1937	3	3	16: 4 pens, 1 dg
TUCK, Jack Manson	13.5.1907	23.3.1967	Waikato	Utility back	1929	3	6	0
TUIGAMALA, Va'aiga Lealuga	4.9.1969		Auckland	Wing	1989-93	19	39	61: 14 tries
TUNNICLIFF, Robert Graham	25.6.1894	7.1.1973	Buller	Hooker	1923	0	1	3: 1 try
TURNBULL, John Steele	2.10.1898	18.1.1947	Otago	Flanker	1921	0	1	0
TURNER, Richard Steven	15.3.1968		North Harbour	No 8	1992	2	2	4: 1 try
TURTILL, Hubert Sydney	1.2.1880	9.4.1918	Canterbury	Fullback	1905	1	1	0
TWIGDEN, Timothy Moore	14.5.1952		Auckland	Threequarter	1979-80	2	15	28: 7 tries
TYLER, George Alfred	10.2.1879	15.4.1942	Auckland	Hooker	1903-06	7	36	27: 5 tries, 6 cons
UDY, Daniel Knight	21.5.1874	29.7.1935	Wairarapa	Hooker	1901, 03	1	9	3: 1 try
UDY, Hart	1860	6.8.1933	Wellington	Forward	1884	0	8	0
UMAGA, Tana Jonathan Falefasa	27.5.1973		Wellington	Wing/centre	1997-2000	27	32	110: 22 tries
URBAHN, Roger James	31.7.1934	27.11.1984	Taranaki	Halfback	1959-60	3	15	9: 3 tries
URLICH, Ronald Anthony	8.2.1944		Auckland	Hooker	1970, 72-73	2	35	30: 9 tries
UTTLEY, Ian Neil	3.12.1941		Wellington	Centre	1963	2	2	0
VALLI, Geoffrey Thomas	3.11.1954		Southland	Fullback	1980	0	1	9: 3 cons, 1 pen
VANISI, Osaiasi Kupu	30.11.1972		Wellington	Flanker	1999	0	1	0
VIDIRI, Joeli	23.1.1973		Counties-Manukau	Wing	1998	2	2	5: 1 try
VINCENT, Patrick Bernard	6.1.1926	10.4.1983	Canterbury	Halfback	1956	2	2	0
VODANOVICH, Ivan Matthew Henry	8.4.1930	2.9.1995	Wellington	Prop	1955	3	3	3: 1 try
VORRATH, Frederick Henry	13.6.1908	1.7.1972	Otago	Utility forward	1935-36	0	12	6: 2 tries
WALLACE, William Joseph	2.8.1878	2.3.1972	Wellington	Utility back	1903-08	11	51	379: 36 tries, 114 cons, 9 pens, 2 dgs, 2 gms
WALSH, Patrick Timothy	6.5.1936		Counties	Utility back	1955-59, 63-64	13	27	23: 7 tries, 1 con
WALTER, John	2.8.1904	25.4.1966	Taranaki	Loose forward	1925	0	7	12: 4 tries
WARBRICK, Joseph Astbury	1862	30.8.1903	Auckland	Threequarter	1884	0	7	12: 3 dgs

ALL BLACKS — THE COMPLETE REGISTER

NAME	DOB	DOD	PROVINCE(S)	POSITION(S)	YEARS	TESTS	GAMES	POINTS
WARD, Edward Percival	28.6.1899	25.9.1958	Taranaki	Utility forward	1928	0	10	3: 1 pen
WARD, Francis Gerald	17.3.1900	11.3.1990	Otago	Wing	1921	0	1	0
WARD, Ronald Henry	1.12.1915	1.8.2000	Southland	Flanker	1936-37	3	4	0
WATERMAN, Alfred Clarence	31.12.1903	22.10.1997	North Auckland	Wing	1929	2	7	18: 6 tries
WATKINS, Eric Leslie	18.3.1880	14.8.1949	Wellington	Hooker	1905	1	1	0
WATSON, James Donald	1872	25.12.1958	Taranaki	Forward	1896	0	1	0
WATSON, William Donald	22.12.1869	25.3.1953	Wairarapa	Forward	1893, 96	0	3	0
WATT, Bruce Alexander	12.3.1939		Canterbury	First five-eighth	1962-64	8	29	27: 4 tries, 5 dgs
WATT, James Michael	5.7.1914	17.9.1988	Otago	Wing	1936	2	2	6: 2 tries
WATT, James Russell	29.12.1935		Southland, Wellington	Wing	1957-58, 60-62	9	42	114: 28 tries, 9 cons, 4 pens
WATTS, Murray Gordon	31.3.1955		Taranaki	Wing	1979-80	5	13	28: 7 tries
WEBB, Desmond Stanley	10.9.1934		North Auckland	Hooker	1959	1	1	0
WEBB, Peter Purves	15.2.1854	28.11.1920	Wellington	Forward	1884	0	8	0
WEBSTER, Thomas Robert Dobson	12.7.1920	6.11.1972	Southland	Fullback	1947	0	4	38: 14 cons, 2 pens, 1 dg
WELLS, John	4.1.1908	7.1.1994	Wellington	Flanker	1936	2	3	0
WELLS, William JG	1872	?	Taranaki	Forward	1897	0	7	0
WESNEY, Arthur William	1.2.1915	23.11.1941	Southland	Centre/fullback	1938	0	3	23: 3 tries, 2 cons, 2 pens, 1 dg
WEST, Alfred Hubert	6.5.1893	7.1.1934	Taranaki	Loose forward	1920-21, 23-25	2	24	20: 6 tries, 1 con
WESTON, Lynley Herbert	1.9.1892	2.11.1963	Auckland	First five-eighth	1914	0	1	0
WHETTON, Alan James	15.12.1959		Auckland	Flanker	1984-91	35	65	104: 26 tries
WHETTON, Gary William	15.12.1959		Auckland	Lock	1981-91	58	101	36: 9 tries
WHINERAY, Wilson James	10.7.1935		Canterbury, Waikato, Auckland	Prop	1957-65	32	77	24: 7 tries, 1 dg
WHITE, Andrew	21.3.1894	3.8.1968	Southland	Flanker	1921-25	4	38	48: 10 tries, 9 cons
WHITE, Hallard Leo	27.3.1929		Auckland	Prop	1953-55	4	16	6: 2 tries
WHITE, Richard Alexander	11.6.1925		Poverty Bay	Lock	1949-56	23	55	33: 11 tries
WHITE, Roy Maxwell	18.10.1917	19.1.1980	Wellington	Flanker	1946-47	4	10	3: 1 try
WHITING, Graham John	4.9.1946		King Country	Prop	1972-73	6	31	4: 1 try
WHITING, Peter John	6.8.1946		Auckland	Lock	1971-74, 76	20	56	20: 5 tries
WICKES, Craig David	26.2.1962		Manawatu	Wing	1980	0	1	0
WIGHTMAN, David Ross	10.8.1929		Auckland	Threequarter	1951	0	4	18: 6 tries
WILLIAMS, Alexander Leonard	18.10.1898	13.6.1972	Otago	Lock	1922-23	0	9	3: 1 try
WILLIAMS, Bryan George	3.10.1950		Auckland	Wing/centre	1970-78	38	113	401: 66 tries, 22 cons, 30 pens, 1 dg
WILLIAMS, Claude Wright	16.5.1916	30.4.1998	Canterbury	Loose forward/lock	1938	0	4	6: 2 tries
WILLIAMS, Graham Charles	26.1.1945		Wellington	Flanker	1967-68	5	18	50: 16 tries, 1 con
WILLIAMS, Peter	22.4.1884	30.8.1976	Otago	Hooker	1913	1	9	3: 1 try
WILLIAMS, Raymond Norman	25.4.1909		Canterbury	Wing	1932	0	1	0
WILLIAMS, Ronald Oscar	20.7.1963		North Harbour	Prop	1988-89	0	10	0

Name	Born	Died	Province	Position	Years	Tests	Matches	Points
WILLIMENT, Michael	25.2.1940	5.9.1994	Wellington	Fullback	1964-67	9	9	70: 1 try, 17 cons, 11 pens
WILLIS, Royce Kevin	28.8.1975		Waikato	Lock	1998-99	11	11	0
WILLOCKS, Charles	28.6.1919	25.8.1991	Otago	Lock	1946-47, 49	5	22	0
WILLOUGHBY, Stanley de lar Poer	21.1.1904	27.9.1985	Wairarapa	Loose forward	1928	0	4	0
WILLS, Murray Clifton	11.10.1941		Taranaki	Flanker	1967	0	5	0
WILSON, Alexander	28.7.1874	6.10.1932	Auckland	Forward	1897	0	8	15: 2 tries, 3 cons, 1 pen
WILSON, Alfred Leonard	15.6.1927		Southland	First five-eighth	1951	0	7	20: 4 tries, 1 con, 2 pens
WILSON, Bevan William	22.3.1956		Otago	Fullback	1977-79	8	12	60: 6 cons, 16 pens
WILSON, Douglas Dawson	30.1.1931		Canterbury	Five-eighth	1953-54	2	14	18: 5 tries, 1 dg
WILSON, Frank Reginald	28.5.1885	19.9.1916	Auckland	Wing	1910	0	2	4: 1 dg
WILSON, Hector William	27.1.1924		Otago	Prop	1949-51	5	13	9: 3 tries
WILSON, Hedley Brett	23.8.1957		Counties	Hooker	1983	0	3	4: 1 try
WILSON, Henry Clarke	2.2.1869	16.12.1945	Canterbury	Fullback	1893	0	7	11: 2 cons, 1 pen, 1 gm
WILSON, Jeffrey William	24.10.1973		Otago	Wing/fullback	1993-99	54	65	274: 45 tries, 11 cons, 8 pens, 1 dg
WILSON, Nathaniel Arthur	18.5.1886	11.8.1953	Wellington	Loose forward	1908, 10, 13-14	10	21	18: 6 tries
WILSON, Norman Leslie	13.12.1922		Otago	Hooker	1949, 51	3	20	6: 2 tries
WILSON, Richard George	19.5.1953		Canterbury	Fullback	1976-80	2	25	272: 5 tries, 48 cons, 51 pens, 1 dg
WILSON, Robert J	?	?	Canterbury	Forward	1884	0	6	4: 2 tries
WILSON, Stuart Sinclair	22.7.1954		Wellington	Threequarter	1976-83	34	85	200: 50 tries
WILSON, Vivian Whitta	6.1.1899	14.8.1978	Auckland	Threequarter	1920	0	7	18: 5 tries, 1 pen
WISE, George Denis	12.5.1904	1.9.1971	Otago	Wing	1925	0	7	15: 5 tries
WOLFE, Thomas Neil	20.10.1941		Wellington, Taranaki	Five-eighth/centre	1961-63, 68	6	14	34: 6 tries, 4 cons, 2 dgs
WOOD, Morris Edwin	9.10.1876	9.8.1956	Wellington, Auckland	Five-eighth	1901, 03-04	2	12	24: 6 tries
WOODMAN, Freddy Akehurst	10.2.1958		North Auckland	Wing	1980-81	3	14	12: 3 tries
WOODMAN, Taui Ben Kawhena	9.5.1960		North Auckland	Wing	1984	0	6	2: 1 con
WOODS, Charles Arthur	5.8.1929		Southland	Hooker	1953-54	0	14	2: 1 con
WRIGHT, Alan Hercules	14.4.1914	2.12.1990	Wellington	Wing	1938	4	4	33: 11 tries
WRIGHT, Donald Hector	20.10.1902	26.12.1966	Auckland	Halfback	1925	0	6	12: 4 tries
WRIGHT, Terence John	21.1.1963		Auckland	Wing/fullback	1986-92	30	64	202: 48 tries, 2 cons, 2 pens
WRIGHT, William Alexander	1.2.1905	19.9.1971	Auckland	Halfback	1926	0	1	0
WRIGLEY, Edward	15.6.1886	2.6.1958	Wairarapa	Second five-eighth	1905	1	1	3: 1 try
WYLIE, James Thomas	26.10.1887	19.12.1956	Auckland	Loose forward	1913	2	12	18: 6 tries
WYLLIE, Alexander John	31.8.1944		Canterbury	Loose forward	1970-73	11	40	42: 12 tries
WYLLIE, Tutekawa	24.10.1954		Wellington	First five-eighth	1980	0	1	4: 1 try
WYNYARD, James Gladwyn	17.8.1914	2.11.1941	Waikato	Loose forward	1935, 36, 38	0	13	15: 5 tries
WYNYARD, William Thomas	1869	15.3.1938	Wellington	Threequarter	1893	0	7	14: 5 tries
YATES, Victor Moses	15.6.1939		North Auckland	No 8	1961-62	3	9	15: 3 tries, 3 cons
YOUNG, Dennis	1.4.1930		Canterbury	Hooker	1955-58, 60-64	22	61	9: 1 try, 3 cons
YOUNG, Francis Beresford	1874	2.11.1946	Wellington	Forward	1896	0	1	0

ALL BLACKS — THE COMPLETE REGISTER